Aging in Prison

Aging in Prison

The Integration of Research and Practice

SECOND EDITION

Martha H. Hurley

CAROLINA ACADEMIC PRESS

Durham, North Carolina

Library of Congress Cataloging-in-Publication Data

Names: Hurley, Martha Henderson, author.
Title: Aging in prison : the integration of research and practice / Martha
  Hurley.
Description: Second Edition. | Durham, NC : Carolina Academic Press, [2018] |
  Revised edition of the author's Aging in prison, [2014] | Includes
  bibliographical references and index.
Identifiers: LCCN 2017044414 | ISBN 9781611638479 (alk. paper)
Subjects: LCSH: Older prisoners--United States.
Classification: LCC HV9469 .H868 2018 | DDC 365/.608460973--dc23
LC record available at https://lccn.loc.gov/2017044414

e-ISBN 978-1-53100-692-1

CAROLINA ACADEMIC PRESS, LLC
700 Kent Street
Durham, North Carolina 27701
Telephone (919) 489-7486
Fax (919) 493-5668
www.cap-press.com

Printed in the United States of America

To David Hurley, Caleb Hurley, and Grace Hurley.

Contents

List of Boxes, Figures, and Tables   xiii
Acknowledgments   xvii

Chapter 1 · Why Study Long-Term and Elderly Prisoners?   3
  Driving Forces for Long-Term and Elderly Increases
    in Prison Populations   4
  Consequences of Long-Term Incarceration   6
  Number of Incarcerated   8
  The High Costs of Incarceration   12
  The Elderly in Prison   17
    Questioning the Need to Incarcerate Elderly Inmates   18
  Why Write This Book?   19
  Purpose and Organization   21
  Websites   22
  References   23

Chapter 2 · Who Are the Long-Term Inmates? What Are the Costs?
            What Are Their Needs?   27
  Defining Long-Term Inmates   29
  Snapshot: National Estimates of the Long-Term Offender Population   29
  Minorities   33
  Women   36
  Costs of Incarceration for Long-Term Inmates   38
  How Does Long-Term Incarceration Affect Male Prisoners?   38
  How Does Long-Term Incarceration Affect Female Prisoners?   41
  What Happens Upon Release?   41
  Conclusions   43

Websites   44
References   44

Chapter 3 · Who Are the Elderly Inmates? What Are the Costs?
          What Are Their Needs?   51
Defining Elderly, Senior or Older Citizens in the General Population   53
Snapshot: National Estimates of the Elderly   54
Challenges in Defining the Elderly Inmate   55
Types of Elderly Inmates   57
Profile of the Elderly Inmate   58
Minority Representation   61
Female Elderly Prisoners   63
The Needs of Elderly Inmates   65
Conclusion   67
Websites   68
References   68

Chapter 4 · Medical Health Issues   75
Why Focus on the Medical Issues of Long-Term and Elderly Inmates?   76
Costs of Medical Care for the Elderly and Long-Term Prisoner   78
What and Who Is to Blame?   80
Health Care Problems among Inmates   81
Communicable Diseases   81
Sexually Transmitted Diseases   82
    Syphilis   82
    Gonorrhea   85
    Chlamydia   86
    Trichomoniasis   86
    HIV/AIDS   87
    Tuberculosis   91
    Hepatitis   94
Chronic Illnesses   96
    Asthma   96
    Diabetes   98
    Hypertension   99
    Heart Disease   100
Disabilities   100
Mortality   101

Effective Approaches for Reducing Costs for Medical Health
   Problems of Long-Term and Elderly Prisoners   108
Conclusion   111
Websites   112
References   112

Chapter 5 · Mental Health Needs   123
Why Focus on the Mental Health Needs of Long-Term
   and Elderly Inmates?   124
Characteristics of Mentally Disordered Prisoners   126
Age and Prisoner Mental Health Problems   128
Most Common Mental Illnesses among Inmates Aged 55 and Up   128
   Late Onset Schizophrenia   128
      Prevalence of Schizophrenia in Correctional Settings   131
   Depression   132
      Prevalence of Depression in Correctional Settings   133
   Dementia/Alzheimer's   134
      Prevalence of Alzheimer's in Correctional Settings   135
   Anxiety Disorders   136
      Prevalence of Anxiety Disorders in Correctional Settings   136
   Suicide   138
   Prevalence of Suicide in Correctional Environments   138
   Causes of Higher Suicide Rates in Correctional Contexts   140
      Long-Term Incarceration   140
      Lack of Social Support   141
      Interpersonal Conflict with Other Inmates   143
      High Rate of Medical and Mental Health Problems   143
      Institutional Contextual Problems   144
Effective Approaches for Dealing with the Mental Health Problems
   of Long-Term and Elderly Prisoners   145
Conclusion   146
Websites   146
References   147

Chapter 6 · Victimization   155
Victimization Research Is Complicated   156
Defining Prisoner Victimization   156
Prevalence and Incidence of Victimization in Prison   158
Special Circumstance — Sexual Victimization   159

Sexual Victimization through the Ages   159
How Does Sexual Victimization Differ in Prison from the Community? 160
Consequences of Victimization   161
What Does All This Mean for Elderly Prisoners?   163
Why Does Victimization Matter?   166
Pre-Prison Trauma   166
Inmate Subculture and Adaptation   167
Age-Related Mental and Physical Decline   168
Nature of Offense   168
Victimization Is Under-Reported   168
What Is the Extent of Victimization?   169
Consequences of Victimization   170
Conclusion   170
Websites   171
References   171

Chapter 7 · Programs and Sentencing Options   177
Driving Forces of the Shift in Sentencing   178
Solutions to the Elderly Prisoner Problem   178
The Do Nothing Argument   179
Early Release   180
Parole Prisoners as Normal   181
Geriatric Release — Considering Age and Disability   182
Home Detention   185
Alternative Living Environments within the Institution   185
Sample of U.S. Prison Programs   187
  True Grit Geriatric Unit in Northern Nevada Correctional
    Center (NNCC)   188
  Florida Programs   188
  The State of Louisiana Hospice Program at Angola   189
  The Maryland Hospice Program   189
  Laurel Highlands in Pennsylvania   189
  The Virginia Special Needs Facility   190
Conclusion   190
Websites   191
References   191
Court Cases   194

Chapter 8 · An Ethic of Care 195
  An Ethic of Care Perspective 198
  The Application of an Ethic of Care for the Elderly in Prison 200
  Conclusion 202
  Websites 203
  References 204
  Court Cases 207

Index 209

List of Boxes, Figures, and Tables

Chapter 1 · Why Study Long-Term and Elderly Prisoners? 3
Box 1-1. 3
Box 1-2. Driving Forces for Increases 5
Table 1-1. Percent of Sentenced Prisoners under the Jurisdiction
of Federal Correctional Authority 7
Table 1-2. World Prison Population Changes 2000 Compared to 2015 8
Figure 1-1. Countries with Highest Incarceration Rates
as of October 2015 9
Figure 1-2. 20 Countries with the Lowest Incarceration Rates
as of October 2015 10
Figure 1-3. 10 Countries with the Highest Prison Population 11
Figure 1-4. Total U.S. Adult Population under Correctional
Supervision 2000–2015 12
Table 1-3. Total Number of Sentenced Prisoners
and Incarceration Rates 2000–2015 13
Table 1-4. The Punishment Rate 14
Figure 1-5. Criminal Justice Spending, 1993–2012 16
Box 1-3. What Would Happen If We Shifted Half
of Nonviolent Offenders from Prison? 17
Table 1-5. Costs and Benefits of Criminal Justice Policies 18
Box 1-4. What Do The Elderly in Prison Deserve? 19

**Chapter 2 · Who Are the Long-Term Inmates? What Are the Costs?
What Are Their Needs?** 27
Figure 2-1. Number of People Serving Life Sentences, 1984–2012 30
Table 2-1. National Trends Average Time Served First Releases 31

Table 2-2. States with the Highest Percent Increases in Time Served
between 1990 and 2009   32
Table 2-3. Pennsylvania Long-Term Inmate Sentences   33
Table 2-4. Changes in Time Served by Offense Type
and Total State Cost 1990–2009   34
Figure 2-2. Time Served All Federal Offenders   35
Figure 2-3. Lifetime Likelihood of Going to Prison   36
Figure 2-4. Rise in Women's Incarceration 1980–2014   37
Table 2-5. Georgia Department of Corrections
Long-Term Female Prisoners   37
Box 2-1. Pains of Imprisonment and Adaptations   40

**Chapter 3 · Who Are the Elderly Inmates? What Are the Costs?
What Are Their Needs?**   51
Figure 3-1. Population 65 Years and Older by Size and Percent
of Total Population: 1900 to 2010   55
Table 3-1. Projections of the Population by Selected Age Groups
and Sex for the U.S.: 2010–2050   56
Figure 3-2. Sentenced State Prisoners by Age   59
Table 3-2. Sentenced State Prisoners by Age   60
Table 3-3. Imprisonment Rate of Sentenced State Prisoners
per 100,000 U.S. Adults for Ages 50 and Older   61
Table 3-4. Sentence Length, Most Serious Offense, and Time Served
for State Prisoners over Age 65   62
Table 3-5. Imprisonment Rate State Prisoners Aged 50 and Older
by Race and Hispanic Origin in 2013   63
Table 3-6. Total Population of Sentenced State Prisoners Aged 50
and Older by Race and Hispanic Origin   64
Table 3-7. Imprisonment Rate Sentenced State Female Prisoners
by Age 1993, 2003, and 2013   65
Table 3-8. Federal Female Prisoner Trends 2007–2010   66
Table 3-9. Federal Female Prisoners by Age
and Sentence Length in 2010   66

Chapter 4 · Medical Health Issues   75
Box 4-1. Why Focus on Medical Issues?   76
Box 4-2. Specialized Care for Aging Prisoners   79
Box 4-3. Most Common Communicable Diseases Among Inmates   81
Table 4-1. Sexually Transmitted Diseases   83

Table 4-2. Primary and Secondary Syphilis by Reporting Source 2011   84
Table 4-3. Gonorrhea-Positivity by Age and Sex,
    Adult Correctional Facilities, 2011   85
Table 4-4. Chlamydia-Positivity by Age and Sex
    in Adult Corrections Facilities, 2011   86
Table 4-5. State and Federal Prisoners with HIV or AIDS
    by Jurisdiction, Yearend 2010, 2011, and 2012   88
Table 4-6. AIDS-Related Deaths among State Prison Inmates
    in Custody, 2001–2014   91
Table 4-7. Rate of HIV or AIDS Cases among State
    and Federal Prisoners, 2001–2012   92
Table 4-8. Prevalence of Ever Having a Chronic Condition
    or Infectious Disease among State and Federal Prisoners
    and the General Population   93
Box 4-4. Symptoms of Tuberculosis   95
Box 4-5. Chronic Illnesses   97
Box 4-6. Complications Associated with Diabetes   98
Table 4-9. Prevalence of Disabilities among State and Federal
    Prisoners and the General Population 2011–2012   101
Table 4-10. Prevalence of Disabilities among State and Federal
    Prisoners by Demographics 2011–12   102
Figure 4-1. Prevalence of Disabilities among State and Federal
    Prisoners and Jail Inmates by Sex, 2011–12   103
Box 4-7. Differences between Cognitive Disabilities
    and Mental Health Disorders   103
Figure 4-2. State Prison Inmate Deaths in Custody, 2001–2014   104
Table 4-11. Mortality Rate per 100,000 State Prisoners
    by Cause of Death, 2001 and 2005–2014   105
Table 4-12. Percent of State Prisoner Deaths by Cause of Death,
    2001 and 2005–2014   106
Table 4-13. Percent of State Prisoner Deaths by Selected
    Decedent Characteristics, 2001 and 2005–2014   107

Chapter 5 · Mental Health Needs   123
Box 5-1. Why Focus on Mental Health Issues?   124
Table 5-1. Recent History and Symptoms of Mental Health Problems
    among Prison and Jail Inmates   127
Table 5-2. Prevalence of Mental Health Problems among Prison
    and Jail Inmates   128

Table 5-3. Mental Health Status and History of Mental Health
    Problems among Inmates, 2011–12   129
Box 5-2. Most Common Mental Illnesses among Inmates
    Aged 55 and Up   129
Table 5-4. Prison and Jail Inmates Who Had Mental Health
    Problems by Gender, Race, and Age   131
Table 5-5. Characteristics of Late Onset and Very Late
    Onset Schizophrenia   132
Box 5-3. Symptoms of Depression in Older Adults   133
Box 5-4. Dementia Defined   134
Box 5-5. Warning Signs of Alzheimer's   135
Box 5-6. Anxiety Disorders   137
Box 5-7. Definitions of Self-Directed Violence   138
Table 5-6. Suicide Rates* among Persons Ages 65 Years and Older
    by Race/Ethnicity and Sex, United States, 2005–2009   139
Box 5-8. Causes of Higher Suicide Rates in Correctional Contexts   141

Chapter 6 · Victimization   155
Box 6-1. Types of Prisoner Victimization   157
Box 6-2. Prison Rape Definition   158
Table 6-1. Adult Prisoners Reporting Sexual Victimization
    by Incident, National Inmate Survey, 2011–12   161
Table 6-2. Prevalence of Sexual Victimization by Incident and Inmate
    Characteristics, National Inmate Survey, 2011–12   162
Table 6-3. Prevalence of Sexual Victimization by Type of Incident
    and Inmate Criminal Justice Status and History,
    National Inmate Survey, 2011–12   164
Table 6-4. Prevalence of Sexual Victimization by Type of Incident
    and Age of Inmate, National Inmate Survey, 2011–12   165
Box 6-3. Visitor Voices: Older Prisoner Reports   169

Chapter 7 · Programs and Sentencing Options   177
Box 7-1. Average Expenditures for Elderly Prisoners in Several States 179
Box 7-2. Solutions to the Elderly Prisoner Problem   179
Box 7-3. List of States with Geriatric Release Policies   183
Box 7-4. BOP Elderly Offender Home Detention Program Eligibility   185

Chapter 8 · An Ethic of Care   195
Box 8-1. Questions that Arise from Dimensions of the Ethic of Care   199

Acknowledgments

The path to writing this book began when the Illinois legislature decided that it was in the state's best interest to examine what happened to long-term prisoners. Without their decision to take a holistic approach to the study of incarceration trends and the impact of prison on long-term prisoners, this book never would have been written.

This book could not have been written without the encouragement of David Hurley. Thank you for continued support of my scholarship.

I would like to acknowledge Beth Hall. Thanks for sticking with me through this process.

I have saved the most important for last—the long-term and elderly prisoners. Your experience of prison deserves far more attention than what can be included in this book. I hope that this edition continues to bring attention to your plight.

Aging in Prison

Chapter 1

Why Study Long-Term and Elderly Prisoners?

Box 1-1.

For 44 years, Dennis Whitney's world has consisted largely of steel bars, razor wire and a metal bed with a three-inch mattress. He has grown old in prison, doing hard time for two murders committed when he was 17. And with time have come the ravages of age: Whitney, 61, has undergone two angioplasties at state expense to clear narrowed or blocked blood vessels, and he needs a third such procedure. The first two cost a total of nearly $9,000 (*USA Today* 2004).

The Estelle Unit in Huntsville has a 60-bed geriatric unit where <u>Raymond Palen</u>, 79, has been housed for four years. He has diabetes, heart problems and arthritis. He moves around with the help of a walker and takes up to nine medications a day (Lee 2011).

Sanges, who is serving a 15-year sentence at Men's State Prison in Georgia, has cerebral palsy and takes multiple medications twice a day. His condition has worsened since he entered prison in 2005 for aggravated assault against his wife of 48 years. Twice while in prison, he was rushed to the hospital for heart problems (Chen 2009).

"It keeps going up and up," said Alan Adams, director of Health Services for the Georgia Department of Corrections. "We've got some old guys who are too sick to get out of bed. And some of them, they're going to die inside. The courts say we have to provide care and we do. But that costs money" (McCaffrey 2007).

Growth in the American penal population is now a fact of life. Many attribute this growth to a shift in attitudes towards rehabilitation in the 1970s (Applegate et al. 1997; Cullen 2005; Cullen and Gilbert 1982; Cullen and Gendreau 1989; Cullen et al. 2009; Latessa 1999; Logan and Gaes 1993). Others point to trans-formations in criminal justice policy that occurred in the aftermath of the Civil Rights Movement, Woodstock, and events such as Vietnam (Cullen and Gilbert 1982). More recent authors have emphasized the role of the War on Drugs in the 80s and 90s as a primary cause (Mauer and King 2007; Meierhoefer 1992).

We live in an American society that incarcerates more people for a longer duration than any other industrialized Western nation (World Prison Brief, n.d).

The United States has the highest incarceration rate in the world. An unintended consequence has been that now, more than at any other time in the past, the country's elderly and long-term offender numbers are substantial (see Box 1-1). This also means that we are returning to the community greater numbers of offenders that suffer from age-related disorders, which restricts their ability to become self-supporting upon release. Offenders that have been incarcerated for long periods of time, and who are released from prison at ages 50 and older, represent a diverse pool. They are diverse in terms of their life experiences prior to incarceration, the offenses that led to their incarceration, their mental and physical responses to incarceration, and their preparedness for returning to society if released (Maschi and Aday 2014). Despite recognizing that long-term and elderly inmates represent a diverse group, and the Obama administration effort to reduce their numbers in the federal system, we still know very little about them beyond brief reviews of their medical and mental health needs.

Driving Forces for Long-Term and Elderly Increases in Prison Populations

The driving forces for long-term and elderly inmate prison population increases are routed in shifts in sentencing policies that have occurred over the last forty years (see Box 1-2). The 1970s was the decade during which the in-carceration rate began its historic ascent. The decade began with Robert Martinson's claims that "the represent array of correctional treatments has no appreciable effect—positive or negative—on rates of recidivism of convicted offenders," followed by subsequent exclamations that "nothing works" to rehabilitate offenders (Martinson 1972; Martinson 1974). Martinson was not alone; other famous criminologists followed in his wake. Renowned Harvard professor, James Q. Wilson, echoed Martinson by stating in his book *Thinking About Crime* that "It requires not merely optimistic but heroic assumptions about the nature of man to lead one to suppose that a person, finally sentenced after (in most cases) many brushes with the law, and having devoted a good part of his youth and young adulthood to misbehavior of every sort, should, by either the solemnity of prison or the skillfulness of a counselor, come to see the error of his ways and to experience a transformation of his character" (Wilson 1975). What is most clear is that by the end of the decade the ideologies driving criminal justice practices were deterrence and incapacitation, resulting in harsher and longer punishments (Farabee 2005). The result of the shift from rehabilitation

---

Box 1-2. Driving Forces for Increases

- Perception that "nothing works" to rehabilitate
- Push to reduce discretion of judges by implementing sentencing guidelines
- Shift from indeterminate to determinate sentences
- Implementation of truth-in-sentencing laws requiring violent offenders to serve 85 percent of their sentences prior to release on parole
- The abolishment of parole
- Enhanced penalties for drug offenders implemented in the 80s
- Implementation of mandatory minimums

---

to stricter sentences and reductions in the use of probation and parole is referred to as the "penal harm" movement in academic circles (Clear 1994).

At the same time that the "nothing works" movement was gaining momentum, criminal justice policy shifted decision-making from the judicial to the legislative branch of government (Cullen and Gilbert 1982). Prior to 1975 American sentencing policy placed power in the hands of judges via indeterminate sentencing strategies. The government was viewed as a benevolent entity that would only hold its citizens in custodial facilities until they were reformed. In the wake of the Civil Rights Movement and the Vietnam protests, liberals began to view the government and its criminal justice process with suspicion. Judges and parole boards were viewed as biased agents of a corrupt government which did not have its citizens' best interests at heart. For such liberals, it was better to implement determinate sentences, to reduce the discretion of judges and parole boards, and to embed sentencing power within the legislature. The result was an eruption in the late 70s, 80s, and 90s of sentence lengthening by legislation, resulting in truth-in-sentencing, mandatory minimums, "three strikes and you're out" laws, and the abolishment of parole in many states. Calls for deterrence and incapacitation remain in vogue among conservative thinkers today (Farabee 2005; Garland 2001).

If Martinson, Wilson, and the liberals of the 70s are responsible for initiating the transition in sentencing practices toward long-term incarceration, the "war on drugs" initiated in the 80s magnified and enhanced legislative mandates, increasing the odds that criminal activity would result in incarceration (Mauer and King 2007; Meierhoefer 1992). In the 1980s, combating drugs became a number one issue for most politicians in the country. Drug use and distribution were blamed for most social problems (Bennett, Dilulio, and Walters 1996); in particular there was an increase in rhetoric suggesting that drugs were responsible for moral decay in the country and, if left unchecked, would lead to a decline in the nation's status internationally (Bennett, Dilulio, and Walters

1996). Such discourse created a moral panic, and culminated in legislative bodies around the country implementing some of the harshest sanctions for drug offenses, sanctions that in some instances were longer for nonviolent drug users than for violent. Much of the "war on drugs" has been fought against low-level users rather than large-scale distributors (Stevenson 2011). According to a Sentencing Project report, a half million people or more were in local, state, or federal custody for drug offenses (Mauer and King 2007). The federal government led the way by introducing mandatory minimums in 1986 as part of the Anti-Drug Abuse Acts of 1986 and 1988 (Mauer and King 2007). Mandatory minimum states naturally increased the number of offenders subject to incarceration for a drug offense, increased sentence lengths, narrowed the difference in the sentences imposed for violent versus nonviolent drug offenses, and often did not distinguish between leadership and middleman roles in the execution of the offense (Meierhoefer 1992).

As depicted in Table 1-1, a review of sentences today reveals that mandatory minimums for drug offenders remains a primary contributor to mass incarceration. Today, two of every three offenders convicted under a mandatory minimum penalty is a drug offender and close to half of all drug offenders are convicted of an offense carrying a 10-year penalty (Guerino, Harrison, and Sabol 2010). The Federal Bureau of Prisons alone houses more than 92,000 inmates who were subject to mandatory minimum penalties. About half (50%) of federal inmates in 2015 were serving time for drug offenses, 36% for public-order offenses (largely weapons and immigration), and less than 10% each for violent and property offenses (Carson and Anderson 2016). While nearly half of federal inmates were serving time for drug offenses, 53% of state prisoners were serving sentences for violent offenses and 16% (223,300 prisoners) were sentenced for drug related offenses.

Consequences of Long-Term Incarceration

Following in the wake of these shifts in policy and practices, the consequences of long-term incarceration have emerged over the past 10 years as a dominating concern among correctional administrators, and state and federal legislative authorities. The explosion in the use of incarceration has come at a significant cost not just for the offenders, but for society as well. We have witnessed four primary consequences resulting from shifts in sentencing policies: 1) massive increases in the number of offenders entering and remaining incarcerated for long periods of time, 2) escalation in the

Table 1-1. Percent of Sentenced Prisoners under the Jurisdiction of Federal Correctional Authority, by Most Serious Offense, Sex, Race, and Hispanic Origin, September 30, 2015

Most Serious Offense	All Prisoners	Male	Female	White	Black	Hispanic
Total	100	100%	100%	100%	100%	100%
Violent	7.4	7.6	4.1	7	10	2.1
Homicide	1.5	1.5	1.3	0.7	2.4	0.3
Robbery	3.7	3.9	1.6	4.7	5.6	0.9
Other	2.1	2.2	1.2	1.6	2	0.9
Property	6	5.2	18.2	9.6	6.1	2.8
Burglary	0.2	0.2	0.1	0.1	0.4	0
Fraud	4.7	4	15.4	7.6	4.6	2.3
Other	1.1	1	2.7	1.9	1.1	0.4
Drug	49.5	48.9	58.6	39.6	51	57.7
Public order	36.3	37.6	18.3	42.4	32.4	37
Immigration	8	8.4	3.3	0.9	0.3	23.4
Weapons	16.3	17.1	4.3	14.8	25.2	7.7
Other	12	12.1	10.7	26.7	6.9	5.9
Other/unspecified	0.8	0.8	0.7	1.5	0.5	0.4
Total number of sentenced prisoners	185,917	173,857	12,060	50,300	69,000	60,800

Source: Carson, E. & Anderson, e. (2016). Prisoners in 2015. U.S. Department of Justice, Bureau of Justice Statistics.https://www.bjs.gov/content/pub/pdf/p15.pdf.

costs associated with long-term incarceration, 3) increases in questions regarding the continued necessity for long imprisonment terms for aging offenders, and 4) significant concern about our ability to meet the needs of, and to provide services for, those inmates incarcerated for long periods of time and then returned to the community.

Table 1-2. World Prison Population Changes 2000 Compared to 2015

	Estimated Prison Population 2000	Estimated Prison Population Oct. 2015	Change in Prison Population since 2000	Change in National Populations 2000–2015
Africa	902,500	1,038,735	+15.1%	+43.8%
Americas	2,690,300	3,780,528	+40.5%	+17.3%
Asia	3,023,500	3,897,797	+28.9%	17.5%
Europe	2,013,600	1,585,348	−21.3%	+3.3%
Oceania	34,400	54,726	+59.1%	+25.2%
World	8,664,300	10,357,134	+19.5%	+18.2%

Source: Walmsley, R. (2015). World Prison Population List, Institute for Criminal Policy Research. Retrieved January 15, 2017 from http://www.prisonstudies.org/sites/default/files/resources/downloads/world_prison_population_list_11th_edition_0.pdf.

Number of Incarcerated

Countries in the Americas house nearly 36% of the world's prison population (see Table 1-2). The United States has long held the record for incarcerating more of its citizens than any other Western industrialized nation. The U.S. incarceration rate standing at 666 per 100,000 in the population is greater than the rate for countries such as Cuba, Russia, England and Wales, Canada, Japan, Nigeria, and India (see Figures 1-1 and 1-2). In terms of the total number of prisoners, the U.S. houses more prisoners than China, Russia, Brazil and India (see Figure 1-3).

Since the early 1970s, the prison population has soared. At the beginning of the 70s, approximately 200,000 citizens were incarcerated. Between 1970 and 1982, the prison population doubled in size, and then tripled by 1999. This pattern of growth persists today. At the national level, correctional statistics reveal an unprecedented number of offenders, more than 7.1 million, under some form of adult correctional supervision (see Figure 1-4). While the 2015 data represent a decline in correctional populations, one in every 37 adults in the U.S. was under the supervision of an adult correctional authority (Kaeble and Glaze 2016). A third of those under supervision were residing in prisons or local jails. This high rate of incarceration has remained relatively stable for more than 10 years.

**Figure 1-1. Countries with Highest
Incarceration Rates as of October 2015**

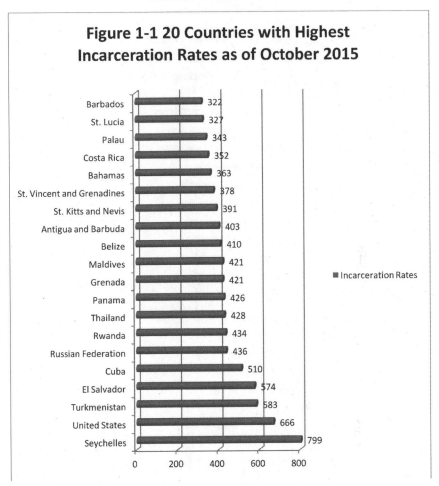

Source: World Prison Brief, Institute for Criminal Policy Research. Retrieved February 15, 2017 from http://www.prisonstudies.org/highest-to-lowest/prison_Population_rate?field_region_taxonomy_tid=All.

Mirroring the incarceration rate, the U.S. imprisonment rate also reflects the overrepresentation of citizens behind prison walls. The 2015 imprisonment rate was 458 sentenced prisoners per 100,000 in the population (see Table 1-3). At the same time, more than half a million inmates were released on parole, with nearly two-thirds of those released offenders expected to recidivate within three years (Carson and Anderson 2016). Another

**Figure 1-2. 20 Countries with the Lowest Incarceration
Rates as of October 2015**

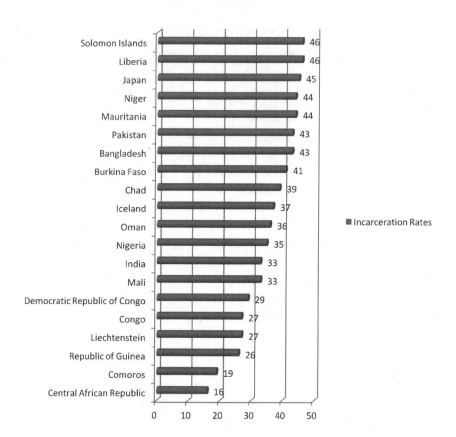

Source: World Prison Brief, Institute for Criminal Policy Research. Retrieved February 15, 2017 from http://www.prisonstudies.org/highest-to-lowest/prison_Population_rate?field_region_taxonomy_tid=All.

startling trend in the data is revealed through analysis of prison release and incarceration data. Since 2000, we have either matched or exceeded the number of releases with prison admissions.

Imprisonment rates are not expected to decline in the future. According to The Pew Center on The States (2007: ii), "imprisonment levels are expected to keep rising in all but four states, reaching a national rate of 562 per 100,000, or one of every 178 Americans. If you put them all together in one place, the incarcerated population in just five years will outnumber the residents of

Figure 1-3. 10 Countries with the Highest Prison Population

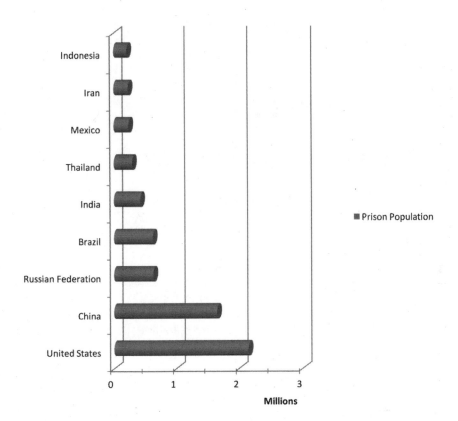

Source: World Prison Brief, Institute for Criminal Policy Research. Retrieved February 15, 2017 from http://www.prisonstudies.org/highest-to-lowest/prison_Population_rate?field_region_taxonomy_tid=All.

Atlanta, Baltimore, and Denver combined." The trends in incarceration continue to reflect a high rate of incarceration that is three times worse than in 1980 (Schmitt, Warner, and Gumpta 2010).

An examination of the punishment rate (ratio of inmates to crime) reveals that all states became more punitive between 1983 and 2013 (The Pew Charitable Trusts 2016). Based on The Pew Charitable Trust's calculation, the U.S. became 165% more punitive between 1983 and 2013 (see Table 1-4). The five most punitive states were in order were Mississippi, Idaho, Louisiana, Virginia, and South Dakota. The states with the lowest punishment rates were

Figure 1-4. Total U.S. Adult Population under Correctional Supervision 2000–2015

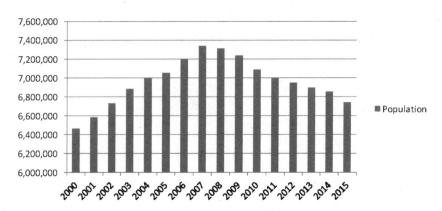

Source: Kaeble, D. and L. Glaze. (2016). Correctional Populations in the United States, 2015. Bureau of Justice Statistics. Retrieved January 15, 2017 from https://www.bjs.gov/content/pub/pdf/cpus15.pdf.

Minnesota, Rhode Island, New Mexico, Washington, and Maine (see Table 1-4). Thus, the U.S. punishment orientation remains high.

The High Costs of Incarceration

The costs associated with the incarceration and supervision of large numbers of inmates are immense. As indicated in Figure 1-5, Real government expenditures on the criminal justice system grew by 74% between 1993 and 2012, to $274 billion (Council of Economic Advisors 2016, p.10). State correctional budgets have risen over the last twenty years. By 2012, federal and state correctional agencies were spending nearly $83 billion per year on adult and juvenile corrections (Council of Economic Advisors 2016, p.43).

In 2008, federal, state and local governments spent close to $75 billion on corrections (Schmitt, Warner, and Gumpta 2010: 102). State prison costs per U.S. resident more than doubled between 1986 and 2001 (Stephan 2004). The average annual operating cost per state inmate in 2001 was $22,650, or $62.05 per day. Among facilities operated by the Federal Bureau of Prisons, it was $22,632 per inmate, or $62.01 per day (Stephan 2004). Recent projections suggest that correctional agencies will need an additional $27.5 billion over

Table 1-3. Total Number of Sentenced Prisoners and Incarceration Rates 2000–2015

Year	Number Sentenced Prisoners	Incarceration Rate
2005	1,462,866	492
2006	1,504,660	501
2007	1,532,850	506
2008	1,547,742	506
2009	1,550,196	504
2010	1,543,206	500
2011	1,538,847	492
2012	1,511,497	480
2013	1,520,403	478
2014	1.507,781	471
2015	1,476,847	458

Source: Carson, E.A. (2016). Prisoners in 2015. U.S. Department of Justice, Bureau of Justice Statistics. Retrieved January 10. 2017 from https://www.bjs.gov/content/pub/pdf/p15.pdf.

the next five years to accommodate both the agency needs and those of the offenders under their supervision (The Pew Center 2007).

Schmitt, Warner, and Gumpta (2010) have calculated the cost savings that would occur upon shifting priorities from incarceration to probation and supervision in the community. "… for each non-violent offender shifted from prison or jail (at an average cost of about $25,500 to $26,000 per year) to probation or parole (at average cost of $1,300 to $2,800 per year), government corrections systems would save $23,000 to $25,000 per inmate per year. Given the mix of prisoners by offense type (see Box 1-3), a 50 percent reduction in non-violent-offender inmates would save the federal government about $2.1 billion per year, state governments about $7.6 billion per year, and local governments about $7.2 billion per year, even after factoring in additional probation and parole costs. Across all three levels of government, these savings total $16.9 billion or about 22.8 percent of the total national spending on

Table 1-4. The Punishment Rate

Punishment Rate Shifts State Rankings
Virginia, Wyoming, Pennsylvania among those higher on punitiveness scale

State	2013 Punishment Rate	Punishment Rank	Imprisonment Rank	2013 Imprisonment Rate
Mississippi	818	1	2	692
Idaho	808	2	11	466
Louisiana	734	3	1	847
Virginia	732	4	17	446
South Dakota	665	5	21	428
Kentucky	644	6	12	462
Oklahoma	622	7	3	659
Wyoming	621	8	22	395
Alabama	610	9	4	647
Texas	591	10	5	602
Pennsylvania	574	11	23	391
Arizona	559	12	6	586
Connecticut	541	13	34	338
Wisconsin	541	14	27	370
West Virginia	533	15	28	367
Michigan	530	16	19	441
Missouri	526	17	10	521
Florida	524	18	9	524
Georgia	511	19	8	533
Arkansas	507	20	7	578
Indiana	506	21	14	454
Ohio	495	22	16	446
Illinois	482	23	26	377
United States	477			417
Colorado	469	24	25	384
Montana	463	25	30	357

Nevada	443	26	13	460
Delaware	432	27	18	442
New York	427	28	38	271
Oregon	426	29	24	385
Vermont	411	30	43	251
Iowa	409	31	37	279
New Jersey	407	32	42	252
Tennessee	407	33	20	438
California	405	34	32	353
Maryland	392	35	33	353
South Carolina	388	36	15	447
North Carolina	372	37	31	356
Kansas	363	38	35	328
Alaska	348	39	29	364
Nebraska	333	40	39	263
New Hampshire	321	41	45	215
North Dakota	317	42	46	211
Hawaii	279	43	40	257
Utah	279	44	44	242
Massachusetts	271	45	48	192
Minnesota	264	46	49	189
Rhode Island	259	47	47	194
New Mexico	253	48	36	321
Washington	237	49	41	256
Maine	231	50	50	148

Source: The Pew Charitable Trust (2016). Punishment Rate Measures Prison Use Relative to Crime. Retrieved February 19, 2017 from http://www.pewtrusts.org/en/research-and-analysis/issue-briefs/2016/03/the-punishment-rate.

Formula: Imprisonment Rate y / (Murder Rate y * Murder Wt y) + (Rape Rate y * Rape Wt y) + (Robbery Rate y * Robbery Wt y) + (Assault Rate y * Assault Wt y) + (Burglary Rate y * Burglary Wt y) + (Larceny Rate y * Larceny Wt y) + (Motor Vehicle Theft Rate y * Motor Vehicle Theft Wt y)

Figure 1-5. Criminal Justice Spending, 1993–2012

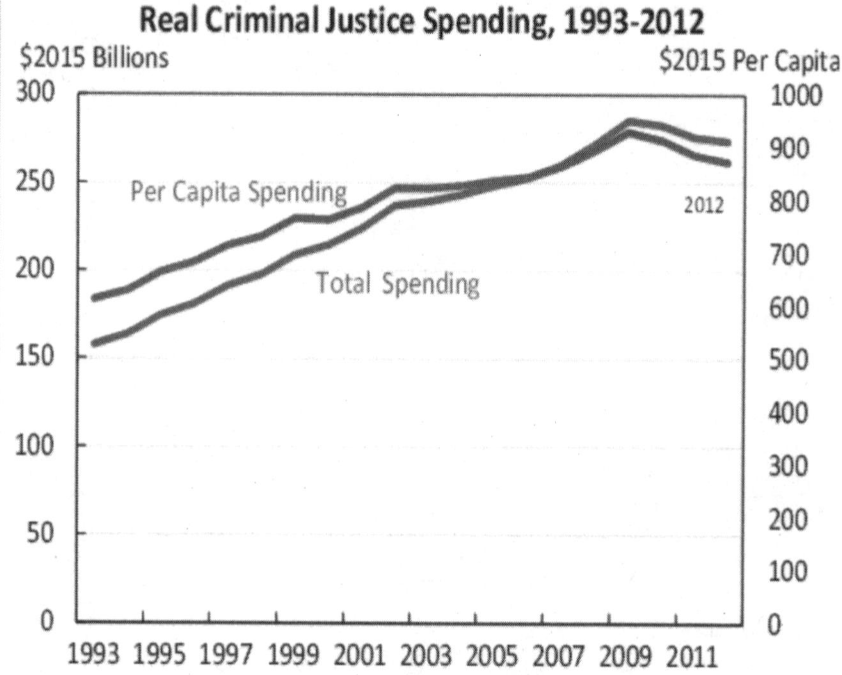
Real Criminal Justice Spending, 1993-2012
$2015 Billions
$2015 Per Capita
300
250
200
150
100
50
0
1000
900
800
700
600
500
400
300
200
100
0
Per Capita Spending
Total Spending
2012
1993 1995 1997 1999 2001 2003 2005 2007 2009 2011

Note: Direct Expenditures in 2015 dollars included, intergovernmental transfers excluded.
Source: Bureau of Justice Statistics, "Expenditure and Employment Extract" series.

Source: Council of Economic Advisers Report: Economic Perspectives on Incarceration and the Justice System. Executive Office of the President of the United States (2016). Retrieved January 18, 2017 from https://obamawhitehouse.archives.gov/sites/whitehouse.gov/files/documents/CEA%2BCriminal%2BJustice%2BReport.pdf.

corrections in 2008" (Schmitt, Warner, and Gumpta 2010: 103). Unfortunately, while such aggregate measures of correctional spending reveal continuous increases, the reality is that, at the state level, correctional budgets are on a downward trend given the numbers of inmates they are expected to house.

More recent assessments of the costs and benefits of punishment policies continue to suggest that the costs of incarceration might outweigh the benefits. The Obama Administration Economic Council report (see Table 1-5) indicates that investment in police and education are more cost effective than policies emphasizing incarceration and sentencing.

Box 1-3. What Would Happen If We Shifted Half of Nonviolent Offenders from Prison?

"... for each non-violent offender shifted from prison or jail (at an average cost of about $25,500 to $26,000 per year) to probation or parole (at average cost of $1,300 to $2,800 per year), government corrections systems would save $23,000 to $25,000 per inmate per year. Given the mix of prisoners by offense type (see Table 3), a 50 percent reduction in non-violent-offender inmates would save the federal government about $2.1 billion per year, state governments about $7.6 billion per year, and local governments about $7.2 billion per year, even after factoring in additional probation and parole costs. Across all three levels of government, these savings total $16.9 billion or about 22.8 percent of the total national spending on corrections in 2008."

Source: Schmitt, J., K. Warner, and S. Gupta. (2010). The High Budgetary Cost of Incarceration. *Real-world Economics Review* (53): 11.

The Elderly in Prison

Life in prison can challenge anyone, but it can be particularly hard for people whose bodies and minds are being whittled away by age. Prisons in the United States contain an ever growing number of aging men and women who cannot readily climb stairs, haul themselves to the top bunk, or walk long distances to meals or the pill line; whose old bones suffer from thin mattresses and winter's cold; who need wheelchairs, walkers, canes, portable oxygen, and hearing aids; who cannot get dressed, go to the bathroom, or bathe without help; and who are incontinent, forgetful, suffering chronic illnesses, extremely ill, and dying (Human Rights Watch 2012: 4).

At the same time that correctional costs are skyrocketing, the number of long-term inmates is increasing, and aging effects are beginning to be noticed. "Human Rights Watch calculates that the number of sentenced federal and state prisoners who are age 65 or older grew an astonishing 94 times faster than the total sentenced prisoner population between 2007 and 2010. The older prison population increased by 63 percent, while the total prison population grew by 0.7 percent during the same period" (Human Rights Watch 2012: 6). These older prisoners bring with them medical expenditures that are three to eight times higher than for non-elderly inmates. Their medical problems are more likely to be chronic, disabling, and terminal. More important, mobility impairments, hearing and vision loss, and cognitive limitations including dementia are the norm for this population rather than the anomaly.

Table 1-5. Costs and Benefits of Criminal Justice Policies

	Number of Studies	Percent of Studies	
		Consider Indirect or Collateral Consequences	Cost-Effective Policy
Police	6	17%	83%
Incarceration	7	43%	29%
Sentencing	5	40%	20%
Education	9	67%	100%

Note: Estimates are derived from economics studies that focus on the United States and conduct cost-benefit analyses. The studies differ in policy setting, outcomes, time frame and methodological approaches. Conclusions about the cost-effectiveness of policies are taken from the analysis and expertise of the authors in each study.

Sources: **Police:** Levitt 1997; Cohen and Ludwig 2003; Evans and Owens 2007; Caetano and Maheshri 2013; Chalfin and McCrary 2013; DeAngelo and Hansen 2014.
Incarceration: Levitt 1996; Spelman 2000; Kuziemko and Levitt 2004; Spelman 2005; Donohue 2009; Hjalmarsson 2009b; Lofstrom and Raphael 2013.
Sentencing: Owens 2009; Helland and Tabarrok 2007; Iyengar 2008; Kuziemko 2013; Mueller-Smith 2015.
Education: Donohue and Siegelman 1998; Reynolds et al. 2001; Lochner, 2004; Lochner and Moretti 2004; Schweinhart et al. 2005; Belfield et al. 2006; CPPRG 2007; Deming 2009b; Oreopoulos and Salvanes 2011; Anderson 2014.

Source: Council of Economic Advisers Report: Economic Perspectives on Incarceration and the Justice System. Executive Office of the President of the United States (2016). Retrieved January 18, 2017 from https://obamawhitehouse.archives.gov/sites/whitehouse.gov/files/documents/CEA%2BCriminal%2BJustice%2BReport.pdf.

What do elderly inmates deserve during incarceration? We are only now analyzing and trying to answer this question. As depicted in Box 1-4, the elderly in prison are entitled to some basic level of care, but this care comes at a high cost.

Questioning the Need to Incarcerate Elderly Inmates

Given the expense associated with incarcerating elderly inmates, a natural question arises as to the utility of incarceration for this population. Just

Box 1-4. What Do The Elderly in Prison Deserve?	
Right to safe conditions of confinement	e.g., not having to live in a dorm with younger persons prone to violence and extortion
Right to decent conditions of confinement	e.g., extra blankets and clothing in winter because it is harder to stay warm e.g., receiving age-appropriate educational, recreational, and vocational opportunities
Right to accommodations for mobility disability	e.g., staff disciplinary responses must be adjusted in recognition of the fact that the inmate is not engaging in willful disobedience
Right to accommodations for mental disability	e.g., providing staff or inmate aides who can help change
Right to personal hygiene care	e.g., clothes and cleanup for a cell when there is an "accident" due to incontinence

what do we achieve as a society by incarcerating offenders age 50 and older? Elderly inmates tend to fall into two categories: 1) offenders whose criminal careers started late in life; and 2) those life-course-persistent offenders who started early, and continue criminal involvement throughout the life course. For this first group of elderly first time offenders, criminality has been traced back to life stressors and lack of opportunity to address needs via prosocial means. The latter group includes an opportunistic group of offenders who will "seize the day" whenever an opportunity for an easy payoff occurs. Regardless of which group we discuss, the research tells us that most offenders age out of crime (Heimer and Matsueda 1994; Giordano et al. 2007; Jolin and Gibbons 1987; Sampson and Laub 1993). If elderly offenders are less likely to recidivate, and are perhaps more expensive than younger inmates, then the time has come for society to reconsider its options with regard to the elderly inmate population.

Why Write This Book?

Over the last few years, many states have experienced dramatic increases in prison populations as a result of changes in sentencing policies. Illinois, for example, followed this national trend and implemented determinate sentences for many offenses in 1978, and stiffer drug penalties as part of the state's "War on Drugs" sanctions in the 1980s. Consequently, such policy changes have contributed to the growth in the number of inmates serving long-term sentences, have increased the number of geriatric inmates, have created more overcrowding, have increased the costs of corrections, and have led to reductions in the ability of state departments of correction to provide rehabilitative programming in institutions.

The problems associated with long-term incarceration were not unique to Illinois. Many other states were grappling with the lengthy incarceration sentences imposed for crimes, and the mental, physical, and economic costs of long-term incarceration policies. These states were also seeking solutions, but had not invested in attempts to understand the nature and scope of the problem. Thus, we felt it important to offer our findings to a broader audience.

Moreover, despite the significant problems associated with long-term incarceration, there was little comprehensive discussion or literature available on the long-term and elderly offender population. While several authors called for changes in policy, few of those changes were based on the research literature available. Many of the articles would provide descriptions of problems, but offered little in the way of what to consider when thinking about changing correctional practices. Thus, this book seeks to fill this gap.

Moreover, while addressing the problems of elderly and long-term prisoners is the fiscally responsible thing to do in this day and age, change is also mandated on moral and ethical grounds. Neglected in discussions about what should be done for long-term, elderly prisoners is that there is an underlying moral and ethical imperative related to our relationships with each other and the provision of care which also substantiates calls for change. The research literature has provided a laundry list of practices that could be implemented to address and improve conditions for elderly prisoners based on expense (Human Rights Watch 2012; ACLU 2012). We need something other than the cost-based analytic approaches to justify alternative sentencing policies and changes in institutional practices for elderly and long-term prisoners as age-related declines in physical and mental health occur. What is missing is a framework which moves beyond a focus on costs to one which strikes at the heart of what 'good care' and ethical care means in practice. Care is (an) activity that includes everything that we do to maintain, continue, and repair our 'world' so that we can live in it as well as possible (Fisher and Tronto 1990; p. 40). From the ethics of care perspective, how we care for one another is an essential feature of what makes us human and gives us a meaningful life by focusing on the actions and practices that constitute the ethic of care. The ethics of care approach serves as an analytical, ethical guide about how and whether we should continue to punish during that most vulnerable period towards the end of human life. Thus, this book situates the need for reform within an ethic of care paradigm.

Purpose and Organization

The purpose of this book is to provide criminal justice professionals, academics, and students with a concise review of the literature available on the issues facing long-term and elderly inmates and the departments of correction that house them. The book also presents background information on the basic issues that policy makers should consider when addressing matters associated with long-term and elderly incarceration practices. The first three chapters present an overview of the long-term and elderly inmate issues. The following five articles review specific programs that have been instituted to address the needs of long-term inmates. Each chapter reviews current research literature on programs and, where possible, discusses some of the barriers to implementing programs in the correctional system at the state and federal level. The book concludes with recommendations concerning the steps that correctional agencies should take when considering changing management practices for long-term and elderly inmates.

Chapter 2 introduces the reader to the fundamental concepts and basic issues associated with long-term inmates. The chapter defines the terminology associated with long-term incarceration and provides a description of the long-term inmate population. The chapter highlights differences between male and female long-term inmates and presents some of the unique policy challenges inherent in these populations.

Chapter 3 examines the problems that exist for elderly inmates. The chapter begins by discussing the difficulties of defining the population of elderly inmates. The chapter reviews the literature that identifies age 50 as the age where an inmate can be considered elderly and its relationship to the much higher age cutoff for the non-incarcerated general population. The chapter offers insight into the differences between elderly male and female inmates and provides an overview of the complex nature of this incarcerated population.

Chapter 4 describes the major medical issues experienced by long-term and elderly inmates, including the disease typology present in the long-term and elderly inmate population. The moral and legal obligations of the state are explored in detail. The chapter also imparts information on current medical practices unique to elderly inmates.

Chapter 5 focuses on the mental health needs of elderly inmates. The chapter describes the most common mental health issues present within the population. The chapter explores differences in mental health between male and female inmates. A significant section of the chapter is devoted to correctional policy regarding mental health.

A common concern among inmate populations is the level and rate of victimization during incarceration. Chapter 6 reviews the level and types of victimization experienced by long-term and elderly inmates.

In Chapter 7, the focus shifts to a review of existing state practices and programs for elderly inmates. Common practices for alleviating costs and justifications for early release are considered.

The final chapter presents a summary of findings. The burdens experienced by long-term and elderly prisoners during their incarceration become the fiscal and social obligations of society at large upon their release. Policies must change if we are to reduce such costs. We cannot and should not subject elderly prisoners to the same programmatic requirements as their younger counterparts. The previous chapters will identify the needs and review some of the approaches; yet the stark reality is that despite this knowledge base few states have fully embraced the changes identified by scholars in the social sciences and medical professions. The reason for this is probably because cost alone does not alleviate political concerns. Perhaps continuing to situate this research evidence as a larger moral imperative will carry some weight and get administrators, advocates, and everyday citizens to push for reform.

Websites

For more information on the costs to incarcerate and correctional policy, visit www.pewtrusts.org.

For more information on world prison population, visit http://www.prisonstudies.org/sites/default/files/resources/downloads/world_prison_population-_list_11th_edition_0.pdf.

For more information on the profile of U.S. prisoners, visit https://www.bjs.gov/.

For more information on U.S. sentencing policy, visit http://www.sentencingproject.org/.

References

ACLU (2012). At America's expense: The mass incarceration of the elderly. American Civil Liberties Union. Retrieved March 12, 2013 from http://www.aclu.org/files/assets/elderlyprisonreport_20120613_1.pdf.

Applegate, B. K., Cullen, F. T., & Fisher, B. (1997). Public support for correctional treatment: The continuing appeal of the rehabilitative ideal. *Prison Journal*, 77(3), 237–258.

Bennett, W. J., DiIulio, J. J., & Walters J. P. (1996). *Body count: Moral poverty and how to win America's war against crime and drugs.* New York, NY: Simon and Schuster.

Bureau of Justice Statistics, Justice Expenditure and Employment Extracts (2011). *Key facts at a glance: Direct expenditures by criminal justice function, 1982–2007.* Retrieved January 9, 2013 from http://bjs.ojp.usdoj.gov/content/glance/tables/exptyptab.cfm.

Carson, E. & Anderson, e. (2016). *Prisoners in 2015.* U.S. Department of Justice, Bureau of Justice Statistics. Retrieved from https://www.bjs.gov/content/pub/pdf/p15.pdf.

Chen, S. (2009). Prison health-care costs rise as inmates grow older and sicker. Retrieved from http://articles.cnn.com/2009-11-13/justice/aging.inmates_1_prison-inmate-largest-prison-systems-medical-costs?_s=PM:CRIME.

Clear, T. R. (1994). *Harm in American penology: Offenders, victims, and their communities.* Albany, NY: State University of New York Press.

Council of Economic Advisers Report: Economic Perspectives on Incarceration and the Justice System. Executive Office of the President of the United States (2016). Retrieved January 18, 2017 from https://obamawhitehouse.archives.gov/sites/whitehouse.gov/files/documents/CEA%2BCriminal%2BJustice%2BReport.pdf.

Cullen, F. T. (2005). The twelve people who saved rehabilitation: How the science of criminology made a difference. *Criminology,* 43(1), 1–42.

Cullen, F. T., & Gilbert, K. E. (1982). *Reaffirming rehabilitation.* Cincinnati, OH: Anderson.

Cullen, F. T., Smith, P., Lowenkamp, C., & Latessa E. (2009). Nothing works revisited: Deconstructing Farabee's rethinking rehabilitation. *Victim and Offenders Journal of Evidence-Based Policies and Practices,* 4, 101–123.

Cullen, F. T., & Gendreau, P. (1989). The effectiveness of correctional rehabilitation: Reconsidering the "nothing works" debate. In L. Goodstein and D. MacKenzie (Eds.), *American Prisons: Issues in Research and Policy* (pp. 23–44). New York, NY: Plenum Press.

Farabee, D. (2005). *Rethinking rehabilitation: Why can't we reform our criminals?* Washington, DC: American Enterprise Institute.

Fisher, B. & Tronto, J. (1990). Toward a feminist theory of caring. In E. Abel and M. Nelson (Eds.) *Circles of Care*, SUNY Press (pp. 36–54). Albany: New York.

Garland, D. (2001). *The culture of control.* Chicago, IL: University of Chicago.

Giordano, P. C., Schroeder, R. D., & Cernkovich, S. A. (2007). Emotions and crime over the life course: A neo-median perspective on criminal continuity and change. *American Journal of Sociology,* 112, 1603–61.

Glaze, L., & Bonczar, T. P. (2006). *Probation and parole in the United States, 2005* (Report No. NCJ 215091). Retrieved from U.S. Department of Justice, Bureau of Justice Statistics website: http://bjs.ojp.usdoj.gov/content/pub/pdf/ppus05.pdf.

Glaze, L. (2011). *Correctional Populations in the U.S., 2010* (Report No. NCJ 236319). Retrieved from U.S. Department of Justice, Bureau of Justice Statistics website: http://bjs.ojp.usdoj.gov/content/pub/pdf/cpus10.pdf.

Guerino, P., Harrison, P., & Sabol, W. (2011). *Prisoners in 2010.* Retrieved from U.S. Department of Justice, Bureau of Justice Statistics website: http://www.bjs.gov/content/pub/pdf/p10.pdf.

Harrison, P. M., & Beck, A. J. (2006). *Prisoners in 2005* (Report No. NCJ 215092). Retrieved from U.S. Department of Justice, Bureau of Justice Statistics webpage: http://bjs.ojp.usdoj.gov/content/pub/ascii/p05.txt.

Heimer, K. & Matsueda, R. L. (1994). Role taking, role commitment, and delinquency: A theory of differential social control. *American Sociological Review,* 59, 365–390.

Human Rights Watch. (2012). Old behind bars: The aging prison population in the United States. Retrieved from http://www.hrw.org/sites/default/files/reports/usprisons0112webwcover_0.pdf.

Jolin, A. & Gibbons, D. (1987). Age patterns in criminal involvement. *International Journal of Offender Therapy and Comparative Criminology* 31, 237–260.

Kaeble, D. and L. Glaze. (2016). Correctional Populations in the United States, 2015. Bureau of Justice Statistics. Retrieved January 15, 2017 from https://www.bjs.gov/content/pub/pdf/cpus15.pdf.

Langan, P. & Levin, D. (2002). *Recidivism of prisoners released in 1994.* Washington, DC: U.S. Department of Justice, Bureau of Justice Statistics.

Latessa, E. (1999). What works in correctional interventions. *Southern Illinois University Law Journal,* 23, 415–426.

Lee, R. (2011, May 16). Elderly inmates are putting a burden on Texas taxpayers: A growing burden. *Houston Chronicle.* Retrieved from http://www.chron.

com/news/houston-texas/article/Elderly-inmates-are-putting-a-burden-on-Texas-1693376.php.

Logan, C. H. & Gaes, G. G. (1993). Meta-analysis and the rehabilitation of punishment. *Justice Quarterly,* 10, 245–263.

Martinson, R. (1972a). Paradox of prison reform. *The New Republic,* 166.

Martinson, R. (1974b). What works?—Questions and answers about prison reform. *The Public Interest,* 22–54.

Mauer, M. & King, R. S. (2007). *A 25-year quagmire: The war on drugs and its impact on American society.* Retrieved from the sentencing project website: http://www.sentencingproject.org/doc/publications/dp_25yearquagmire.pdf.

McCaffrey, S. (2007). Aging Inmates Clogging Nation's Prisons. Associated Press. Retrieved from http://abclocal.go.com/wpvi/story?section=news/national_world&id=5682003.

Meierhoefer, B. S. (1992). *The general effect of mandatory minimum prison terms: A longitudinal study of federal sentences imposed.* Washington, DC: Federal Judicial Center. Retrieved from http:://www.fjc.gov/public/pdf.nsf/lookup/geneffmm.pdf/$file/geneffmm.pdf.

Sampson, R. & Laub, J. (1993). *Crime in the making: Pathways and turning points through life.* Cambridge, MA: Harvard University Press.

Schmitt, J., Warner, K., & Gupta, S. (2010). The high budgetary cost of incarceration. *Real-world Economics Review,* No. 53. Retrieved from Center for Economic and Policy Research website: http://www.cepr.net/index.php/publications/reports/the-high-budgetary-cost-of-incarceration/.

Stephan, J. (2004). *State Prison Expenditures, 2001* (Report No. NCJ 202949) Washington, DC: U.S. Department of Justice, Bureau of Justice Statistics. Retrieved from http://bjs.ojp.usdoj.gov/content/pub/ascii/spe01.txt.

Stevenson, B. (2011). Drug Policy, Criminal Justice, and Mass Imprisonment. Global Commission on Drug Policies. Retrieved from http://www.globalcommissionondrugs.org/wp-content/themes/gcdp_v1/pdf/Global_Com_Bryan_Stevenson.pdf.

The Pew Charitable Trusts, Public Safety Performance Project. (2007). *Public Safety, Public Spending: Forecasting America's Prison Population 2007–2011.* Retrieved from http://www.pewstates.org/uploadedFiles/PCS_Assets/2007/Public%20Safety%20Public%20Spending.pdf.

United States Sentencing Commission. (2011). *Executive Summary: Report to Congress: Mandatory minimum penalties in the Federal Criminal Justice System* (p. xxxiii). Washington, DC: Author. Retrieved from http://www.ussc.gov/Legislative_and_Public_Affairs/Congressional_Testimony_and_Reports/Mandatory_Minimum_Penalties/20111031_RtC_PDF/Executive_Summary.pdf.

USA Today (2004). Elderly Inmates Swell Prisons, Driving Up Health Care Costs. USA Today. Retrieved from http://usatoday30.usatoday.com/news/nation/2004-02-28-elderly-inmates_x.htm.

Walmsley, R. (2015). World Prison Population List, Institute for Criminal Policy Research. Retrieved January 15, 2017 from http://www.prisonstudies.org/sites/default/files/resources/downloads/world_prison_population_list_11th_edition_0.pdf.

Wilson, James Q. (1975). *Thinking About Crime* (p. 170). New York, NY: Basic Books.

World Prison Brief, Institute for Criminal Policy Research. Retrieved February 15, 2017 from http://www.prisonstudies.org/highest-to-lowest/prison_Population_rate?field_region_taxonomy_tid=All.

Chapter 2

Who Are the Long-Term Inmates? What Are the Costs? What Are Their Needs?

Three decades after the war on crime began, the United States has developed a prison-industrial complex—a set of bureaucratic, political, and economic interests that encourage increased spending on imprisonment, regardless of the actual need (Schlosser 1998: 4).

When the War on Drugs began, few considered possible secondary and tertiary effects beyond the more immediate impact of lowering the crime rate. Mandatory sentences combined with "get tough" legislation showed a secondary effect, however—a dramatic increase in the incarceration rate, primarily among women and minorities. While numerous authors have commented on this by product of the "get tough" stance, few have taken into account the other side of the equation, namely the long-term effect of longer sentences and mandatory life imprisonment. So not only did we incarcerate more people, we incarcerated them for longer, and more often for life. This very foreseeable but often overlooked consequence created an elderly, long-term prison population with all of the concomitant mental health and geriatric side effects.

This is uniquely an American problem. The United States comprises only five percent of the world's population, yet houses 25 percent of the world's prisoners (Petteruti 2011). Until the mid-1970s, the American imprisonment rate had been stable for at least half a century at approximately 100 inmates per 100,000 in both state and federal populations (Blumstein and Cohen 1973). Between 1970 and 2006, the incarceration rate grew from 96 per 100,000 to 501 per 100,000 (Greenfeld and Langan 1987; Sabol, Couture, and Harrison 2007). Consequently, one in 99 adults finds himself or herself behind bars (Warren

2008). The outcome of our high incarceration rate is that at present nearly 1.6 million people are incarcerated in state and federal prisons and eight states plus the Federal Bureau of Prisons are operating at more than 100 percent of their rated capacity (Carson and Sabol 2012). Resolution of these increases in imprisonment is not expected any time soon, given an expansion rate of two percent per year in federal and state prison populations (Justice Policy 2009).

An inescapable fact is that we continue to spend on imprisonment without reflection, i.e., regardless of whether it is in our best interest to do so (Aos 2008; Schlosser 1998; Wright, 2010). Schlosser (1998: 4) quoted the head of the National Criminal Justice Commission as saying that "If crime is going up, then we need to build more prisons; and if crime is going down, it's because we built more prisons—and building even more prisons will therefore drive crime down even lower." This logic seems somewhat tautological and misplaced considering the United States incarceration rate remains high despite falling crime rates (Aos 2008). Critics question the value of imprisonment, noting that the current system of incarceration is overly punitive and produces fewer benefits than were assumed in the 1980s and 1990s (Johnson and Raphael 2010; Liedka, Piehl, and Useem 2006; Okafo 2009; Vincent and Hofer 1994).

How did we get here—to a juxtaposition where we incarcerate more people, incarcerate them for longer, and incarcerate them with little perceived benefit? Schlosser (1998) contends the prison industrial complex grew essentially as a result of the politics of fear. Coming out of the 1970s liberals and conservatives, albeit for different reasons, agreed that it was in the best interest of the country to implement determinate sanctions (see Cullen and Gilbert (1982) for complete overview), and to limit discretionary decision making for release (Allen 1981; Garland 2001; Schulhofer 1993). Other academics and politicians in the 1980s and 1990s made claims that America had fallen into moral decay, and that citizens would fall prey to predators unless firm steps were taken to remove them from society (Baum 1997; Bennett, DiIulio, and Walters 1996; DiIulio 1996; Gray 2000; Schlosser 1998). Add to the mix the determinate sanctions advocated by the War on Drugs, and the end result is that offenders are serving longer sentences for an ever-increasing number of offenses (Camp and Camp 2000).

To understand the current predicament, we must define and explore the history over the last forty years. There is pertinent literature on long-term inmates bearing on the changing nature of this population. The long-term incarceration trends over the last thirty years also illuminate the present situation. Both literature and trends lead to a definition of exactly what constructs constitute a long-term inmate. By reviewing the distribution of long-term inmates across the country, we can establish a context for discussion of the costs of incarceration and the problems long-term inmates face upon release.

Defining Long-Term Inmates

The challenge of defining any subset of humans is determining who belongs and who does not. Population boundaries within corrections institutions are difficult to set because to be effective the boundary must narrow the scope in such a way as to delineate an accurate number of individuals within a specific correctional population. Another major impediment in defining correctional populations is that specific populations vary tremendously in their stability. Some populations remain relatively static, while others fluctuate dramatically over the same time period. From an ecological perspective, prisons are an open system whose population varies in size depending on the time period studied, the type of institution, and the goals of the research project. For example, the number of death row inmates will change more slowly than the number of inmates with long sentences for other types of violent crimes. Unfortunately, a uniform definition for long-term inmate does not exist (Flanagan 1992). The lack of a uniform definition has hampered the ability of scholars and advocates to discuss the challenges and to make corresponding policy modifications.

The size of the long-term inmate population varies significantly across time as a result of changes in sentencing and release practices (see Figure 2-1). Vincent and Hofer (1994) place much of the blame for increases in long-term inmates, and the corresponding diversity among this population on the shift to mandatory sentences. A review of correctional populations prior to the 1980s reveals that the majority of offenders serving long sentences were incarcerated for very serious violent offenses such as murder and kidnapping. An examination of the inmate population today uncovers a much more heterogeneous population comprised of young, nonviolent, and often repeat offenders (Flanagan, Clark, Aziz, and Szelest 1989; MacKenzie and Goodstein 1985). The current economic crisis is also likely to result in shifts in the nature of long-term incarceration as correctional officials respond to reductions in state budgets, focus on maximizing operational efficiency, and change practices in the search for cost savings (Scott-Hayward 2009).

Snapshot: National Estimates of the Long-Term Offender Population

At the start of 2012, 492 out of every 100,000 U.S. residents were sentenced to more than one year in prison (Carson and Sable 2012), and about 1 in every 107 adults was incarcerated in prison or jail (Glaze and Parks 2012). While the

Figure 2-1. Number of People Serving Life Sentences, 1984–2012

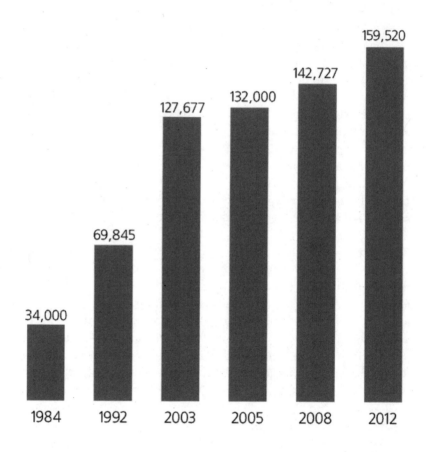

Number of People Serving Life Sentences, 1984-2012

THE SENTENCING PROJECT

greatest share of offenders serve two years or less, a small but significant percentage of offenders are serving prison sentences of five years or more.

Table 2-1 presents the national average time served by type of crime for first time releases. Offenders are serving the longest sentences nationally for serious violent crimes. According to the Pew Center the aggregate average

Table 2-1. National Trends Average Time Served First Releases

Offense	'93	'94	'95	'96	'97	'98	'99	'00	'01	'02	'03	'04	'05	'06	'07	'08	'09
Violent offenses	36	36	37	39	41	43	45	47	49	49	31	31	50	50	50	52	52
Homicide	60	60	61	64	67	73	75	83	89	93	83	87	101	103	107	110	118
Nonnegligent manslaughter	81	79	79	84	89	96	97	104	112	117	110	113	133	136	143	148	159
Murder	93	88	88	94	98	104	101	111	119	124	113	118	140	144	154	160	175
Nonnegligent manslaughter	50	51	60	62	66	74	81	85	92	97	96	101	108	109	109	109	111
Negligent manslaughter	36	39	41	41	42	46	49	51	54	58	45	46	55	55	53	53	55
Unspecified homicide	58	69	55	69	55	35	36	44	49	43	39	58	68	66	70	68	72
Kidnaping	41	43	43	43	48	50	52	53	58	55	33	34	56	59	60	62	65
Rape	57	57	59	60	63	67	72	76	82	81	68	68	86	87	92	95	94
Other sexual assault	33	35	36	39	40	42	41	42	44	45	35	36	48	49	49	51	52
Robbery	38	38	38	40	43	46	48	50	55	55	40	40	57	56	56	57	57
Assault	23	24	26	27	30	31	33	32	34	32	20	20	32	32	32	33	32
Other violent	20	20	20	22	21	21	23	23	24	24	17	16	23	24	23	25	24
Property offenses	17	19	20	22	24	25	24	24	26	24	14	14	22	22	21	21	21
Drug offenses	16	17	18	20	21	22	22	22	23	23	15	15	22	21	21	21	21
Public-order offenses	13	14	16	17	18	19	19	20	20	19	13	14	20	20	21	21	21

Source: National Corrections Reporting Program, 1990–2009. Bureau of Justice Statistics.

Table 2-2. States with the Highest Percent Increases in Time Served between 1990 and 2009

State	Percent Increase
Florida	166
Virginia	91
North Carolina	86
Oklahoma	83
Michigan	79
Georgia	75

Source: Modified from Table. 1, pg. 13 in the Pew Center on the States. (2012). Time Served: The high cost, low return of longer prison terms.

time served across the states increased by 36 percent between 1990 and 2009 (The Pew Center on the States 2012). Six states (Florida, Virginia, North Carolina, Oklahoma, Michigan and Georgia) experienced 75 percent or greater increases in average sentence lengths during this same time period (see Table 2-2).

Analyses of state-by-state sentence lengths reveals large numbers incarcerated with prison sentences of 20 years or more. A few state-level examples are discussed here. As depicted in Table 2-3, Pennsylvania experienced increases in all but one of its long-term prisoner categories. A 2015 study conducted by the Texas Department of Criminal Justice revealed that more than 31,892 prisoners were serving sentences of 21 to 60 or more years, 6,296 had life sentences, 768 had life without parole, and 249 prisoners were sitting on death row (Texas Department of Criminal Justice 2015). Twenty-six percent of the South Carolina prison population is serving sentences of 20 years or more according to 2016 data (South Carolina Department of Corrections 2016).

In a number of states inmates who commit violent, property, and drug offenses serve more time for these offenses now than they did back in the early 1990s (The Pew Charitable Trusts 2015). As revealed in Table 2-4, inmates in California, Florida, Georgia, Michigan, North Carolina, Oklahoma, Pennsylvania, and Virginia on low end 17% longer sentences for property crime to 181 percent longer sentences for property crime. In Florida, the time served for violent offenses increased 137% between 1990 and 2009 and a 194 percent.

Table 2-3. Pennsylvania Long-Term Inmate Sentences

Minimum Sentence	2010	2011	2012	2013	2014	2015
10–20 years	4,670	4,839	4968	5091	5192	5249
Over 20 years	1,908	2,055	2207	2387	2567	2709
Lifers	4,829	4,971	5121	5254	5352	5431
Capital Cases	216	205	197	190	186	181
Total	11,623	12,070	12,493	12,922	13,297	13,570
Percent total inmate population in PA	22.6%	23.4%	24.4%	24.15%	26.2%	27.2%

Source: Source: Pennsylvania Department of Corrections (2015). Annual Statistical Reports 2010–2015, Retrieved from http://www.cor.pa.gov/About%20Us/Statistics/Documents/Report.

The greatest disparities occur at the federal level. As revealed in Figure 2-2, federal offenders who elect to go to trial and are convicted receive in many instances sentences that are more than double what they would have been sentenced to serve had they plead guilty in 1988. More important, Figure 2-2 reveals that the average increase in sentence length for convicted federal offenders ranged from a 321% increase for public order crimes to 39 percent for property offenses (The Pew Charitable Trusts 2015).

Minorities

Noting the racial composition of long-term prisoners is critical because not every racial and ethnic group or gender has the same geriatric medical needs, we first must understand the groups that comprise the long-term population. Long-term incarceration disproportionately affects African-Americans and Hispanics (Beckett and Western 2001; Blumstein 1982, 1993; Garland, Spohn, and Wodahl 2008; Lynch 2007; Mauer 1999; Mauer and King 2007). People of color make up 37% of the U.S. population but comprise 67% of the prison population (The Sentencing Project 2017). Nearly 900,000 of the 1.5 million individuals incarcerated are African-American or Hispanic (Carson and Anderson 2016). While the imprisonment rate decreased for all races from 2014–2015, the imprisonment rate for African-Americans at 1,745 per 100,000 U.S. residents over the age of 18 remained higher than any other racial or ethnic group (Carson and An-

Table 2-4. Changes in Time Served by Offense Type and Total State Cost 1990–2009

State	Offense Type	Change in Time Served 1990–2009	Average Cost of Keeping in Prison Longer	Number of Offenders Released in 2009	Total State Cost of keeping Offenders Released in 2009 in Prison Longer
California	All offenses	51% more time	$46,396	47,599	$2.2B
	Violent	63% more time			
	Property	16% more time			
	Drug	41% more time			
Florida	All offenses	166%	$38,477	36,678	$1.4B
	Violent	137%			
	Property	181%			
	Drug	194%			
Georgia	All offenses	75%	$28,563	18,768	$536.1M
	Violent	41%			
	Property	68%			
	Drug	85%			
Michigan	All offenses	79%	$53,247	8,862	$471.9M
	Violent	97%			
	Property	35%			
	Drug	74%			
North Carolina	All offenses	86%	$37,231	11,168	415.8M
	Violent	55%			
	Property	20%			
	Drug	38%			
Oklahoma	All offenses	83%	$25,636	7,953	$203.9M
	Violent	34%			
	Property	93%			
	Drug	122%			
Pennsylvania	All offenses	32%	$39,440	8,027	$316.6M
	Violent	44%			
	Property	17%			
	Drug	44%			
Virginia	All offenses	91%	$39,800	13,036	$518.8M
	Violent	68%			
	Property	62%			
	Drug	72%			

Source: Modified table The Pew Charitable Trusts. (2012). Time Served: The High Cost, Low Return of Longer Prison Terms. Retrieved February 20, 2017 from http://www.pew trusts.org/~/media/legacy/uploadedfiles/wwwpewtrustsorg/reports/sentencing_and_correc tions/prisontimeservedpdf.pdf.

Figure 2-2. Time Served All Federal Offenders

Figure 1

Average Time Served Rose Sharply for All Federal Offense Types From 1988 to 2012

Increases ranged from 321% for public order crimes to 39% for property offenses

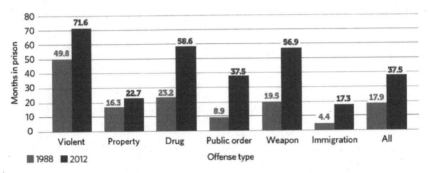

1988 2012   Offense type

Notes: Data show average time served by inmates released from prison in 1988 and 2012. Public order offenses include tax law violations, bribery, perjury, racketeering, extortion, and other crimes.

Source: The Pew Charitable Trusts. (2015). Prison Time Surges for Federal Inmates. Washington, D.C.: The Pew Charitable Trusts. Retrieved January 18, 2017 from http://www.pew trusts.org/en/research-and-analysis/issue-briefs/2015/11/prison-time-surges-for-federal-inmates.

derson 2016). In contrast, the rate of imprisonment for Whites was 312 per 100,000 U.S. residents over the age of 18. Hispanics, who represent 15 percent in the general population, are over represented within prison ranks as well with an imprisonment rate of 820 per 1000,000 adults over the age of 18. The rate of imprisonment for African-American men is 6.5 times higher than the rate for whites, and the Hispanic rate is 2.5 times higher (Mauer and King 2007; Sabol et al. 2009; Wacquant 2001). The harsh reality is that African-Americans are overrepresented in prison in every state in the union (Human Rights Watch 2002).

A consequence of disparities in the incarceration rate is that Black offenders are more likely to receive longer sentences of imprisonment (see Figure 2-3) than nonwhites. Much of the disparity in sentences can be traced to the War on Drugs (Mauer 1999, 2009; Lynch 2007; Tonry and Melewski 2008). Moreover, Blacks and Hispanics are sentenced to prison as a result of drug offenses at a much higher rate than whites (Mauer 2009; Tonry and Melewski 2008). Mauer (2009) indicates that this problem occurs because minorities are targeted for long sentences as a result of the crack cocaine laws in the federal system. For example, African-Americans comprise 14 percent of illicit drug users; but make

Figure 2-3. Lifetime Likelihood of Going to Prison

Lifetime Likelihood of Imprisonment of U.S. Residents Born in 2001

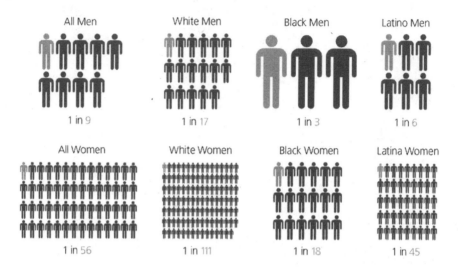

Source: Bonczar, T. (2003). *Prevalence of Imprisonment in the U.S. Population, 1974-2001.* Washington, DC: Bureau of Justice Statistics.

THE SENTENCING PROJECT

up more than 34 percent of drug arrests, and represent 53 percent of offenders sentenced to prison for drug crimes (Mauer 2009).

Women

The War on Drugs has also had an adverse effect on women. Since 1980, the rate at which women are sentenced to prison has nearly doubled the rate for men (see Figure 2-4) increasing by more than 50% between 1980 and 2014 (Mauer, Potler, and Wolf 2004; The Sentencing Project 2017). A 2006 Bureau of Justice Statistics study reported that since 1995, the total number of male prisoners had grown 34 percent and the number of female prisoners increased 57 percent (Harrison and Beck 2006, p.4). At present, the imprisonment rate for women stands at 82 per 100,000 adult female residents in the U.S. (Carson and Anderson 2016). Similar to the data for their male counterparts, imprisonment rates are dramatically higher for minorities. The imprisonment rate for Black non-Hispanic females (103 per 100,000) is nearly two times greater than that for white non-Hispanics (52 per 100,000) (Carson and Anderson

Figure 2-4. Rise in Women's Incarceration 1980–2014

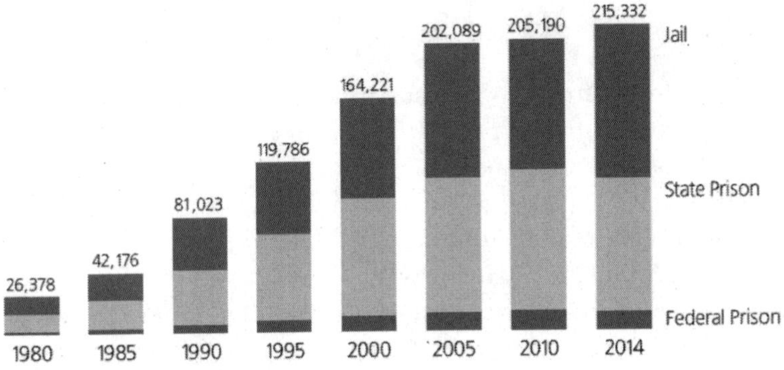

Source: The Sentencing Project (2017). Incarcerated Women and Girls. Washington, DC: The Sentencing Project. Retrieved February 16, 2017 from http://www.sentencingproject. org/wp-content/uploads/2016/02/Incarcerated-Women-and-Girls.pdf.

2016, p. 30). Nearly three out of five women in federal prison and a third of the women in state prisons are incarcerated for drug-related offenses resulting in lengthy prison terms (Carson and Anderson 2016). Consequently, at the end of 2011, there were 105,596 sentenced women prisoners under the jurisdiction of state and federal correctional agencies (Carson and Anderson 2016). These women are serving long-terms of imprisonment (see Table 2-5). In Georgia, for example, more than 16 percent of incarcerated women are serving sentences of 10 years or more (Georgia Department of Corrections 2013).

Table 2-5. Georgia Department of Corrections Long-Term Female Prisoners

Sentence	Count	Percent
10.1–12 years	157	4.06
12.1–15 years	191	4.93
15.1 to 20 years	170	4.39
20.1 and up	93	2.40
Life	322	8.32
Life without Parole	18	.46
Death	1	.03

Source: Georgia Department of Corrections. (2013). Inmate Statistical Profile. Retrieved from http://www.dcor.state.ga.us/Research/Monthly/Profile_all_inmates_2012_12.pdf.

Costs of Incarceration for Long-Term Inmates

The costs for incarcerating offenders for long periods of time continue to rise. More than $51 billion per year is now spent annually by states to cover expenses (National Association of State Budget Officers, State Expenditure Report 2010). One in 14 state general fund dollars is spent on corrections with close to 90 percent of these funds directed toward prison expenditures (Pew Center on the States 2012). Henrichson and Delaney (2012: 9) report that the average cost per inmate in fiscal year 2010 averaged $31,286, and ranged from a low of $14,603 to a high of $60,076. Given that states are keeping offenders in prison longer, the costs mount commensurately. The Pew Center on the States (2012) has estimated that the total cost if offenders released in 2009 were kept in prison longer would exceed $10 billion. With the cost soaring up to $2.2 billion in California and nearly $1.4 billion in Florida (see Table 2-4 for state calculations). Even if offenders were kept in prison for only an additional nine months, at the current average cost of $85 per day, the cost for that additional time would be over $20,000. Now consider just what this means when we are talking about housing inmates for an additional 10 years (the cost soars to over $300,000, without adjustment for inflation).

How Does Long-Term Incarceration Affect Male Prisoners?

Whether long-term incarceration has a deleterious impact is contingent on whose research study is examined and the phase of incarceration in which the data was collected (Acevedo and Bakken 2001; Flanagan 1980; Sapsford 1978; Zamble 1992). The harmful effects of imprisonment were first identified in the work of Goffman (1961), Sykes (1958), and Sykes and Messinger (1960), all of whom concluded that the pains of imprisonment lead to a mode of adaptation characterized by violence and fear. Research studies on samples of prisoners serving 15 years or less indicates that incarceration may not result in permanent psychological damage (Bolton, Smith, Heskin, and Banister 1976; Haney 2001; Rasch 1981; Sapsford 1978). Others assert that it is not necessarily the amount of time served but how the time is served that matters. It is the nature of the prison (level of violence, rated capacity, level of security, types of prisoners housed, etc.), and the level of deprivation that the prisoner encounters that determine the psychological impact (Haney 2001).

Ample research now indicates that the consequences of long-term incarceration vary depending on the phase of incarceration. First-time prisoners and those early in their sentences experience negative emotional states and psychological problems (Paulus and Dzindolet 1993; Rubeck, Carr, and Hopper 1986; Schmid and Jones 1993; Zamble 1992; Zamble and Porporino 1988). MacKenzie and Goodstein (1985) found long-term prisoners who were early in their sentence reported significantly more anxiety, depression, psychosomatic illness, and fear than other long-term inmates who were closer to the end of their sentences. Over time, the fear, anxiety, and emotional distress dissipate, leading for many long-term inmates to a relative period of stability behind bars (Paulus and Dzindolet 1993; Rubeck, Carr, and Hopper 1986; Schmid and Jones 1993). While perhaps more stable during the middle phase of their sentence, long-term prisoners report greater feelings of apathy and decreased desire for work (Porporino 1991). As time passes and release dates from long prison terms approach, however, some long-term prisoners become even more passive, less involved, depressed and potentially more hostile (Buskel and Kilman 1980; Sappington 1996; Porporino 1991). Zamble (1992) found that involvement in infractions was significantly lower in the last period of the study compared to the first period for long-term male inmates. Unfortunately, while long-term inmates are less involved in prison misconduct, when they do become involved, their infractions tend to be more serious than those of the short-term inmates. The link to fewer but more serious disciplinary infractions holds true for both males and females (Casey-Acevedo and Bakken 2001; Flanagan 1980).

Gresham Sykes in 1958 argued that the "… deprivations and frustrations (of prison life) pose profound threats to the inmate's personality or sense of personal worth." Such problems are magnified among long-term prisoners. Haney (2001) identified eight psychological harms caused by institutional life and the deprivations experienced by prisoners (see Box 2-1). Life behind bars is highly routinized and structured, with little opportunity provided for independent thinking. Long-term prisoners may become so severely institutionalized that "… they no longer know how to do things on their own, or how to refrain from doing those things that are ultimately harmful or self-destructive" (Haney 2001). Moreover, as a result of hyper-vigilance, fear, and the corresponding psychological distancing that allows prisoners to cope with fear, long-term prisoners become alienated from themselves and society. Long-term prisoners, in particular, are vulnerable to social withdrawal, isolation and depression (Haney 2001; Sapsford 1978; Taylor 1961). Long-term inmates may also be conditioned to over respond when faced with frustration-inducing situations upon release. Thus, they are more likely to respond aggressively to per-

Box 2-1. Pains of Imprisonment and Adaptations

Pains of Imprisonment	Adaptations
Skyes 1958 Deprivation of Liberty Deprivation of Goods and Services Deprivation of Heterosexual Relationships Deprivation of Autonomy Deprivation of Security	**Haney 2001** Dependence on institutional structure and contingencies. Hypervigilance, interpersonal distrust and suspicion. Emotional over-control, alienation, and psychological distancing. Social withdrawal and isolation. Incorporation of exploitative norms of prison culture. Diminished sense of self-worth and personal value. Post-traumatic stress reactions to the pains of imprisonment.

ceived minor slights (Haney 2001). Additionally, their internalized value system of being tough, handling one's own problems, and hiding stress and fear is ironically likely to inhibit ex-prisoners from engaging in help-seeking behaviors upon release, which is the one antidote for their social withdrawal, isolation and depression.

Prisons are violent places with numerous mechanisms for victimization. We now know that victimization in prison, regardless of phase of imprisonment, is directly associated with a host of negative physical and mental health problems. More important, the longer an individual is incarcerated the greater the odds of becoming a victim. As detailed later in this book, victims of violence in prison are at significant risk for acquiring communicable diseases such as TB and sexually transmitted diseases (Dumond 2003; Mariner 2001). Victimization in prison also impacts psychological functioning with victims describing symptoms consistent with PTSD, rape trauma, depression, and suicidal ideations. Thus, a byproduct of longer incarceration seems to be older parolees with more emotional, psychological, and physical ailments.

How Does Long-Term Incarceration Affect Female Prisoners?

Less attention has been paid to the issues and needs of long-term female felons. A review of the research conducted to date reveals that long-term female prisoners experience some of the same negative consequences as their male counterparts (Dowden and Smallshaw 2000; Goodstein, Robinson, and Campbell 1989; Grant and Johnson 2000). Female lifers exhibit high rates of psychological dysfunction such as excessive worry, depression and suicidal ideations during incarceration (Dowden and Smallshaw 2000). Significant differences in adjustment to incarceration have also been noted based on the combination of time served and inmate expectations about sentence length (Goodstein, Robinson, and Campbell 1989; Grant and Johnson 2000). Grant and Johnson (2000) compared lifers serving sentences for first degree murder, lifers serving sentences for second degree murder, and female prisoners serving fixed sentences of 10 years or more. The females with the longest sentences, the first-degree murderers, had lower criminogenic needs and were better adjusted than female prisoners serving shorter sentences. Thus, shorter sentences among female prisoners was associated with maladjustment early during prison sentences, a result very similar to that found by MacKenzie and Goodstein (1985) and Zamble (1992) among male prisoners. Goodstein et al. (1989) found that long-term female prisoners perceived greater problems with incarceration as a result of the deprivations related to social support, isolation, and lack of programming experienced whereas shorter-term prisoners were more concerned about safety and security. Female long-term prisoners, just as their male counterparts, engage in fewer but more serious disciplinary infractions (Casey-Acevedo and Bakken 2001; Flanagan 1980). Among female lifers, involvement in violent offenses in prison occurred in a U-shaped pattern, with the fewest infractions occurring during the early parts of their sentences, followed by increases in the middle of their sentences, with a subsequent decrease in infractions prior to release. Thus, female long-term prisoners are remarkably similar to their male counterparts in terms of adjustment to imprisonment.

What Happens Upon Release?

The pains of imprisonment and the corresponding adaptations in behavior among long-term prisoners may impede their ability to adjust upon release into the community. According to Haney (2001), "the psychological consequences of incarceration may represent significant impediments to post-prison adjustment. They may interfere with the transition from prison to home, impede an ex-convict's successful re-integration into a social network and employment setting, and may compromise an incarcerated parent's ability to resume his or her role with family and children." We ask a great deal of ex-offenders released after serving sentences of 10 years or more. We release them without addressing the harms experienced during incarceration. We expect them to be able to make decisions independently when all aspects of daily living prior to this point have been prescribed for them. We ask them to immediately throw off the shackles of the prison world in order to embrace a world where they are restricted as to where they may live, with whom they can come into contact, and the jobs for which they are qualified to apply. Thus, it should come as no surprise that many, when released after long periods of incarceration, fail to adjust. Immediately upon release, former felons require housing, employment, health care, and funds to live. Such items may be more readily available to short-term prisoners who have maintained contact with the outside world and who have not internalized inmate values and modes of adaptation. For the long-term prisoner, however, the ability to cope, make good decisions, and be successful upon release is limited.

In addition to the problems identified, long-term female prisoners experience additional problems upon release. More often than not, long-term female prisoners entered prisons with little education, extensive histories of substance abuse or dependence, high rates of sexual and domestic abuse, and self-esteem problems (Amnesty International 1999; Young and Reviere 2006). Because female prisoners experience higher rates of inmate-on-inmate sexual victimization, and may be victimized by staff, there is a greater likelihood that they are returning to society with additional emotional scars associated with sexual abuse (Beck and Harrison 2010). Relationships matter for female prisoners. Not surprisingly, those women who are better able to maintain familial relationships have better outcomes upon release (Bloom, Owen, and Covington 2003). The lengthy prison sentences also result in less frequent contact with family making reunification difficult upon release (Lynch and Sabol 2001). A broad body of literature indicates that female inmates suffer from more extensive mental health issues and physical health problems during incarceration than do their male counterparts. Moreover, they are less likely to participate in treatment programs (Richie 2001; Young and Reviere 2006).

A major assumption about incarceration has been that its use would result in reductions in the crime rate over time. The belief was that if we locked up serious high rate offenders and their violent counterparts for long periods of time, then as a society we would see the crime rate drop (Currie 1985; Petersilia

1992; Zimring, Hawkins, and Ibser 1995; Zimring 2001). Even though we are locking up more people for longer periods of time, still nearly two-thirds of state prisoners recidivate within three years of release (Beck and Shipley 1989; Hughes and Wilson 2003; Langan and Levin 2002; Petersilia 2003). While prisoner recidivism is less for federal ex-felons than for state prisoners, 18 percent of federal ex-felons released in 1994 returned to prison within three years (Sabol et al. 2000).

The problem of recidivism is exacerbated by the length of time imprisoned. The longer the period of time incarcerated prior to release, the greater are the odds that ex-offenders will return to an incarcerated state (Johnson and Grant 2000). In one study, serving more time in prison was associated with a three percent increase in recidivism compared to those serving less time (Gendreau et al. 2000). With regard to federal releasees, 25 percent of ex-offenders who served five years or more returned to prison within three years of release (Sabol et al. 2000). While the benefits of long-term incarceration are at best questionable, the consequences of long-term incarceration suggest that we have made it harder for ex-offenders who served long sentences to reintegrate back into society and have perhaps increased their likelihood of reoffending.

Conclusions

The notion that long-term prison sentences will have positive effects on American society has proven a failure. Rather than reap benefits from mass incarceration, our prisons now overflow with men and women who are ill prepared for a return to society upon release. The impact of incarceration on long-term prisoners' physical and emotional health is complex. There remains much that we do not know. The long-term prison population is diverse, and because of this diversity "unitary prescriptions for managing long-term prisoner populations are doomed to failure if they fail to account for the variety that exists within this group" (Flanagan 1992: 21).

Policies developed to manage long-term prisoners must be goal-directed and evidence-based (Flanagan 1992). Determining the best approach for addressing the needs of long-prisoners will require that correctional agencies develop better information systems to track the characteristics and needs of long-term prisoners (Cowles 1990; Unger and Buchanan 1985). It is also important to consider whether it is in the best interest of our society to hand out long prison sentences when evidence indicates that most offenders age out of crime (Gottfredson and Hirschi 1990; Horney, Osgood, and Marshall 1995; Moffit 1993; Sampson and Laub 1993). A plethora of evidence now exists which shows the same propensity for individual participation in criminal activity that peaks during young adulthood, and then declines steadily (Farrington 1986; Nagin and Land 1993; Piquero, Brame, and Lynam 2004). If these theorists are correct, then long-term incarceration does little more than serve as a warehouse for individuals whose criminal proclivities are on the decline at least from the very first day of their incarceration.

Websites

For more information on the Georgia Department of Corrections, visit http://www.dcor.state.ga.us.

For more information on the Pennsylvania Department of Corrections, visit http://www.cor.pa.gov.

For more information on the costs to incarcerate and correctional policy, visit www.pewtrusts.org.

For more information on the profile of U.S. national trends, visit https://www.bjs.gov/.

References

Allen, F. (1981). *The decline of the rehabilitative ideal.* New Haven, CT: Yale University Press.

Amnesty International. (1999). *Not part of my sentence: Violations of the human rights of women in custody.* Washington, DC: Amnesty International.

Aos, S. (2008, July). Evidence-based policy options to reduce crime, criminal justice costs and prison construction. *Alternatives to incarceration.* Symposium conducted at the meeting of the U.S. Sentencing Commission of Washington DC.

Aubertin, N. (1992). The challenge of managing long-term inmates in minimum-security institutions. *Forum on Corrections Research, 4,* 1–2. Retrieved from http://_www.csc-scc.gc.ca/_text/_pblct/_forum/_e042/_042o_e.pdf.

Baum, D. (1997). Smoke and mirrors: *The war on drugs and the politics of failure.* Backbay Books.

Beckett, K., & Western, B. (2001). Governing social marginality. In D. Garland (Ed.), Mass Imprisonment: Social Causes and Consequences. London: Sage.

Bennett, W. J., DiIulio, J. J. Jr., & Walters, J. P. (1996). *Body count.* New York, NY: Simon & Schuster.

Bloom, B., Owen, B., & Covington, S. (2003). *Gender-responsive strategies: Research, practice, and guiding principles for women offenders.* Washington, DC: National Institute of Corrections.

Blumstein, A. (1982). On racial disproportionality of the United States' prison populations. *Journal of Criminal Law and Criminology, 73,* 743–760.

Blumstein, A. (1993). Racial disproportionality of U.S. prison populations revisited. *University of Colorado Law Review, 64,* 743–760.

Blumstein, A., & Cohen, J. (1973). A theory of the stability of punishment. *Journal of Criminal Law and Criminology, 64*(2), 198–206.

Bolton, N., Smith, F. V., Heskin, K. J., & Banister, P. A. (1976). Psychological correlates of long-term imprisonment IV: A longitudinal analysis. *British Journal of Criminology, 16,* 36–47.

Bonta, J., & Gendreau, P. (1990). Reexamining the cruel and unusual punishment of prison life. *Law and Human Behavior, 14,* 347–372.

Bonta, J., Law, M., and Hanson, R. K. (1998). The prediction of criminal and violent recidivism among mentally disordered offenders: A meta-analysis. *Psychological Bulletin, 123,* 123–142.

Camp, C. G., & Camp, G. M. (2000). *The 2000 corrections yearbook: Adult corrections.* Criminal Justice Institute: Middletown, CT.

Carson, E. & Anderson, e. (2016). *Prisoners in 2015.* U.S. Department of Justice, Bureau of Justice Statistics. Retrieved from https://www.bjs.gov/content/pub/pdf/p15.pdf.

Carson, E. A., & Sable, W. J. (2012). *Prisoners in 2011.* Retrieved from the U.S Department of Justice, Bureau of Justice Statistics website: http://_bjs.ojp.usdoj.gov/_content/_pub/_pdf/_p11.pdf.

Casey-Acevedo, K., & Bakken, T. (2001). The effect of time on the disciplinary adjustment of women in prison. *International Journal of Offender Therapy and Comparative Criminology, 45,* 489–497.

Casey-Longoria, P. (2000). Cooperative effort brings success to transitioning long-term offenders. *Corrections Today, 62,* 94–96.

Cullen, F. T., & Gilbert, K. (1982). *Reaffirming Rehabilitation.* Cincinnati, OH: Anderson.

Currie, E. (1985). *Confronting crime: An American challenge.* New York: Pantheon.

DiIulio, J. J. Jr., (1995, December 16). Moral Poverty. *Chicago Tribune.*

Dowden, C., & Smallshaw, K. (2000). The effective management of women serving life sentences. *Forum on Corrections Research, 12,* 39–41.

Farrington, D. (1986). Age and crime. In vol. 7 of *Crime and Justice: A Review of Research,* ed. M. Tonry and N. Morris. Chicago: University of Chicago Press.

Flanagan, T. (1980). Time served and institutional misconduct. *Journal of Criminal Justice, 8,* 357–367.

Flanagan, T., Clark, D., Aziz, D., & Szelest, B. (1989). Compositional changes in a long-term prisoner population. *The Prison Journal, 80,* 15–34.

Flanagan, T. J. (1992). Long-term incarceration: Issues of science, policy and correctional practice. *Forum on Corrections Research, 4,* 19–24.

Garland, David. (2001). *The culture of control.* New York, NY: Oxford University Press.

Garland, B., Spohn, C., & Wodahl, E. J. (2008). Racial disproportionality in the American prison population: Using the Blumstein method to address the critical race and justice issue of the 21st century. *Justice Policy Journal,* 5(2), 1–42.

Gottfredson, M., & Hirschi, T. (1990.) *A General Theory of Crime.* Stanford University Press.

Graham, E. (2000). Residential program for lifers: Six keys to success. *Forum on Corrections Research, 12,* 6–7.

Grant, B. A., & Johnson, S. L. (2000). Women offenders serving long sentences in custody. *Forum on Corrections Research, 12,* 25–28.

Gray, M. (2000). *Drug Crazy: How we got into this mess and how we can get out.* New York, NY: Routledge.

Greenfeld, L., & Langan, P. (1987). "Trends in prison populations." Paper prepared for the National Conference on Punishment for Criminal Offenses, Ann Arbor, MI, November.

Grove, W. M., & Meehl, P. E. (1996). Comparative efficiency of informal (subjective impressionistic) and formal (mechanical, algorithmic) prediction procedures: The clinical-statistical controversy. *Psychology, Public Policy, and Law, 2,* 293–323.

Guerino, P., Harrison, P., & Sabol, W. (2011). *Prisoners in 2010.* Retrieved from U.S. Department of Justice, Bureau of Justice Statistics website: http://www.bjs.gov/content/pub/pdf/p10.pdf.

Haney, C. (2001). The psychological impact of incarceration: Implications for post-prison adjustment. *From Prison to Home: The Effect of Incarceration and Reentry on Children, Families, and Communities.* Retrieved from http://aspe.hhs.gov/hsp/prison2home02/Haney.htm#N_12_.

Harris, V. R. (1992). The management and review of life sentence prisoners in England and Wales. *Forum on Corrections Research, 4,* 1–9. Retrieved from http://_www.csc-scc.gc.ca/_text/_pblct/_forum/_e042/_042q_e.pdf.

Harrison, P. M., & Beck, A. J. (2006). *Prisoners in 2005* (Report No. NCJ 215092). Retrieved from U.S. Department of Justice, Bureau of Justice Statistics webpage: http://bjs.ojp.usdoj.gov/content/pub/ascii/p05.txt.

Henrichson. C., & Delaney, R. (2012). *The price of prisons: What incarceration costs taxpayers.* New York NY: Vera Institute of Justice.

Horney, J., Osgood, W., & Marshall, H. (1995). Criminal careers in the short-term: Intra-individual variability in crime and its relation to local life circumstances. *American Sociological Review, 60,* 655–673.

Human Rights Watch. (2002). *Race and incarceration in the United States.* New York: Human Rights Watch.

Hughes, T., & Wilson, D. (2003). *Reentry trends in the United States: Inmates returning to the community after serving time in prison.* Washington, DC: Bureau of Justice Statistics, U.S. Department of Justice.

Johnson, R., & Raphael, S. (2012). How much crime reduction does the marginal prisoner buy? *Journal of Law and Economics, 55(2),* 275–310. doi:10. 1086.664073.

Johnson, S. L., & Grant, B. A. (2000). Release outcomes of long-term offenders. *Forum on Corrections Research, 12,* 16–20.

Justice Policy Institute. (2009). *Effective investments in public safety: Mass incarceration and longer sentences fail to make us safer.* Washington, DC: Justice Policy Institute.

Landenberger, N. A., & Lipsey, M. W. (2005). The positive effects of cognitive-behavioral programs for offenders: A meta-analysis of factors associated with effective treatment. *Journal of Experimental Criminology, 1,* 451–476.

Liedka, R. V., Piehl, A., & Useem, B. (2006). The crime-control effect of incarceration: Does scale matter? *Criminology & Public Policy, 5,* 245–276.

Lynch, M. J. (2007). *Big prisons, big dreams: Crime and the failure of America's penal system.* New Brunswick, NJ: Rutgers University Press.

MacKenzie, D. L., & Goodstein, L. (1985). Long-term incarceration impacts and characteristics of long-term offenders. *Criminal Justice and Behavior, 12(4),* 395–414.

MacKenzie, D. L., Robinson, J. W., & Campbell, C. S. (1989). Long-term incarceration of female offenders: Prison adjustment and coping. *Criminal Justice and Behavior, 16,* 223–238.

Mauer, M. (1999). *Race to incarcerate.* New York: New Press.

Mauer, M., & King, R. S. (2007). *Uneven justice: The rates of incarceration by race and ethnicity.* Washington, DC: The Sentencing Project.

McGinnis, K. L. (1990). Programming for long-term inmates. *Prison Journal, 70,* 119–120.

Mossman, D. (1994). Assessing predictions of violence: Being accurate about accuracy. *Journal of Consulting and Clinical Psychology, 62,* 783–792.

Nagin, D. & Land, K. (1993). Age, criminal careers, and population hetero-geneity: Specification and estimation of a non-parametric, mixed Poisson model. *Criminology*, 31, 327–362.

National Association of State Budget Officers. (2011). *State expenditure report: Examining fiscal 2009–2011 state spending.* Retrieved from http://_www.nasbo.org/_sites/_default/_files/_2010%20State%20Expenditure%20Report.pdf.

Nellis, A. (2013). Life goes on: The historic rise in life sentences in America. Washington, DC: The Sentencing Project.

Okafo, N. (2009) *Reconstructing justice in a post colony.* Burlington, VT: Ashgate Publishing.

Petteruti, A. (2011). Finding Direction: Expanding Criminal Justice Options by Considering Policies of Other Nations. Justice Policy Institute. Washington, DC. Retrieved from http://_www.justicepolicy.org/_uploads/_justicepolicy/_documents/_finding_direction-full_report.pdf.

Petersilia, J. (1992). California's prison policy: Causes, costs, and consequences. The Prison Journal, 72, 8–36.

Petersilia, J. (2003). When prisoners come home: Parole and prisoner reentry. New York: Oxford University Press.

Piquero, A., Brame, R., & Lynam, D. (2004). Studying criminal career length through early adulthood among serious offenders. *Crime and Delinquency*, 50, 412–435.

Poporino, F. J. (1991). *Differences in response to long-term imprisonment: Implications for the management of long-term offenders.* Correctional Service of Canada: Ottawa, Ontario.

Rasch, W. (1981). The effects of indeterminate sentencing: A study of men sentenced to life imprisonment. *International Journal of Law and Psychiatry*, 4, 417–431.

Richie, B. (2001). Challenges incarcerated women face as they return to their communities: Findings from life history interview. *Crime and Delinquency*, 47(3), 368–389.

Ruback, R., & Carr, T. (1984). Crowding in a woman's prison: Attitudinal and behavioral effects. *Journal of Applied Psychology*, 14, 57–68.

Sabbath, M. J., & Cowles, E. L. (1990). Using multiple perspectives to develop strategies for managing long-term inmates. *Prison Journal, 70*, 58–72.

Sabol, W., Adams, W., Parthsarathy, B. & Yuan (2000). *Offenders returning to federal prisoner, 1986–1997.* Washington, DC: Bureau of Justice Statistics, U.S. Department of Justice.

Sampson, R., & Laub, J. (1993). *Crime in the Making Pathways and Turning Points Through Life.* Harvard University Press.

Sapsford, R. J. (1978). Life sentence prisoners: Psychological changes during sentence. *British Journal of Criminology, 18,* 128–145.

Schlosser, E. (1998, December). The prison-industrial complex. *Atlantic Magazine.* Retrieved from http://_www.theatlantic.com/_magazine/_archive/_1998/_12/_the-prison-industrial-complex/_304669/_.

Schulhofer, S. J. (1993). Rethinking mandatory minimums. *28 Wake Forest Law Review 199.* Retrieved from http://_www.lexisnexis.com/_hottopics/_lnacademic/_?.

Scott-Hayward, C. (2009). The fiscal crisis in corrections rethinking policies and practices. New York, NY: Vera institute of Justice.

Simourd, D. J. (2004). Use of dynamic risk/_need assessment instruments among long-term incarcerated offenders. *Criminal Justice and Behavior, 3,* 306–323.

South Carolina Department of Corrections (2016). Sentence length distribution of SCDC total inmate population on June 30,2016. Retrieved from http://www.doc.sc.gov/research/InmatePopulationStatsTrend/ASOFTrendSentenceLengthDistributionFY12-16.pdf.

Sykes, G. (1958). The *society of captives: A study of a maximum security prison.* Princeton University Press.

Taylor, A. (1961). *Social isolation and imprisonment.* Psychiatry, 24, 373.

Texas Department of Criminal Justice (2015). Statistical report. Retrieved from http://www.tdcj.texas.gov/documents/Statistical_Report_FY2015.pdf.

The Pew Center on the States. (2012). *Time Served: The high cost, low return of longer prison terms.* Retrieved from http://_www.pewstates.org/_uploadedFiles/_PCS_Assets/_2012/_Prison_Time_Served.pdf.

The Sentencing Project (2017). *Criminal Justice Facts.* Washington, DC: The Sentencing Project. Retrieved from http://www.sentencingproject.org/criminal-justice-facts/.

Toch, H., & Adams, K. (1989). *Coping: Maladaptation in prisons.* New Brunswick, NJ: Transaction Books.

Unger, C. A., & Buchanan, R. A. (1985). *Managing long-term inmates: A guide for the correctional administrator.* National Institute of Corrections: Aurora, CO.

Unger, C. A., & Buchanan, R. A. (1983). *Long-term offenders in Pennsylvania.* Kansas City, MO: Correctional Services Group, Inc.

Vincent, B. S., & Hofer, P. J. (1994). *The consequences of mandatory minimum prison terms: A summary of recent findings.* Washington, DC: The Federal Judiciary Center.

Wacquant, L. (2001). Deadly symbiosis: When ghetto and prison meet and mesh. *Punishment and Society,* 3, 95–134.

Warren, Jenifer. (2008). *One in 100: Behind Bars in America*. Washington, DC: Pew Charitable Trusts.

West, H. C., Sabol, W. J. & Greenman, S. J. (2010). *Prisoners in 2009*. Washington, D.C.: U.S. Department of Justice.

Wright, P. (2010). *The new prison industrial-complex state budgets and technology in the age of declining state revenue*. Retrieved from the Centre for Research on Globalization website http://www.globalresearch.ca/index.php?context=va&aid=18993.

Young, V., & Reviere, R. (2006). *Women behind bars: Gender and race in U.S. prisons*. Boulder, Co: Rienner Press.

Zamble, E. (1992). Behavior and adaptation of long-term prison inmates: Descriptive longitudinal results. *Criminal Justice and Behavior, 19*, 409–425.

Zimring, F. (2001). Imprisonment rates and the new politics of criminal punishment. In D. Farland (Ed.), *Mass imprisonment: Social causes and consequences* (pp. 145–149). Thousand Oaks, Ca: Sage Publications.

Zimring, F., Hawkins, G., & Ibser, H. (1995). Estimating the effects of increased incarceration on crime in California. California Policy Seminar Brief 7: 10.

Chapter 3

Who Are the Elderly Inmates?
What Are the Costs?
What Are Their Needs?

Prisons are primarily designed for the young and able-bodied; it takes additional effort on the part of corrections officials to meet the needs and respect the rights of the old and infirm (Human Rights Watch 2012: 43).

The increase in long-term sentencing combined with mandatory sentences for both first time and repeat offenders coalesced with an aging baby boomer generation, making elderly inmates one of the fastest growing segments of the prison population (Craig-Moreland 2002). While the elderly in prison do not comprise the largest share of inmates, this residential population requires more health care and special programming than younger inmates. Hence the cost of providing care for elderly inmates at some point may overwhelm already strained correctional budgets. These hidden and rising costs should create major anxiety in every correctional administrator and serve as a major concern for criminal justice policy-makers. To date most correctional agencies remain ill-equipped and/or ill-prepared to deal with the influx of these special needs inmates (Bernat 1989; Chaiklin and Fultz 1983; Morton and Anderson 1982; Morton 2001; Vito and Wilson 1985).

The increase in elderly inmates is due to the amalgamation of several factors. First and foremost, as the general population grows older that change in the societal age structure is subsequently mirrored within the prison population. As the U.S. population ages, the number of older Americans eligible for incarceration increases as well. Ergo the greater the chance that a corresponding increase in arrests and crime for this age group will occur.

There appear to be other factors beyond a demographic shift at work because the number of older persons in prison is growing faster than the numbers of elderly people in the general population. As Human Rights Watch (2012, p. 37) noted "The number of persons entering state prison as new court commitments at the age of 55 years or older grew 109 percent between 1995 and 2009." The "get tough" laws associated with 1980s sentencing practices emerge as a second factor. These laws increased the amount of time served by inmates due to longer mandatory sentences while curtailing early release mechanisms such as parole (Human Rights Watch 2012; Kerbs and Jolley 2009). Forty percent of state prisoners who were 51 or older in 2009 were serving sentences of more than 20 years or life sentences (Human Rights Watch 2012). Hence, they will become elderly while incarcerated.

The third factor is that mandatory arrest laws did not just increase the amount of time served they also increased the number of people who served time. This is a major contributing factor for why the United States has one of the highest incarceration rates in the world. The "get tough" laws had an especially detrimental effect on special populations, i.e., the young, the old and the mentally ill. By limiting judicial discretion the courts could no longer tailor the sentence to the needs and characteristics of the offender, meaning all populations were uniformly sanctioned harsher than before. Previously during sentencing the judge had more leeway in modifying the sentence or punishment of the convicted based on characteristics of the offender such as age, medical needs, and the threat they posed to the community. Mandatory sentences and sentencing guidelines greatly curtailed the discretion the judges could exercise. And consequently, these laws forced judges to impose often long sentences on elderly and nonviolent offenders that made little criminological sense. Concern over the growth of the elderly inmate population and their treatment led Human Rights Watch (2012) to do a major investigation of prison facilities around the country.

In response to issues surrounding the treatment of elderly inmates, most states are now reviewing their policies and practices. A number of advocacy groups have also grown increasingly concerned about the loss of human dignity and correctional administrator's ability to provide safe, secure, and sanitary conditions of confinement (Human Rights Watch 2012). Likewise, Vogel (2012) notes that the number of inmate lawsuits related to issues and conditions of elderly inmate have increased.

This chapter focuses on defining and describing the scope of the problem across the country. The chapter begins by demarcating the relevant constructs of elderly, geriatric and older person. Then a review of the distribution of the elderly in the general population and an analysis of the extent of the elderly incarcerated population within the United States is presented. Also included is a discussion of the costs of incarceration and problems elderly inmates face upon release.

Defining Elderly, Senior or Older Citizens in the General Population

The concepts elderly, geriatric, and older persons have no uniform recognized definitions within the general population of the United States. Hence determining exactly who are and should be considered an elderly, senior, or older citizen is challenging and correspondingly there is more than one approach. Academics have argued that such terms should not be defined simply based on chronological age; this seems, however, to be the primary defining factor among most definitions (Flynn 1992; Lemieux, Dyeson, and Castiglione 2002; Morton 2001). Even chronological age definitions are problematic as the requirements for qualifying for state, local and federal senior citizen services vary depending on the initial age used to define senior amongst government agencies. For example, the Social Security Administration (SSA) utilizes a definition for age-based retirement established by when you were born. SSA establishes the age for full retirement benefits for people born after 1960 to be 67; but for individuals born in 1937 or earlier the full retirement benefits age is 65. SSA does, however, allow anyone at least 62 years old to retire with reduced benefits. This arbitrary government benchmark created by SSA is used by many to ascertain the initial age at which someone should be considered an elderly, senior or older citizen. The Supplemental Nutrition Assistant Program (SNAP), however, defines a qualifying elderly person as someone age 60 or older. The Older American Act which is used to determine whether elder abuse has occurred legislatively also defines some at least 60 years old as elder or senior citizen. Outside of the government the American Association of Retired Persons better known as the AARP extends their membership to 50 year olds. For other federal grant program assistance, applicants must be at least 70 years old to qualify. Thus, depending on the program and the organization the qualifying chronological age for being categorized as senior or elderly and receiving age-based benefits could be 50, 60, 62, 65, or 70.

Others suggest age should not be determined solely chronically but in terms of overall physiology, i.e., that genetic factors combined with environmental aspects such as lifestyle and career choices have major impacts on life expectancy. Morton (2001) advanced this notion by suggesting that rather than relying on chronological age to determine elderly or senior definitions should be based on individual levels of functioning reflected in the mental and physical abilities of the individual. Such definitions shift focus away from chronological age to disability level or what they can or cannot do without assistance.

The Americans with Disabilities Act (ADA) defines disability as a mental or physical disability that limits one or more major life activities (caring for oneself, performing manual tasks, seeing, hearing, eating, sleeping, walking, standing, lifting, bending, speaking, breathing, learning, reading, concentrating, thinking, communicating, and working) and bodily functions (functions of the immune system, normal cell growth, digestive, bowel, bladder, neurological, brain, respiratory, circulatory, endocrine, and reproductive functions). This medical or ability based distinction of elderly adds another dimension to chronological definitions that is often overlooked.

Snapshot: National Estimates of the Elderly

The United States elderly population continues to increase at a rapid rate (see Figure 3-1). More people in 2010 were over the age of 65 than at any other time in history (Werner 2011). According to the U.S. Census Bureau between 2000 and 2010 the population aged 65 and older increased at a faster rate (15.1 percent vs. 9.7 percent) than the total U.S. population (Werner 2011). By 2030 one if five Americans is projected to be 65 or older (Colby and Ortman 2015). This trend of growth will continue well into the future. Projections indicate that by 2050 more than 88 million Americans will be age 65 or older (see Table 3-1).

At the same time that the American elderly population is increasing in numbers, they are also living longer. In 1900 the average life span in the U.S. was 49 (Shresthra 2006). At present the life expectancy at birth for the total population is 78.6 years of age (Murphy, Xu, and Kochanek 2011). A typical male can expect to live until the age of 76 and a female until the age of 81. A person aged 55 in 2006 could expect to live an additional 26.5 years (Arias 2010). Longevity is not evenly distributed in the population. Females can expect to live longer than males and Whites longer than African-Americans (Arias 2010).

Moreover, not only is there a gender and racial component to longevity this uneven distribution is also replicated in differential cost for health care. According to the Agency for Healthcare Research and Quality (AHRQ) analysis, "Only 10 percent of the U.S. population accounted for nearly two-thirds of all health care costs in 2008." The AHRQ further noted that of this 10 percent ap-

**Figure 3-1. Population 65 Years and Older by Size and
Percent of Total Population: 1900 to 2010**

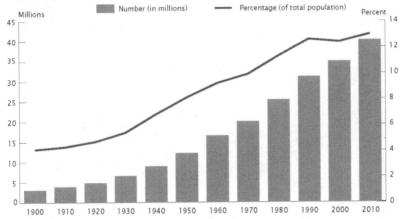

Population 65 Years and Older by Size and Percent of Total Population:
1900 to 2010
(For more information on confidentiality protection, nonsampling error, and definitions, see *www.census.gov
/prod/cen2010/doc/sf1.pdf*)

Sources: U.S. Census Bureau, decennial census of population, 1900 to 2000; 2010 Census Summary File 1. (For more information on confidentiality protection, nonsampling error, and definitions, see www.census.gov/prod/cen2010/doc/sf1.pdf.)

proximately 60 percent were female and 40 percent were 65 years old or older. Males between the ages of 18 to 29, the most crime prone demographic group only accounted for 3 percent of this total.

Challenges in Defining the Elderly Inmate

Currently, there is no standard definition of what constitutes an elderly inmate (Flynn 1992; Lemieus, Dyeson and Catiglione 2002; Morton 2001). This makes the issue even more convoluted for correctional officials, legislative bodies and advocacy groups; all of whom are expected to address this issue while its very scope remains unspecified. Morton (1992) and Aday (2003) recommend 50 as the initial age defining elderly inmates. Other researchers have indicated 55 as the age cutoff for inmates (Jones, Connelly and Wagner 2001).

There are three primary justifications for using an age cutoff below 60 years of age. First, by 2030 the prison population aged 55 or older is expected to account for one-third of all incarcerated people in the U.S. (Osborne Association

Table 3-1. Projections of the Population by Selected Age Groups and Sex for the U.S.: 2010–2050

(Resident population as of July 1. Numbers in thousands.)

Sex and age	2010	2015	2020	2025	2030	2035	2040	2045	2050
BOTH SEXES	310,233	325,540	341,387	357,452	373,504	389,531	405,655	422,059	439,010
Under 18 years	75,217	78,106	81,685	84,866	87,815	90,722	93,986	97,669	101,574
Under 5 years	21,100	22,076	22,846	23,484	24,161	25,056	26,117	27,171	28,148
5 to 13 years	37,123	39,011	40,792	42,490	43,858	45,170	46,743	48,664	50,697
14 to 17 years	16,994	17,019	18,048	18,892	19,796	20,496	21,126	21,834	22,728
18 to 64 years	194,787	200,597	204,897	208,678	213,597	221,266	230,431	239,933	248,890
18 to 24 years	30,713	30,885	30,817	32,555	34,059	35,695	37,038	38,234	39,538
25 to 44 years	83,095	85,801	89,724	92,612	95,242	97,962	101,392	106,366	110,862
45 to 64 years	80,980	83,911	84,356	83,510	84,296	87,608	92,000	95,333	98,490
65 years and over	40,229	46,837	54,804	63,907	72,092	77,543	81,238	84,456	88,547
85 years and over	5,751	6,292	6,597	7,239	8,745	11,450	14,198	16,985	19,041
100 years and over	79	105	135	175	208	239	298	409	601
16 years and over	243,639	255,864	268,722	282,014	295,595	309,084	322,265	335,328	348,811
18 years and over	235,016	247,434	259,702	272,585	285,688	298,809	311,669	324,389	337,437
15 to 44 years	126,644	129,351	134,078	139,325	144,157	149,051	154,301	160,992	167,455

Source: Population Division, U.S. Census Bureau. Release Date: August 14, 2008.

2014, p. 2). If the projections are accurate, then this figure is large enough that it should be cause for alarm. Second, whether it is a result of their lifestyle prior to incarceration or of aging in prison, inmates appear to experience the effects aging earlier than the general population (Mitka 2004). As will be detailed later, inmates often enter prison having existed in a world where medical care was minimal, substance abuse rates were high, and nutritional deficits were widespread. These problems culminate in an accelerated aging process for inmates. Inmates who are 50 years of age chronologically appear physiologically to be 60–65 years of age as a result of health problems (Mitka 2004). This is backed up by medical data that suggest long term prisoner life expectancy is shorter than their non-incarcerated counterpart (Binswanger et al. 2007; Binswanger et al. 2009; Spaulding et al. 2011). Negative health outcomes are even more startling post-release where female ex-offenders have higher rates of death than men (Binswanger et al. 2007) and where white male ex-offenders had mortality rates twice that of other white men (Binswanger et al. 2009).

Third, beyond a thoughtful discussion the lack of a working definition has a frank side effect for prison officials and policy-makers. The inability to establish a common understanding both of the scope and the characteristics of this population severely hampers the ability of those responsible to budget and to plan for both the present and future cost and needs of these inmates. For instance, the lack of a definition impedes prisoner administrators from preventing or limiting the onset of medical decline. In a recent report researchers at the Urban Institute stated that "… it is imperative to develop and adopt a consistent definition of 'older prisoners'" (Kim and Peterson 2014, p. 21). A clear functional definition or classification would allow prison administrators to plan more effectively for the future cost of this population.

Types of Elderly Inmates

If you stopped a citizen on the street and asked them to describe the elderly inmate, they would probably describe a weak, docile, and infirm inmate. While some inmates conform to this description, the elderly inmate population in reality is heterogeneous in nature (Johnson 1988; Kerbs and Jolley 2009; Kerbs 2000). There exist three types of elderly inmate; each group exhibiting differences in offending patterns and varying in how well they adapt to prison life.

The most recognizable group is long-term inmates who have grown old in prison. These inmates often were incarcerated in the 1980s and 1990s and are serving life sentences (Abner 2006; Cox and Lawrence 2010; Kerbs and Jolley 2009). The increase in their numbers is often attributed to changes in sentencing policies established during this time period and resulting in keeping inmates in prison for longer periods of time. Research indicates that during the early years of their confinement this population experience significant adjustment problems but as the years have gone by they have tended to adjust to the prison environment and become model citizens (Lipman et al. 1985).

The second group is comprised of first time offenders, incarcerated late in life. As the U.S. elderly population has increased significantly, corresponding increases in first time offenders falling between 50 and 65 has increased (Kerbs and Jolley 2009). These inmates for the most part comprised of males who have committed violent offenses, often against family members (Aday 1994). Correctional administrators have also witnessed increases in the elderly first time offender population as a result of changes in sex offender statutes and increases in reporting of older individuals for sex offenses (Flynn 1998; 2000). Many of these violent and sexual predators were likely sentenced around 60 years of age and their offenses occurred without premeditation (Teller and Howell 1981; Williams 1989). Included in this category is a smaller group of first-time white-collar crime, drug, and alcohol offenders (Fry 1988). These elderly first time offenders often experience problems adjusting to the life behind bars (Lipman, Lowery, and Sussman 1985).

The final category is the recidivists or life-course persistent offenders. The life-course persistent offender started out involved in the criminal lifestyle early in life, has spent much of his/her life involved with the criminal justice system, and prison is a revolving door. These individuals continue their criminal involvement across different situations and conditions leading them to become institutionally dependent (Kerbs 2000; Kerbs and Jolley 2009; Moffitt 1993).

Profile of the Elderly Inmate

How many inmates currently fit the elderly designation? The answer to this question is important because it establishes the scope of the problem and aids advocates and policy-makers in determining the best approach for handling problems. Collecting and presenting data has the added advantage of creating greater public awareness and facilitating resource acquisition during incarceration and upon release. To examine the scope of the elderly inmate population

Figure 3-2. Sentenced State Prisoners by Age

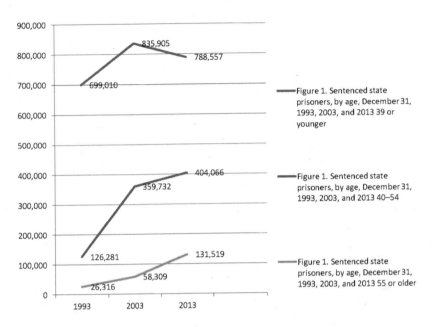

Source: Carson, E.A. (2016). Aging of the State Prison Population, 1993–2013. U.S. Department of Justice, Bureau of Justice Statistics, p. 1. Retrieved January 17, 2017 from https://www.bjs.gov/content/pub/pdf/aspp9313.pdf.

it is useful to review national, state-level, and county-wide data on the demographics of this population.

Nationally we witnessed significant increases in the elderly prison population over the last five years. Between 2007 and 2010 the number of state and federal prisoners who were age 65 or older grew by 63 percent (*2007—16,100 and 2010—26,200*). An analysis of federal and state data for those aged 55 and older is even more revealing. In 2007 there were 76,600 prisoners aged 55 or older by 2010 the number had grown to 124,400 or a 62.4% increase (Bureau of Justice Statistics). More recent figures (see Figure 3-2 and Table 3-2) show that by 2013 there were more than 131,000 prisoners aged 55 or older (Carson and Anderson 2016). Many of whom were admitted into state custody at age 55 or older rather than turning that age after incarceration. In fact the Human Rights Watch report indicates that the number of prisoners aged 55 or older grew at over a six times faster pace than the rest of the prison population (282 percent vs. 42.1 percent).

Table 3-2. Sentenced State Prisoners by Age
December 31, 1993, 2003, 2013

Age	Number	Percent	Number	Percent	Number	Percent
18–19	27,500	3.2	22,800	1.8	14,300	1.1
20–24	164,700	19.2	197,100	15.7	163,000	12.3
25–29	208,400	24.3	216,800	17.2	213,300	16.1
30–34	180,400	21	203,200	16.2	218,000	16.5
35–39	117,900	13.7	195,900	15.6	179,900	13.6
40–44	72,800	8.5	179,300	14.3	155,200	11.7
45–49	34,800	4.1	117,700	9.4	136,600	10.3
50–54	18,700	2.2	62,700	5	112,200	8.5
55–59	12,600	1.5	31,300	2.5	68,000	5.1
60–64	7,700	0.9	15,000	1.2	34,400	2.6
65 or older	6,000	0.7	12,000	1	29,100	2.2
40–54	126,300	14.7%	359,700	28.6%	404,100	30.5%
55 or older	26,300	3.1	58,300	4.6	131,500	9.9
Total	857,675	100%	1,256,442	100%	1,325,305	100%
Mean age	31.7 years		35.2 years		37.8 years	
Median age	30		34		36	

Source: Carson, E.A. (2016). Aging of the State Prison Population, 1993–2013. U.S. Department of Justice, Bureau of Justice Statistics, p. 2. Retrieved January 17, 2017 from https://www.bjs.gov/content/pub/pdf/aspp9313.pdf.

The imprisonment rate of for those 50 years of age and older has also increased over time. According to Table 3-3 the rate of imprisonment for state prisoners 65 and older in 2013 is three and half times higher than in 1993 (Carson and Anderson 2016). These elderly prisoners are serving significantly longer sentences. The Human Rights Watch (2012) reports that:

- 20% of the prisoners between 61 and 70 are serving sentences of more than 20 years (p. 26);
- 17% of prisoners who entered in 2009 when they were age 51 or older have sentences ranging from more than 20 years to life (p. 27);

Table 3-3. Imprisonment Rate of Sentenced State Prisoners per 100,000 U.S. Adults for Ages 50 and Older

Age	1993	2003	2013
Total	448	575	543
50–54	144	326	497
55–59	117	194	318
60–64	75	122	188
65 or older	18	33	64
40–54	259	562	628
55 or older	49	90	154
Number of prisoners	857,675	1,256,442	1,325,305

Source: Carson, E.A. (2016). Aging of the State Prison Population, 1993–2013. U.S. Department of Justice, Bureau of Justice Statistics, p. 4. Retrieved January 17, 2017 from https://www.bjs.gov/content/pub/pdf/aspp9313.pdf.

- In New York, 28% of prisoners age 60 or older have been in prison continuously for more than 20 years (p. 32);
- In Pennsylvania 66% of older inmates were serving a maximum sentence of 10 years or more (p. 33);
- Among the 16 states in the Southern Legislative Conference, at least 30% of the elderly inmates in each of the states are serving sentences of at least 20 years or more (p. 33).

Recent figures (see Table 3-4) provided by the Bureau of Justice Statistics indicate that approximately 31% of prisoners aged 65 and older were serving life sentences and less than 1% were housed on death row in the U.S. (Carson and Anderson 2016). Half of these offenders had already served 121 months or more. Such lengthy sentences were primarily a result of the commission of violent, property, or drug-related crimes.

Minority Representation

Not surprisingly, the imprisonment rate for minorities aged 50 and older is quite high (see Table 3-5). Whether one examines those aged 50–54, 5–

Table 3-4. Sentence Length, Most Serious Offense, and Time Served for State Prisoners over Age 65

Sentence length	100%
Less than life or death	68.8
Life	30.6
Death	0.6
Most serious offense by sentence length	
Violent offenses	100%
Less than life or death	69.1
Life	30.4
Death	0.6
Estimated number of prisoners	20,600
Property offenses	100%
Less than life or death	92.6
Life	7.4
Death	0
Estimated number of prisoners	1,700
Drug offenses	100%
Less than life or death	96
Life	4
Death	0
Estimated number of prisoners	1,400
Time served to date	100%
12 months or less	9.9
13–24 months	7.6
25–36 months	6.4
37–60 months	9.3
61–120 months	16.5
121 months or more	50.4

Source: Carson, E.A. (2016). Aging of the State Prison Population, 1993–2013. U.S. Department of Justice, Bureau of Justice Statistics, p. 5. Retrieved January 17, 2017 from https://www.bjs.gov/content/pub/pdf/aspp9313.pdf.

Table 3-5. Imprisonment Rate State Prisoners Aged 50 and Older by Race and Hispanic Origin in 2013

Age	White	Black	Hispanic
	2946	1,704	741
50–54	306	1,537	589
55–59	188	1,010	432
60–64	115	567	295
65 or older	45	164	120
40–54	387	1,868	715
55 or older	93	509	256
	468,600	497,000	274,200

Source: Carson, E.A. (2016). Aging of the State Prison Population, 1993–2013. U.S. Department of Justice, Bureau of Justice Statistics, p. 11. Retrieved January 17, 2017 from https://www.bjs.gov/content/pub/pdf/aspp9313.pdf.

59, 60–64, or 65 and older, the African-American imprisonment rate ranges from three to ten times higher than their White counterparts. In this analysis, Hispanics also do not fare well in terms of their likelihood of imprisonment. A comparison of the sentenced state prisoner total population numbers reveals an astonishing amount of growth for African-American and Hispanic groups (see Table 3-6).

Female Elderly Prisoners

There has also been a significant increase in the number of female elderly prisoners. The imprisonment rate for females in 2013 is four times greater than in 1993 (see Table 3-7). California experienced a 35 percent increase in the past decade (Williams et al. 2006). In Florida, 5.6 percent (910) of the geriatric prisoner population was female (Florida Department of Corrections 2012). On June 30th, 2012, in South Carolina approximately 15 percent of black female prisoners are aged 50 or older and the figure for white females is 13 percent (South Carolina Department of Corrections 2012).

Table 3-6. Total Population of Sentenced State Prisoners Aged 50 and Older by Race and Hispanic Origin

Age at Yearend	1993			2003			2013		
	White	Black	Hispanic	White	Black	Hispanic	White	Black	Hispanic
Total	302,600	380,900	150,500	423,200	503,000	254,300	468,600	497,000	274,200
50–54	10,300	5,000	2,800	25,000	23,700	9,400	47,300	41,800	17,000
55–59	6,800	3,000	2,400	14,500	9,600	4,500	28,700	25,000	9,800
60–64	4,300	2,300	800	7,800	3,700	2,200	15,500	11,100	5,000
65 or older	3,000	2,700	200	6,500	2,800	1,700	16,000	6,500	4,200
40–54	57,700	44,600	19,600	139,100	142,900	56,700	160,400	148,500	71,800
55 or older	14,100	8,000	3,400	28,800	16,100	8,400	60,200	42,500	18,900

Source: Carson, E.A. (2016). Aging of the State Prison Population, 1993–2013. U.S. Department of Justice, Bureau of Justice Statistics, p. 8. Retrieved January 17, 2017 from https://www.bjs.gov/content/pub/pdf/aspp9313.pdf.

Table 3-7. Imprisonment Rate Sentenced State Female Prisoners by Age 1993, 2003, and 2013

Age	1993	2003	2013
Total	49	74	73
18–19	18	22	13
20–24	80	96	87
25–29	132	135	155
30–34	104	146	163
35–39	74	158	134
40–44	43	123	111
45–49	24	72	93
50–54	15	35	60
55–59	9	17	30
60–64	4	9	16
65 or older	1	2	4
40–54	29	79	87
55 or older	3	7	13
Number of prisoners	48,485	82,801	91,581

Source: Carson, E.A. (2016). Aging of the State Prison Population, 1993–2013. U.S. Department of Justice, Bureau of Justice Statistics, p. 10. Retrieved January 17, 2017 from https://www.bjs.gov/content/pub/pdf/aspp9313.pdf.

Federal prisons admitted 690 female prisoners over the age of 50 in 2010 (see Table 3-8 and Table 3-9). This trend suggests that the number of elderly female prisoners continues to rise.

The Needs of Elderly Inmates

Because the average cost for incarcerating a geriatric prisoner is two to three times that of younger prisoner, more attention has been paid to the needs and issues associated with the imprisoning the elderly (Kerbs 2000; Williams et al. 2006). Growing old in prison is associated with numerous impairments. These

Table 3-8. Federal Female Prisoner Trends 2007–2010

Age at Time of Commitment	Statistic	2007	2008	2009	2010
51–60 years	N	541	551	547	557
61–70 years	N	108	105	119	120
71–80 years	N	7	6	12	13
> 80 years	N	0	0	2	0
Total Records	N	71,933	71,663	74,336	73,972

Citation: BJS' Federal Justice Statistics Program website (http://bjs.ojp.usdoj.gov/fjsrc/).
Data Source: Bureau of Prisons—Extract from BOP's online Sentry System: 2007, (as standardized by the FJSRC) 2008, (as standardized by the FJSRC) 2009, (as standardized by the FJSRC) 2010 (as standardized by the FJSRC).

prisoners experience advanced rates of physical and emotional decline, more than those in the same age group in the general population (Colsher et al. 1992; Kerbs and Jolley 2009). For example, geriatric prisoners report high rates of functional impairment and often require help with the daily living activities (Colsher et al. 1992; Williams et al. 2006). There is an increased risk that the elderly in prison will be diagnosed with serious chronic and acute illnesses such as diabetes, heart disease, cancer, etc. (Colsher et al. 1992; Mitka 2004; Voelker 2004). Numerous studies have found that elderly prisoners experience higher rates of other geriatric conditions related to mobility, vision, hearing, and incontinence (Mitka 2004; Voelker 2004). In addition to advanced rates of

Table 3-9. Federal Female Prisoners by Age and Sentence Length in 2010

FY 2010 Prisoners Entering Federal Prison	
Age at Time of Commitment	N (Percent)
51–60 years	557 (80.7%)
61–70 years	120 (17.3%)
71–80 years	13 (1.9%)
Total N:	690

Citation: BJS' Federal Justice Statistics Program website (http://bjs.ojp.usdoj.gov/fjsrc/).
Data Source: Bureau of Prisons—Extract from BOP's online Sentry System, FY 2010 (as standardized by the FJSRC).

physical decline, relationships between age and mental health disorders, for instance dementia, depression, anxiety, have been established (Kerbs 2000; Williams et al. 2006).

As a result of age-related degeneration, geriatric prisoners may require special consideration while incarcerated. "Prisons are primarily designed for the young and able-bodied; it takes additional effort on the part of corrections officials to meet the need and respect the rights of the old and infirm" (Human Rights Watch 2012: 43). Prisons are rule-bound institutions and as such most have the same behavioral and work requirements for prisoners regardless of age (Anno et al. 2004). Because of age-related memory problems and other mental health issues, geriatric prisoners may be unable to engage in the same level of prison work as their younger counterparts (Fazel et al. 2001). Moreover, the majority of correctional institutions do not include environmental modifications for the functional impairments demonstrated by geriatric prisoners (Williams et al. 2006). For example, many lack bathroom handrails and have a limited number, if any, ramps for wheel chairs. Most institutions do not take into consideration the risks associated with housing the elderly among the general population of inmates (Human Rights Watch 2012; Kerbs and Jolley 2009; Terhune 1999). Elderly prisoners may be find it difficult to rest in the top bunk and may be more easily victimized by younger cellmates (Human Right Watch 2012). Additionally, as functioning deteriorates elderly prisoners may need help getting dressed, eating, cleaning up after themselves (Terhune 1999). Consequently, the elderly prisoner may be unable to cope with institutional life without an aide to help under these circumstances (Faiver 1998; Kerbs and Jolley 2009).

Conclusion

Elderly prisoners represent one of the fastest growing segments of the inmate population. Many academics, policymakers, and concerned citizens now question the utility of spending so much to incarcerate the elderly (see for example, article written by Chettiar, Bunting, and Schotter 2012). Still others discuss this problem in terms of a national epidemic (ACLU 2012). In order to determine the best approach for addressing the problems associated with geriatric prisoners, we need to conduct an in-depth examination of the physical and mental health plight for those aged 50 and above who reside behind institutional walls.

Websites

For more information on the elderly population projections, visit http://www.census.gov.

For more information on human rights issues and aging prisoners, visit https://www.hrw.org/.

For more information on the profile of elderly prisoners, visit https://www.bjs.gov/.

References

Abner, C. (2006). *Graying prisons: States face challenges of an aging inmate population*. Retrieved from http://www.csg.org/knowledgecenter/docs/sn0611 GrayingPrisons.pdf.

ACLU (2012). At America's expense: The mass incarceration of the elderly. American Civil Liberties Union. Retrieved March 12, 2013 from http://www.aclu.org/files/assets/elderlyprisonreport_20120613_1.pdf.

Aday, R. H. (1994). Aging in prison: A case study of new elderly offenders. *International Journal of Offender Therapy and Comparative Criminology, 38,* 79–91.

Aday, R. H., & Nation, P. (2001). *A case study of older female offenders.* Nashville, TN: Tennessee Department of Corrections.

Aday, R. H. (2003). *Aging prisoners: Crisis in American corrections.* Wesport, CT: Praeger Publishers.

Aday, R. H., & Webster, E. L. (1979). Aging in prison: The development of a preliminary model. *Offender Rehabilitation, 3,* 272–282.

Agency for Health Care Research and Quality (2012). Most health care costs incurred by few Americans. Retrieved from http://www.ahrq.gov/news/nn/nn011212.htm.

American Correctional Association (1992). *Directory: Juvenile and adult correctional departments, institutions, agencies and paroling authorities.* Laurel, MD: The Association.

Anno, B. J., Graham, C., Lawrence, J. E., Shansky, R., Bisbee, J., & Blackmore, J. (2004). *Correctional health care: Addressing the needs of elderly, chronically ill, and terminally ill inmates.* Aurora, CO: National Institute of Corrections.

Arias, E. (2010). *United States life tables, 2006.* (National vital statistics reports, vol. 58 no. 21). Hyattsville, MD: National Center for Health Statistics. Retrieved from Center for Disease Control and Prevention website: http://www.cdc.gov/nchs/data/nvsr/nvsr58/nvsr58_21.pdf.

Binswanger, I., Stern, M., Deyo, R., et al. (2007). Release from prison—A high risk of death for former inmates. *New England Journal of Medicine,* 356(2), 157–165.

Binswanger, I., Krueger, P., & Steiner, J. (2009). Prevalence of chronic medical conditions among jail and prison inmates in the USA compared with the general population. *Journal of Epidemiological Community Health,* 63(11), 912–919.

Bonta, J., Law, M., & Hanson, R. K. (1998). The prediction of criminal and violent recidivism among mentally disordered offenders: A meta-analysis. *Psychological Bulletin, 123,* 123–142.

Carson, E. & Anderson, e. (2016). *Prisoners in 2015.* U.S. Department of Justice, Bureau of Justice Statistics. https://www.bjs.gov/content/pub/pdf/p15.pdf.

Caverley, S. J. (2006). Older mentally ill inmates: A descriptive study. *Journal of Correctional Health Care, 12,* 262–268.

Chettiar, IM, Bunting, W., & Schotter, G. (2012). At America's Expense: The mass incarceration of the elderly. New York University Law and Economic Working Papers, Paper 301.

Colby, S. & Ortman, J. (2015). *Projections of the size and composition of the U.S. population: 2014 to 2060 population estimates and projections.* U.S. Census Bureau. Retrieved from https://www.census.gov/content/dam/Census/library/publications/2015/demo/p25-1143.pdf.

Colsher, P. L., Wallace, R. B., Loeffelholz, P. L., & Sales, M. (1992). Health status of older male prisoners: A comprehensive survey. *American Journal of Public Health, 82,* 881–884.

Corrections Yearbook (2000). Criminal Justice Institute: South Salem, NY.

Cox, J. (1982). *Self-perceptions of health and aging of older females in prison: An exploratory groups case study.* (Unpublished doctoral dissertation). Southern Illinois University, Carbondale, IL.

Cox, J., & Lawrence, J. E. (2010). Planning services for elderly inmates with mental illness. *Corrections Today, 72*(3), 52–57. Retrieved from http://www.aca.org/fileupload/177/ahaidar/1_Cox_Lawrence.pdf.

Craig-Moreland, D. E. (2002). The needs of elderly offenders. In Palacios, W.R., Cromwell, P. F. & Dunham, R. G. (Eds.), *Crime & justice in America: Present realities and future prospects* (pp. 370–373). Upper Saddle River, NJ: Prentice Hall.

Crawley, E. (2005). Institutional thoughtlessness in prisons and its impacts on the day-to-day prison lives of elderly men. *Journal of Contemporary Criminal Justice, 21,* 350–363.

Crawley, E. & Sparks, R. (2005). Older men in prison: Survival, coping and identity. In Liebling, A. & Maruna, S. (Eds.), *The effects of imprisonment* (pp. 343–365). Cullompton, UK: Willan.

Criminal Justice Institute. (2000). *Corrections Yearbook.* (2000). South Salem, NY: Author.

Faiver, K. L. (1998). Special issues of aging. In Faiver, K. (Ed.), *Health care management issues in corrections* (pp. 123–132). Lanham MD: American Correctional Association.

Falter, R. G. (1999). Selected predictors of health service needs of inmates over age 50. *Journal of Correctional Health Care, 6,* 149–175.

Fazel, S., Hope, T., O'Donnell, I. et al. (2001). Health of elderly male prisoners: Worse than the general population, worse than younger prisoners. *Age Aging, 30,* 403–407.

Flanagan, T. (1983). Correlates of institutional misconduct among state prisoners. *Criminology, 21,* 29–39.

Florida Department of Corrections (2013). Elderly Inmates. Retrieved from http://www.dc.State.fl.us/pub/annual/1011/ar-additional-facts-elderly.html.

Flynn, E. E. (1992). The graying of America's prison population. *The Prison Journal, 72,* 77–98.

Flynn, E. (1998). *Managing elderly offenders: A national assessment.* Washington, DC: National Institute of Justice.

Flynn, E. (2000). Elders as perpetrators. In M. Rothman & B. Sunlop (Eds.), *Elders, crime, and the criminal justice system: Myths, perceptions and reality in the 21st century* (pp. 207–228). New York, NY: Springer Publishing Company.

Fry, L. (1988). The concerns of older inmates in a minimum security prison setting. In McCarthy, B. & Langworthy, R, (Eds.), *Older offenders: Perspectives in criminology and criminal justice* (pp. 157–163). New York, NY: Praeger.

Gal, M. (2002). The physical and mental health of older offenders. *Forum on Corrections Research, 14,* 15–19.

Genders, E., & Player, E. (1990). Women lifers: Assessing the experience. *The Prison Journal, 80,* 46–57.

Gentry, H. (1987). *A comparison of the chronic rule violator, the occasional rule violator and the non-violator in the Texas department of corrections.* (Unpublished master's thesis). Sam Houston State University, Huntsville, TX.

Goetting, A. (1984). The elderly in prison: A profile. *Criminal Justice Review, 9,* 14–24.

Greco, R. (1996). I'm in prison, my mind is not! *Perspective on Aging, 25,* 25–27.

Grove, W. M., & Meehl, P. E. (1996). Comparative efficiency of informal (subjective, impressionistic) and formal (mechanical, algorithmic) prediction procedures: The clinical-statistical controversy. *Psychology, Public Policy, and Law, 2,* 293–323.

Harrison, M. T. (2006). True Grit: An innovative program for elderly inmates. *Corrections Today, 68,* 46–49.

Harrison, P. M., & Beck, A. J. (2004). *Prisoners in 2003.* Washington, DC: Bureau of Justice Statistics.

Hooyman, N., & Kiyak, H. A. (1999). *Social gerontology.* Boston, MA: Allyn & Bacon.

Human Rights Watch. (2012). Old behind bars: The aging prison population in the United States. Retrieved from http://www.hrw.org/sites/default/files/reports/usprisons0112webwcover_0.pdf.

Jensen, G. (1977). Age and rule breaking in prison: A test of socio-cultural interpretations. *Criminology, 14,* 555–568.

Johnson, E. H. (1988). Care for elderly inmates: Conflicting concerns and purposes in prisons. In B. McCarthy & R. Langworthy (Eds.), *Older offenders: Perspectives in criminology and criminal justice* (pp. 157–163). New York, NY: Praeger.

Kaye, L. W. (1997). *Self-help support groups for older women.* Washington, DC: Taylor & Francis.

Kerbs, J. J. (2000). The older prisoner: Social, psychological, and medical considerations. In D.B. Dunlop & M.B. Rothman (Eds.), *Elders, Crime, and the Criminal Justice System: Myths, perceptions and reality in the 21st century* (pp. 207–228). New York, NY: Springer Publishing Company.

Kerbs, J. J., & Jolley, J. M. (2009). Challenges posed by older prisoners: What we know about America's aging prison population. In R. Tewksbury and D. Dabney (Eds), *Prisons and jails: A reader* (pp. 389–411). New York, NY: McGraw Hill.

Kim, K. & Peterson, B. (2014). *Aging behind bars: Trends and implications of graying prisoners in the federal system.* Urban Institute.

Kratcoski P. C., & Babb, S. (1990). Adjustment of older inmates: An analysis by institutional structure and gender. *Journal of Contemporary Criminal Justice, 6,* 139–156.

Lemieuz, C. M., Dyeson, T. B., & Castiglione, B. (2002). Revisiting the literature on prisoners who are older: Are we wiser? *The Prison Journal, 82,* 440–458.

Lipman, A., Lowery, S., & Sussman, M. (1985). *Crime and the elderly.* Tampa, FL: International Exchange Center on Gerontology, University of South Florida.

Loeb, S. J., & Steffensmeier, D. (2006). Older male prisoners: Health status, self-efficacy beliefs, and health-promoting behaviors. *Journal of Correctional Health Care, 12,* 269–278.

Marquart, J. W., Merianos, D. E., & Doucet, G. (2000). The health-related concern of older prisoners: Implications for policy. *Ageing and Society, 20,* 79–96.

McShane, M. D., & Williams, F. P. (1990). Old and ornery: The disciplinary Experiences of elderly prisoners. *International Journal of Offender Therapy and Comparative Criminology, 34,* 197–212.

Meyer, J. (2001). *Age 2000:* Retrieved from U.S. Census Bureau website: http://www.census.gov/prod/2001pubs/c2kbr01-12.pdf.

Mitka, M. (2004). Aging prisoners stressing health care system. *Journal of the American Medical Association (JAMA), 292*(4), 423–424.

Moffitt, T. E. (1993). Adolescent-limited and life-course persistent antisocial behavior: A developmental taxonomy. *Psychological Review,* 100, 674–701.

Moore, E. O. (1989). Prison environments and their impact on older citizens. *Journal of Offender Counseling, Services &Rehabilitation, 2,* 175–191.

Morton, J. B. (1992). *An Administrative overview of the older inmate.* Washington, DC: U.S. Department of Justice.

Morton, J. B., & Anderson, J. C. (1982). Elderly offenders: The forgotten minority. *Corrections Today, 44,* 14–20.

Mossman, D. (1994). Assessing predictions of violence: Being accurate about accuracy. *Journal of Consulting and Clinical Psychology, 62,* 783–792.

Murphy, S., Xu, J., & Kochanek, K. (2011) Deaths: Preliminary data for 2010. *National Vital Statistics Reports, 60(4).* Retrieved from http://www.cdc.gov/nchs/data/nvsr/nvsr60/nvsr60_04.pdf.

Osborne Association (2016). The high cost of low risk: The crisis of America's aging prison population. Retrieved from http://www.osborneny.org/images/uploads/printMedia/Osborne_Aging_WhitePaper.pdf.

Sabbath, M. J., & Cowles, E. L. (1988). Factors affecting the adjustment of elderly inmates to prison. In B. McCarthy & R. Langworthy (Eds.), *Older offenders: Perspectives in criminology and criminal justice* (pp. 157–163). New York, NY: Praeger.

Shrestha, L. (2006). *Life expectancy in the United States.* Retrieved from United States Senate website: http://aging.senate.gov/crs/aging1.pdf.

Spaulding, A., Seals, R., McCallum, V., Perez, S., Brzozowski, A., & Streenlan, N. (2011). Prisoner survival inside and outside of the institution: Implications for health-care planning. *American Journal of Epidemiology,* 173 (5): 479–487. Retrieved from http://aje.oxfordjournals.org/content/early/2011/01/14/aje.kwq422.full.pdf+html.

Stewart, J. (2000). The reintegration effort for long-term infirm and elderly federal offenders (RELIEF) program. *Forum on Corrections Research, 12,* 35–38.

Taylor, P. J., & Parrott, J. M. (1988). Elderly offenders: A study of age-related factors among custodially remanded prisoners. *British Journal of Psychiatry, 152,* 340–346.

Teller, F. E., & Howell, R. J. (1981). The older prisoner: Criminal and psychological characteristics. *Criminology, 18,* 549–555.

Terhune, C., Cambra, S., Steinberg, J. et al. (1999). Older inmates: The impact of an aging population on the correctional system. An Internal Planning Document for the California Department of Corrections.

Vega, M., & Silverman, M. (1988). Stress and the elderly convict. *International Journal of Offender Therapy and Comparative Criminology, 32,* 153–162.

Voelker, R. (2004). New Initiatives target inmates' health. *JAMA, 291,* 1549–1551.

Walsh, C. E. (1990). *Needs of older inmates in varying security settings.* (Doctoral Dissertation). Rutgers the State University of New Jersey, University Microfilms International, Newark, NJ.

Werner, C. (2011). *The Older Population: 2010.* Retrieved from U.S. Census Bureau website: http://www.census.gov/prod/cen2010/briefs/c2010br-09.pdf.

Williams, G. C. (1989). *Elderly offenders: A comparison of the chronic and new offenders.* (Unpublished thesis). Middle Tennessee State University, Murfreesboro, TN.

Wilson, D. G, & Vito, G. F. (1986). Imprisoned elders: The experience of one Institution. *Criminal Justice Policy Review, 1,* 399–421.

Chapter 4

Medical Health Issues

We are in the midst of a dramatic rise in prisoner age, a trend that will continue to skyrocket unless there is equally dramatic reform. This fastest-growing group of prisoners is also our most expensive. Because of the health care and physical needs of aging prisoners, our prisons find themselves ill equipped to handle their aging prisoner population—prisoners who cost twice as much to incarcerate as younger prisoners (Chettiear and Bunting 2012).

As elderly inmates enter prison or long-term inmates age in prison and become elderly there is a corresponding medical cost directly related to their geriatric care. Accordingly the increasing price of inmate healthcare is one of the primary driving forces of the rising costs of incarceration (Kim and Peterson 2014; The Pew Center on the States 2012). These health costs and challenges are further exacerbated for long-term and elderly offender populations. Healthwise, inmates appear 10 years older than their non-incarcerated counterparts, i.e. 50-year-old inmates appear to physiologically be 60 years old (Maschi and Aday 2014; Petersilia 2001). Hence, in many jurisdictions, inmates 50 years of age are considered elderly (Morton 2001; Petersilia 2001). The inescapable truth is that many long-term inmates will age in prison and become elderly. Not surprisingly these two concepts of long-term inmates and elderly inmates are deeply intertwined. Research indicates that both length of incarceration combined with the age of the inmate increase the intensity and severity of medical and mental health complications among prisoners (Petersilia 2001; The Pew Charitable Trusts and John D. and Catherine T. MacArthur Foundation 2014). Moreover, elderly inmates present more serious and chronic health issues than younger, shorter-term prisoners (Morton 2001) or individuals in the community (Fruedenberg 2001; Hammett, Roberts, and Kennedy 2001; Robillard et al. 2003). The end result is an accelerated aging process resulting in correctional expen-

---

Box 4-1. Why Focus on Medical Issues?

• They are entitled to a certain level of care.
• The majority of long-term and elderly inmates will be released from prison, posing a health risk to society at large if released without having received adequate medical care.
• There are significant social costs associated with their health that are transferred to the communities that they return to.

---

ditures that are now in the billions per year across the country (The Pew Charitable Trusts and John D. and Catherine T. MacArthur Foundation 2014).

The true rate of medical problems within correctional environments can be difficult to determine. The best available data is provided as a result of institutional reporting of the medical problems self-reported by inmates or that are a result of inmate deaths during incarceration. (See for example the Deaths in Custody Reporting Program sponsored by the Bureau of Justice Statistics http://bjs.ojp.usdoj.gov/index.cfm?ty=dcdetail&iid=243#Documentation.) Unger and Buchanan (1985) noted that long-term inmates aging in prison were uniquely different in terms of health concerns than those inmates serving shorter sentences. It was not until the late 1980s, however, that the needs of elderly offenders and the complications and inability of prison system to meet that need began to be studied (Morton 2001). This chapter highlights some of the more common issues surrounding long-term and elderly offender health care.

Why Focus on the Medical Issues of Long-Term and Elderly Inmates?

There are four primary reasons why a focus on elderly and long-term inmate medical needs is of critical importance to address. First and foremost prisons are not designed for healthy living. Despite reductions in overall correctional admissions, many prisons operate at full capacity or significantly above capacity, and often resort to double or triple celling. Such practices increase health risks via the use of shared razor blades, drug use, tattooing, and increased opportunities for consensual and nonconsensual sexual relations (Restum 2005; Sieck and Demba 2011). As a result of the placement of large numbers of inmates in a confined space, prisoners have opportunities to pass on their infectious diseases to other prisoners, staff, and their own friends and family who visit. Moreover, given the large number of offenders entering prisons, correctional systems are often challenged in their ability to effectively screen for diseases upon admission and may only catch debilitating diseases after they have become aggressive and are life-threatening (Restum 2005). This fact has caused some to assert that prisoners receive poorer care (Winter 2011) for serious and chronic medical conditions.

Second, inmates do not lose all of their rights upon the closing of the prison gates. They are as U.S. citizens entitled to a certain level of dignified care (Anno 2001; Vaughn and Smith 1999). This is especially true given their increased risk of contracting communicable diseases during their incarceration (Kinsella 2004). Since the state is responsible for their custody, it consequently falls to the state to provide an adequate level of health care. Courts have repeatedly held that correctional agencies must provide adequate health care for inmates (Kinsella 2004).

Third, the majority of long-term and elderly inmates will be released from prison posing a health risk to society at large if released without having received adequate medical care. (Jones, Connelly, and Wagner 2001; Petersilia 2003; Robillard et al. 2003; Travis and Visher 2005). Inmates with untreated communicable diseases may transmit those diseases to family members and others in the community upon release. As Shuter (2002: 167) states, a "common feature of all of these infections is the ability of a small core group of individuals possessing specific sociodemographic and/or physiologic characteristics to exert a disproportionate force in the spread of illness through communities." For example, recent research indicates that untreated communicable diseases have been associated with outbreaks of tuberculosis, HIV and Aids, and hepatitis in the community (Crosland, Poshkus, and Rich 2003; Glaser and Greifinger 1993; Hammett, Harmon, and Rhodes 2002; Hammett, Roberts, and Kennedy 2001; Robillard et al. 2003).

Finally, because long-term and elderly inmates upon release experience an accelerated aging process and suffer from more health problems than similarly aged individuals in the community, there are significant social costs associated with their health that are transferred to the communities that they return to (Jones, Connelly, and Wagner 2001; Meyer 2003; Webster et al. 2005). Often these released inmates must immediately seek state sponsored medical care such as emergency rooms or free clinic care in order to have their medical needs addressed (Crosland, Poshkus, and Rich 2003; Hammett, Harmon, and Rhodes 2002; Hammett, Roberts, and Kennedy 2001). At least one research article suggested that a released offender committed crime in order to return to prison and receive care when he was unable to have his medical concerns addressed in the community (Hammett, Roberts, and Kennedy 2001).

Rest assured that the problems and risks associated with inmate healthcare have not gone unnoticed. "Although public sentiment in an era of more restricted health care may resist the idea of expanding the scope and intensity of medical services in correctional facilities, the public health community in this Nation resoundingly endorses the aggressive diagnosis and treatment of prisoners as a critical, cost-effective measure to improve health both inside and outside the facilities" (Shuter 2002: 167).

Costs of Medical Care for the Elderly and Long-Term Prisoner

The cost of medical care is growing annually by 10%, and these costs will only accelerate as the prison population ages (Lamb-Mechanick and Nelson 2000; The Pew Charitable Trusts 2008; State Health Care Expenditure Report 2001). States housing the largest share of older inmates "incur higher per-inmate health care spending" (The Pew Charitable Trusts and John D. and Catherine T. MacArthur Foundation 2014, p. 1). A 2012 Vera Institute report estimates that it costs at least 40 states upwards of $335 million to provide health and hospital care for the prison population (Henreichson and Delaney 2012). In Ohio the estimated yearly cost per inmate for health care is around $4,780 and the cost of pharmaceuticals alone for 2010 in the state cost $28.5 million (Geisler 2011). Massachusetts reports spending close to $100 million a year on prisoner health care (Puleo and Chedekel 2011). The Legislative Analyst Office in California spends on average for each inmate per year $8,768 for medical care, $988 for pharmaceuticals, and $748 for dental care. In Florida the reported health care costs for elderly inmates are three times the cost for younger inmates (The Florida House of Representatives 1999). In at least ten states the largest share of costs (37% of their budget) is utilized to provide general medical care—doctors, nurses, physician assistants, and medical supplies (The Pew Charitable Trusts and John D. and Catherine T. MacArthur Foundation 2014, p. 6). To a large extent these costs across such states are directly attributable to the aging and long-term inmate population (see page 12 of the Pew Charitable Trusts and John D. and Catherine T. MacArthur Foundation 2014 report).

As the inmate population continues to age, a larger and larger share of correctional budgets must be expended to address the physical and emotional needs of elderly and long term inmates (Drake 2005; Kinsella 2004). At present there are more than 245,000 prisoners aged 50 and older (ACLU 2012). On average these aging prisoner costs taxpayers about twice as much (an estimated $16 billion per year) as the average prisoner (ACLU 2012; Rudolph 2012). This figure represents an average cost of $68,000 per year for an inmate older than 50 compared

---

Box 4-2. Specialized Care for Aging Prisoners

1. Assisted Living — There are elderly inmates who don't just need daily medications, they also need assisted living. They need help going to the toilet, brushing their teeth, and some need to be wheeled around if they want to attend church, or move from room to room.
2. Nursing Home Care — Elderly inmates, who are totally dependent, require the same level of care as the elderly who are not incarcerated.
3. Alzheimer's Disease — We all understand the effects of Alzheimer's. Imagine suffering from Alzheimer's disease in a facility that is understaffed to handle mental illness. It can cost prisons a lot to have mental health specialists commuting to their facilities each day.
4. Geriatric Prison Units — Some prisons have such a high number of elderly inmates that they have to build special geriatric prison units for their elderly prisoners. Naturally, it is the states, and their taxpayers, who foot the bill.
5. General Medicine — Elderly inmates need more medications than younger inmates. Sometimes, generic medicine is provided, but other times, elderly prisoners are given the same name brand medications that any person receives from a normal pharmacy.

Source: Roberts, C. (2012). Elderly Inmates—The Cost of Dealing with an Elderly Prison Population. Universal Senior Living. Available at http://www.universalseniorliving.com/article/elderly-inmates-cost-dealing-elderly-prison-population.

$34,000 per year for the average prisoner (ACLU 2012; Rudolph 2012). The average cost of housing an inmate over 60 in the United States was reported as approximately $70,000 (USA Today). A figure confirmed in the state of Illinois in a John Howard Association Report and asserted to be a consequence of having to pay for the complications associated with chronic medical conditions among the elderly (John Howard Association 2012). "Moreover, while only 11% of North Carolina's prisoners are age 50 and older, the $25 million it costs the state each year to provide healthcare to these aging prisoners constitutes nearly 30% of the state's total correctional healthcare budget" (ACLU 2012). In the state of Washington, older offenders accounted for 10.6% of the total inmate population, yet accounted for 25% of off-site medical trips; 16% of on-site medical visits, and 51% of expenditures for overall hospital costs (Drake 2005: 4).

There are several factors that have driven up the costs for elderly and long term inmates. Because prisoners are entitled to adequate health care, most prison systems now must provide assisted living quarters, nursing home type care, treat Alzheimer's, create geriatric prison units, and provide more general medical care specific to aging populations (Roberts 2012; Williams et al. 2010; Williams et al. 2011; Williams et al. 2012).

What and Who Is to Blame?

A prominent theoretical debate among correctional theorists occurs over whether inmate adaptation to prison is a result of characteristics that they brought with them (imported) into prison or ensues because of the deprivations experienced (Dhami, Ayton, and Loewenstein 2007; Thomas 1977). A similar debate exists with regard to the medical problems of long-term and elderly inmates (Kerbs 2002a; 2002b; Kerbs 2006). Some theorize that the fact that inmates experience an accelerated aging process is primarily a result of their lifestyle prior to incarceration (Jones, Connelly, and Wagner 2001). Offenders are well-known for their participation in risky lifestyles characterized by smoking, use of alcohol, illicit use of drugs, risky sexual behavior, poor diet, and limited medical care (Webster et al. 2005; Sampson and Lauritsen 1990; Shaffer 2004). Their often impoverished pre-prison environments are considered breeding grounds for infectious diseases (Restrum 2005). All of which are factors that are thought to contribute to the majority of deaths in the country (Danaei, Ding, Mozaffarian, Taylor, Rehm, Murray, and Ezzati 2009).

Inmates themselves may be responsible for the deterioration in their health after incarceration by engaging in risky behaviors after incarceration. Most notably are institutional behaviors associated with drug use (Kang, Deren, and Andia 2005; Niveau 2006; Seal. Belcher, and Morrow 2004; Sieck and Demba 2011); sexual relations (Hensley, Tewksbury and Wright 2001; Kerbs 2002; Okie 2007; Seal, Margolis, and Morrow 2008; Sieck and Demba 2011); and tattooing (Kerbs 2002; Hellard and Aitken 2004; Sieck and Demba 2011).

Another possible explanation for the increased health problems that inmates exhibit is that the rise in medical problems is a direct reflection of inadequacies within the institutional medical care system. From this perspective the current health system is presumed to be so substandard as to heighten the medical problems by focusing on triage rather curing (Leonard 2012). Correctional systems across the country have long failed to provide adequate and sufficient health care is well documented in the literature (*Estelle v. Gamble 1976; Newman v. Alabama 1974;* Useem and Kimball 1989). In 2008 the ACLU filed a class action lawsuit against the director of the Nevada Department of Corrections for failing to provide prescribed medications and x-rays ordered by an outside physician, to treat Herpetic Iritis which could cause blindness, failing to treat Hepatitis C, arbitrarily discontinuing medications and running out of prescribed dosages of medications (ACLU 2008).

Box 4-3. Most Common Communicable Diseases Among Inmates

HIV/AIDS
Syphilis
Gonorrhea
Chlamydia
Trichomoniasis
Tuberculosis (TB)
Hepatitis (B and C)

Source: National Commission on Correctional Healthcare (2012). The Health Status of soon-to-be-released Inmates. Retrieved http://www.nchc.org.

Health Care Problems among Inmates

Although there is more information about what the medical problems of inmates are than ever before, this information has not always translated into better health care solutions. The greatest share of medical problems among prisoners is reported by offenders incarcerated for more than 72 months and who are older (Maruschak and Beck 2001). This section discusses the prevalence and incidence of medical problems among long-term and elderly inmates. The National Commission on Correctional Health Care (2002) has identified three categories of health care concerns that are salient among inmates: communicable diseases, chronic diseases, and mental health issues. A fourth category, general disabilities, has also been added. Each of these categories contains specific illnesses that should be considered by correctional administrators as priorities. It is difficult to determine the exact number of inmates who experience these disorders; but several sources of data exist which provide estimates related to prevalence and incidence (Hammett, Harmon and Rhodes 2002).

Communicable Diseases

Communicable diseases are illnesses capable of being transmitted from man to man, animal to man, or from the environment (water, air, food, etc.) to man. Most often they are referred to as contagious or infections illnesses. Twenty-one percent of prisoners and 14% of jail inmates self-reported ever having an infectious disease (Maruschak, Berzofsky and Unangst 2016). The percentage of prisoners reporting a communicable disease is much higher than the percentage who self-report in the general public. The most common occurring communicable diseases within incarcerated populations are HIV/AIDS, syphilis, gonorrhea, chlamydia, trichomoniasis, tuberculosis, and hepatitis (B and C) (NCCHC 2002). The public health implications for high rates of communicable diseases within inmate populations have been detailed elsewhere (Hammett, Harmon, and Rhodes 2002; Shuter 2002; Sieck and Demba 2011).

Sexually Transmitted Diseases

The prevalence of those with STDs, human immunodeficiency virus (HIV) infection and acquired immunodeficiency syndrome (AIDS) is higher among inmates of correctional facilities than among the general population (Hammett, Harmon, Rhodes 2002). A review of recent literature indicates that an increasing problem for these populations is that they have had little prior access to primary health care or health interventions, and may have engaged in or fallen victim to risky behavior increasing their chance of infection. Approximately 6% of prisoners in 2011–2012 self-reported ever having an STD compared to 3.4% of the population outside prison walls (Maruschak, Berzofsky and Unangst 2016). Table 4-1 provides information about the nature, symptoms, and long-term impact of the most common occurring sexually transmitted diseases within correctional institutions. Below, information on the prevalence for each disease is presented.

Syphilis

Syphilis is a sexually transmitted disease (STD) caused by the bacterium Treponema pallidum. Syphilis occurs during vaginal, anal or oral sex as a result of direct contact with a syphilitic sore or chancre. Syphilis progresses in stages and symptoms often will go away with or without treatment (see Table 4-1). According to the Centers for Disease Control, the late stage of syphilis occurs in approximately 15% of people and can appear 10–20 years after the infection is acquired (Centers for Disease Control 2011). Moreover, the genital sores caused by syphilis make it easier to transmit the HIV infection and increases the risk of acquiring HIV while infected with syphilis. Diagnoses of syphilis are primarily made using blood tests. The national picture reveals that during 2011, there were 46,042 new cases of syphilis reported (Centers for Disease Control 2011). Racial minorities are disproportionately affected by syphilis with the highest rates among African-Americans.

Table 4-1. Sexually Transmitted Diseases

	Syphilis	Gonorrhea	Chlalmydia	Trichomoniasis Most Common Curable STD
Transmission	Vaginal, anal, or oral sex	Vaginal, anal, or oral sex	Vaginal, anal, or oral sex	During sex, usually transmitted from a penis to a vagina, or from a vagina to a penis, but it can also be passed from a vagina to another vagina
Symptoms	Primary stage — sores Secondary stage — skin rashes and/or sores in the mouth, vagina, or anus Late stage — difficulty co-ordinating muscle movements, paralysis, numbness, gradual blindness, and dementia	May have no symptoms at all Males — burning sensation when urinating, or a white, yellow, or green discharge from the penis Females — some women painful or burning sensation when urinating, increased vaginal discharge, or vaginal bleeding	Most infected people have no symptoms Males — discharge from their penis or a burning sensation when urinating Females — some women abnormal vaginal discharge or a burning sensation when urinating	70% of infected do not have any symptoms Males — itching or irritation inside the penis, burning after urination or ejaculation, or some discharge from the penis Females — itching, burning, redness or soreness of the genitals, discomfort with urination, or a thin discharge with an unusual smell that can be clear, white, yellowish, or greenish
Long-Term Complications	Paralysis, blindness, dementia. Late stage damage to internal organs — brain, nerves, eyes, heart, vessels, liver, bones, joints Life threatening	Men epididymitis in tubes attached to the testicles PID, inability to get pregnant, ectopic pregnancy Life threatening if spread to blood	Rare for men PID, inability to get pregnant, ectopic pregnancy	Genital inflammation that makes it easier to get infected with the HIV virus, or to pass the HIV virus

Table 4-2. Primary and Secondary Syphilis by Reporting Source 2011

Percentage

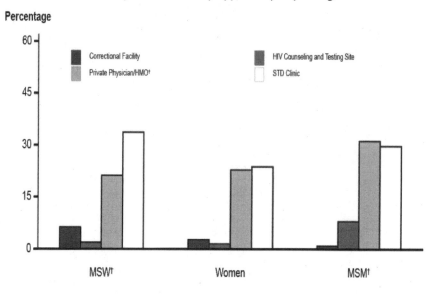

Syphilis is one of the most common STDs found among incarcerated populations. NCCHC estimates that somewhere between 46,000 and 70,000 inmates tested positive for syphilis and more than 200,000 prisoners were released back into the community with the condition. Consequently, they estimated that 2.6–4.3% of the inmate population suffers from syphilis. More recent estimates from the Centers for Diseases Control (2011) that adult correctional institutions accounted for 6 percent of syphilis cases among men who have sex with women only, 3 percent among women, and approximately 1 percent of cases among men who have sex with men (see Table 4-2). The reported rates of syphilis are higher in correctional environments than in the non-incarcerated population. Syphilis transmission within prison contexts has been attributed to the mixing of prisoners with unscreened jail populations, transfers of infected inmates between institutions, and multiple sexual partners (Wolfe, Xu, Patel, et al. 2001). "In the prison setting with no routine universal screening program, the lifetime cost of syphilis in the hypothetical cohort would approach $2 million.... Implementing a routine universal screening program that included treatment of persons identified as infected would cost $160,648. Disease costs associated with routine universal screening would be only $140,065. Thus, a routine universal screening program might save almost $1.7 million compared to the no-screening option...." (Kraut, Haddix, Carrande-Kulis, and Greifinger 2002).

Table 4-3. Gonorrhea-Positivity by Age and Sex, Adult Correctional Facilities, 2011

Men						Positivity						Women
20	16	12	8	4	0	Age	0	4	8	12	16	20
				1.7		<20		4.3				
				1.4		20-24		2.2				
				0.7		25-29		1.8				
				0.5		30-34		1.3				
				0.4		≥35		0.8				
				1.0		Total		1.8				

Gonorrhea

Gonorrhea is a sexually transmitted disease (STD) caused by infection with the Neisseria gonorrhea bacterium. Gonorrhea is transmitted through sexual contact with the penis, vagina, mouth, or anus of an infected person. Most men and women are asymptomatic (see Table 4-1 for symptoms if present). Untreated gonorrhea has been associated with infertility, arthritis, and may be life threatening. Gonorrhea can cause individuals to more easily contract and transmit HIV/AIDS (CDC Gonorrhea Fact Sheet 2011). According to the Centers for Disease Control, more than 700,000 people in the United States get new gonorrheal infections (Centers for Disease Control 2011). The highest rates of gonorrhea are among teenagers, young adults, and African-Americans. Because most facilities do not perform intake screening for gonorrhea or chlamydia on asymptomatic men, the prevalence of disease is difficult to estimate (Hammett, Harmon and Maruschak 1999). NCCHC (2002: 18) estimated approximately 1.0% of inmates have gonorrhea and that at least 77,000 prisoners were released back into the community with the condition. According the Centers for Disease Control report on Gonorrhea in adult correctional institutions, the positivity rate for gonorrhea was 1 percent for men and 1.8 percent for women (see Table 4-3). Recent neighborhood studies have indicated that Neighborhoods with high rates of returning offenders experience higher rates of gonorrhea (Thomas, Levandowski, and Isler et al. 2007).

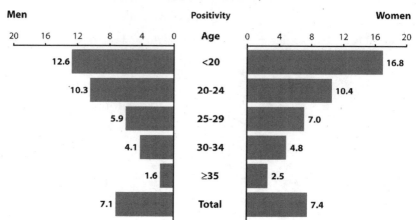

Table 4-4. Chlamydia-Positivity by Age and Sex in Adult Corrections Facilities, 2011

Men						Age						Women
12.6						<20						16.8
10.3						20-24						10.4
5.9						25-29						7.0
4.1						30-34						4.8
1.6						≥35						2.5
7.1						Total						7.4

Chlamydia

Chlamydia is a sexually transmitted disease (STD) caused by infection with Chlamydia trachomatic and is transmitted through contact with the penis, vagina, mouth or anus of an infected person. Chlamydia is most frequently occurring STD with more than 1.4 million cases reported and estimates as high as 2.8 when unreported cases are considered (Centers for Disease Control 2011). Most men and women with chlamydia are asymptomatic. Chlamydia can be easily cured with antibiotics. Chlamydia has been associated with infertility, chronic pelvic pain, arthritis. In the general population rates of chlamydia are highest among non-Hispanic blacks and men who have sex with men (Centers for Disease Control 2011). Because chlamydia is associated with genital inflammation, the diseases may also increase risk of transmitting and acquiring the HIV infection. The rate of chlamydia for asymptomatic male inmates is difficult to discern. Most correctional facilities do not perform routine chlamydia checks on male inmates. In 1997 an estimated 43,000 inmates tested positive for chlamydia and 186,000 prisoners were released into the community with the condition (NCCH 2002). The chlamydia positivity rates for males in adult correctional institutions was 7 percent and 7.4 percent for women in 2011 (see Table 4-4).

Trichomoniasis

Trichomoniasis is a sexually transmitted disease (STD) caused by infection with a protozoan parasite called Trichomonas vaginalis. Trichomoniasis transmitted by sexual contact. In women the most commonly infected body part is the lower genital tract (vulva, vagina, or urethra). In men the most commonly infected body part is the inside of the penis (urethra) (Centers for Disease Control 2011). The disease is usually transmitted from penis to vagina, vagina to penis, or vagina to vagina. See Table 4-1 for symptoms. An estimated 3.7 million people have the infection, which is most common in women and minorities (Centers for Disease Control 2011).

HIV/AIDS

HIV (human immunodeficiency virus) is a virus that attacks the immune system and destroys white blood cells. Ultimately, HIV can lead to acquired immune deficiency syndrome (AIDS). A person can be infected with HIV by coming into contact with the blood, semen, vaginal secretions, or breast milk of an infected person. HIV is most commonly transmitted through anal or vaginal sexual behaviors or sharing needles with an infected person.

The prevalence of human immunodeficiency virus (HIV) infection among incarcerated persons in the United States is approximately four to five times greater than the prevalence among persons in community settings (Centers for Disease Control and Prevention 2006; Jafa, McElroy, Fitzpatrick et al. 2009; Kerbs 2006; Kerbs 2002; Varghese and Peterman 2001). Degroot, Hammett, and Scheib (1996) found HIV positive rates 10 to 100 times higher among inmates than the general population. The percentage of inmates in state institutions testing positive for HIV range from 1.8 to more than 6 percent (Brewer, Vlahov, Taylor, et al. 1988; Horsburgh, Jarvis, McArthur et al. 1990; Macalino, Vlahov, Sanford-Colby et al. 2004). Still other researchers have estimated that up to one-fourth of people living with the HIV infection in the United States pass through correctional facilities each year (Spaulding, Stephenson, Macalino, et al. 2002). Since 1983, nearly 5 percent of HIV/AIDS cases in the United States have been reported from correctional facilities (Vlahov, Putnam, et al. 2006). Sabin, Frey, Horsley, et al. (2001) examined rates from 1992–1998 for 459,155 inmates and found at least 3 percent (16,797) testing positive. The majority (56%) of those cases were newly identified again suggesting high rates of prevalence within correctional contexts. At yearend 2012, state and federal prisons held a reported 18,945 inmates who had HIV or AIDS, down from 20,093 at yearend 2010 (Noonan 2016). The estimated rate of HIV/AIDS among prisoners in custody dropped from 145 HIV/AIDS cases per 100,000 inmates in 2011 to 143 per 100,000 in 2012 (Maruschak, Berzofsky and Unangst 2016). Four states (California, Florida, New York, and Texas) held more than half of all state prisoners with HIV/AIDS with more than 1,000 inmates with HIV/AIDS (see Table 4-5). The HIV positivity rate among female prisoners is three times higher than the rate for male prisoners (Degroot 2001; Degroot, Hammett, and Scheib 1996; Maruschak 1999).

Table 4-5. State and Federal Prisoners with HIV or AIDS by Jurisdiction, Yearend 2010, 2011, and 2012

Jurisdiction	2010	2011	2012
U.S. total	20,093	19,536	18,945
Federal	1,578	1,610	1,601
State	18,515	17,926	17,344
Alabama	252	274	266
Alaska	/	/	/
Arizona	164	165	181
Arkansas	128	110	105
California	1,098	1,165	1,089
Colorado	181	198	201
Connecticut	301	301	249
Delaware	73	76	81
Florida	2,920	2,679	2,583
Georgia	912	903	891
Hawaii	18	21	13
Idaho	20	/	14
Illinois	487	457	/
Indiana	/	/	/
Iowa	36	37	37
Kansas	33	61	5
Kentucky	87	62	91
Louisiana	665	536	532
Maine	15	3	11
Maryland	722	572	485
Massachusetts	206	208	186
Michigan	233	428	370
Minnesota	47	50	70

Mississippi	254	255	287
Missouri	273	292	295
Montana	7	18	11
Nebraska	20	20	22
Nevada	133	123	115
New Hampshire	12	4	5
New Jersey	420	372	303
New Mexico	27	37	29
New York	3,080	3,010	2,950
North Carolina	720	692	718
North Dakota	9	1	2
Ohio	381	376	405
Oklahoma	155	137	131
Oregon	63	60	63
Pennsylvania	703	706	695
Rhode Island	47	32	35
South Carolina	412	387	328
South Dakota	11	12	11
Tennessee	219	213	226
Texas	2,394	2,320	2,200
Utah	35	24	24
Vermont	3	7	6
Virginia	306	307	279
Washington	75	71	75
West Virginia	25	18	29
Wisconsin	128	120	135
Wyoming	5	6	2

Source: Maruschak, L., Berzofsky, M., and Unangst, J. (2016). Medical Problems of State and Federal Prisoners and Jail Inmates, 2011–2012. Bureau of Justice Statistics.

The cost for treating HIV infected inmates is high. In 2009 the average cost per newly diagnosed HIV infection ranged from $2,451 to $25,288 for correctional institutions (Shrestha, Sansom, and Richardson-Moore, et al. 2009). Varghese and Peterman (2001) estimated life-time treatment costs of $186,900. This figure is likely much greater today.

There are some common characteristics for inmates testing positive for HIV/AIDS. The highest proportions of inmates testing positive for HIV are African-Americans and inmates over 30 years of age (Centers for Disease Control 2006; Horsburgh, Jarvis, McArthur et al. 1990). Research also indicates a relationship between longer prison sentences and rates of HIV infection (Centers for Disease Control 2006; Kerbs 2002; 2006).

A major concern related to HIV/AIDS for incarcerated populations is whether prisons themselves are to blame for the high rates of infection (Kerbs 2002; 2006). In 1997, it was estimated that 35,000–47,000 inmates were infected with HIV (NCCH 2002). By the mid-1990s evidence began to support the fact that transmission of HIV/AIDS was occurring after inmates went to prison. Mutter, Grimes, Labarthe (1994) examined 556 prisoners in Florida prisons who had been incarcerated since 1977. Of the eighty-seven prisoners who were tested for HIV infection, 21% were found to be positive. An extensive body of literature now exists which suggests that the primary method of transmission of HIV/AIDS in prison is related to risky behaviors which occur during incarceration. Male-to-male sexual behaviors have been connected with HIV infection in several studies (Centers for Disease Control 2006; Kerbs 2002; 2006; Macher, Kibble and Wheeler 2006). Another behavior associated with HIV transmission is tattooing (Centers for Disease Control 2006; Kerbs 2002; 2006).

The rate of deaths in prison as a result of AIDS has decreased. In 2001 the HIV/AIDS cases per 100,000 inmates was 23 by 2010 this rate was 6 per 100,000 inmates (Maruschak 2012). In 2014 the mortality rate for AIDS was lowered to 5 per 100,000 inmates (Noonan 2016). Fewer inmates died in 2014 (64 deaths) of AIDS related illnesses compared to 2001 when there were 275 inmate deaths (see Table 4-6). As has been a trend for several years more male inmates than female inmates died from AIDS related complications in 2014 (Noonan 2016). It is also not surprising that minorities and older inmates would have higher rates than nonminorities and younger inmates given the higher concentration of the disease among African-Americans. Despite the increases the number of deaths over the between 2013 and 2014, the overall rate of HIV or AIDS cases is among state and federal prisoners is down (see Table 4-7).

**Table 4-6. AIDS-Related Deaths among State Prison
Inmates in Custody, 2001–2014**

Year	Number of Deaths
2001	275
2008	99
2009	98
2010	73
2011	57
2012	74
2013	52
2014	64

Source: Noonan, M. (2016). Mortality in State Prisons, 2001–2014—Statistical Tables. Bureau of Justice Statistics.

Tuberculosis

Tuberculosis doesn't stop at any border or any locked gate.
— Jeremy Goldhaber-Fiebert, a faculty member at Stanford Health
Policy, a research center at the university's Freeman Spogli Institute for International Studies. (Gorlick 2012)

According to the Centers for Disease Control, one-third of the world's population is infected by tuberculosis (TB). TB is caused by Mycobacterium tuberculosis, which spreads in airborne droplets when people with the disease cough, sneeze, speak or sing. According to the Centers for Disease Control, the bacteria usually attack the lungs, but can attack any part of the body such as the kidney, spine, and brain (http://www.cdc.gov/tb/topic/basics/default.htm). The TB bacteria can live in the body and not cause an individual to become sick. People with healthy immune systems often are able to fight off the bacteria. If the immune system is unable to stop the growth of the bacteria, then the person will develop TB disease, which is highly infectious.

Tuberculosis rates among institutional populations are much higher than what is found among the general population (Angie, Malgosia, Michael, Hans, et al. 2000; Dara, Grzemska, Kimerling, Reyes, and Zagorskiy 2009; Hammett, Roberts and Kennedy 2001; Hutton, Cauthen, and Bloch 1993; MacNeil and Lobato 2005). In 1997 an estimated 131,000 inmates tested positive for latent

Table 4-7. Rate of HIV or AIDS Cases among State and Federal Prisoners, 2001–2012

Year	HIV/AIDS Cases per 10,000 Prisoners
2001	196.172
2002	189.791
2003	184.713
2004	175.52
2005	172.315
2006	166.396
2007	159.557
2008	157.439
2009	152.004
2010	146.762
2011	144.87
2012	143.2

Source: Maruschak, L, Berzofsky, M. and Unangst, J. (2016). Medical Problems of State and Federal Prisoners and Jail Inmates, 2011–2012. Bureau of Justice Statistics, National Prisoner Statistics Program, 2001–2012.

TB infection (NCCH 2002). While it is clear that the rate of TB is higher in prisons than in the community, a more accurate estimate of the increased incidence of TB is found among prison populations (Baussano, Williams, Numm, Beggiato, Fedeli, and Scano 2010).

The number of inmates who have tuberculosis depends on whose study you read. When prisoners were asked about ever having tuberculosis, approximately 6 % reported (see Table 4-8) ever having tuberculosis compared to .05 % of the general population (Maruschak, Berzofsky and Unangst 2016). The average incidence of TB in prisons was found to be 26.4 times higher among incarcerated populations than in the general population (Baussano, Williams, Numm, Beggiato, Fedeli, and Scano 2010). Hammett, Roberts and Kennedy. (2001) estimate that nearly 40 percent of active TB among individuals were among individuals who were incarcerated in the previous year. Earlier estimates conducted by Hutton, Cauthen, and Bloch 1993 indicated that inmates were 3.9 times more likely to have TB than the general population.

Table 4-8. Prevalence of Ever Having a Chronic Condition or Infectious Disease among State and Federal Prisoners and the General Population

Chronic Condition/Infectious Disease	State and Federal Prisoners Percent	General Population Percent
Ever had a chronic condition	43.9	31
Cancer	3.5	/
High blood pressure/hypertension	30.2	18.1
Stroke-related problems	1.8	0.7
Diabetes/high blood sugar	9	6.5
Heart-related problems	9.8	2.9
Kidney-related problems	6.1	/
Arthritis/rheumatism	15	/
Asthma	14.9	10.2
Cirrhosis of the liver	1.8	0.2
Ever had an infectious disease	21	4.8
Tuberculosis	6	0.5
Hepatitis	10.9	1.1
Hepatitis B	2.7	/
Hepatitis C	9.8	/
STDs	6	3.4
HIV/AIDS	1.3	0.4

Source: Maruschak, L, Berzofsky, M. and Unangst, J. (2016). Medical Problems of State and Federal Prisoners and Jail Inmates, 2011–2012. Bureau of Justice Statistics, National Prisoner Statistics Program, 2001–2012.

There are three primary causes for the high rates of TB found behind correctional walls. First, as discussed earlier, many of these offenders have not received adequate medical care prior to incarceration, may be infected with diseases such as HIV, or have used illicit substances, all of which make them more susceptible to TB (White, Tulsky, Portillo, Menendez, and Goldenson 2001). Second, most prisons are designed with poor ventilation and are overcrowded, making airborne diseases much more prevalent (Jones, Craig, Valway, Woodley, and Schaffner 1999; Koo, Baron, and Rutherford 1991; MacIntryre, Kendig, Kummer, Birago and Graham 1997). Lastly, correctional facilities are well known for shuffling inmates within and between institutions, exacerbating risk.

There is also evidence that the spread of tuberculosis within the general population has been associated with the return of released inmates back into the community (Baussano I, Williams BG, Nunn P, Beggiato M, Fedeli U, et al. 2010; Hutton, Cauthen, and Bloch 1993). We have known since the 1970s that outbreaks of TB were directly related to the length of time incarcerated and release back into the community (Stead 1978). Bellin, Fletcher and Safyer (1993) reported an association of tuberculosis infection with confinement in the New York jail system. In addition to the increased risk for the families and friends of released inmates, correctional workers and their families are also exposed to TB as a result of working in this closed environment.

Hepatitis

Hepatitis means inflammation of the liver. According to Binswanger, Krueger, and Steiner (2009) and more recently Maruschak, Berzofsky and Unangst (2016) compared with the general population, jail and prison inmates had higher odds of hepatitis (see Table 4-8). This condition can be caused by alcohol, chemicals, drugs and viruses that attack the liver and can lead to death. The two most common forms of hepatitis among correctional populations are Hepatitis B and C. Hepatitis B is generally considered to be an adult disease because it's known to be transmitted through unsafe sex, shared needles, sharing of razors, sharing of toothbrushes, tattooing, or contact with blood or sores. The majority of people with Hepatitis B are asymptomatic. If they do experience symptoms, then most commonly reported indicators are jaundice, fatigue, loss of appetite, and nausea. In 2009, an estimated 38,000 persons in the United States were newly infected with HBV (Centers for Disease Control 2012b).

Rates of Hepatitis B infection among inmates vary. The National Commission on Correctional Health Care (2002) estimates that 2.0% of the inmate population in 1997 was infected with Hepatitis B. Similar results were found among prisoners who self-reported ever having Hepatitis B in 2011 (Maruschak, Berzofsky and Unangst 2016). Macalino, Vlahov, Sanford-Colby et al. (2004) reported prevalence rates of 20.2 percent among Rhode Island adult correctional inmates between 1998 and 2000. Khan, Simard, Bower et al. (2005) recounted prevalence rates of 20.1 percent in their cross-sectional study. A Maryland study found 25.2% prevalence rates among detainees and prisoners had antigen or core or surface antibodies to HBV (Soloman, Flynn, Muck, et al. 2004).

Box 4-4. Symptoms of Tuberculosis

A bad cough (lasts 3 weeks or longer)
Coughing up blood
Weakness
Weight loss
No appetite
Chills
Fever
Night Sweats

Source: Centers for Diseases Control—http://www.cdc.gov/tb/topic/basics/signsand symptoms.htm.

Hepatitis C virus (HCV) infection is the most common chronic blood infection in the United States; approximately 3.2 million persons are chronically infected (Centers for Disease Control 2012). Individuals with HCV rarely experience symptoms during the early phase. Rates of Hepatitis C infection varies among prisoners. NCCHC (2002) estimated that close to 18% of inmates tested positive for HCV, which represents a prevalence rate 9 to 10 higher than in the United States Population. Macalino, Vlahov, Sanford-Colby et al. (2004) reported prevalence rates of 23.1 percent among Rhode Island adult correctional inmates between 1998 and 2000. Maryland Correctional facilities rates for HCV prevalence was 29.7% (Soloman, Flynn, Muck, et al. 2004). In the most recent study among prisoners incarcerated in 2012 approximately 10% of prisoners self-reported ever having Hepatitis C (see Table 4-8). The actual incidence of HCV among inmate populations is unknown because the majority of institutions use risk based models to identify which inmates to test. Macalino, Dhawan, Rich (2005) argue that risk-based testing underestimates the hepatitis C virus (HCV) prevalence in correctional settings. Between 16–41% of those incarcerated have some evidence of HCV infection and between 12–35% suffer from chronic HCV infection (Centers for Disease Control 2003).

There are some common characteristics associated with positive HBV and HBC tests in prison. Prior incarceration has long been associated with increased rates of Hepatitis infection (Hammett et al. 2002). According to Khan, Simard, Bower et al. (2005) inmates testing positive were more likely to have injected drugs, been incarcerated for more than 14 years, and to have had more than 25 female sex partners. Soloman, Flynn, Much, et al. (2004) found the following inmate characteristics associated with positive HCV rates—women, whites, older age groups, those who were HIV seropositive, and individuals with past or present infection with HBV were significantly more likely to be positive for HCV.

Chronic Illnesses

Chronic illnesses are medical conditions that are of a prolonged duration and affect physical and emotional functioning. The majority of these conditions cannot be prevented by a vaccine nor cured by a one-time infusion of medication. They require continual medical treatment and become more common with age (Kinsella 2004). Half of all prisoners in state and federal institutions report having a chronic condition (Maruschak, Berzofsky and Unangst 2016). The National Institute of Corrections lists arthritis, diabetes, Hepatitis C, hypertension, ulcer disease, prostate problems, myocardial infarction and cancer among the most common chronic diseases among elderly inmates. Common features of these illnesses include: long development periods for which no symptoms may be observed, prolonged duration which can often lead to other health complications, and habitually are associated with functional impairment or disability (Hung, Ross, Boockvar, and Siu 2011). Disabilities, such as the inability to walk, see and hear are also prevalent among older citizens in the general population and occur in even greater numbers among the incarcerated population (National Commission on Correctional Health Care 2002). For example, a recent study conducted by Harzke, Baillargeon, Pruitt, Pulvino, Parr, and Kelly (2010) that nearly two thirds of all inmates over age 55 had a least one of the following chronic conditions: asthma, diabetes, heart disease, or hypertension. "An elderly inmate will experience an average of three chronic illnesses during his or her term" (Abner 2006: 10). Chronic disease results in: amputation, blindness, pain, debilitation, disability, and dependence, depression, lost physical function, decreased mobility and death. As prison populations continue age corresponding increases in chronic illnesses and corresponding disabilities should be anticipated. The Federal prison system reported in 2000 significant rates of chronic illnesses with 5,639 (4.4%) inmates with asthma, 4,616 (3.6%) in a diabetic clinic, 3,358 (2.6%) in a cardiac clinic, and 10,011 (7.8%) in a hypertension clinic" (Maruschak and Beck 2001). The next section describes some of the common chronic illnesses experienced by long term and elderly prisoners and presents institutional prevalence rates where possible. Recent studies of self-reported chronic illnesses among prisoners indicate that these rates remain high ten years later (Maruschak, Berzofsky and Unangst 2016).

Asthma

Asthma is a disorder of the lungs, which causes the airways of the lungs to swell and narrow causing wheezing, shortness of breath, chest tightness, and

---

Box 4-5. Chronic Illnesses

Defined—medical conditions that are of a prolonged duration and affect physical and emotional functioning.

- Asthma
- Diabetes
- Hypertension
- Cancer
- Visual Impairment/Blindness
- Deafness and Hearing Impairment
- Obesity

---

coughing (Centers for Disease Control 2011). Asthma attacks can be triggered by inhaling allergens such as pet hair/dander, dust, mold, changes in the weather, tobacco smoke, pollen, cockroaches, etc. Most people with asthma have attacks separated by symptom-free periods. There is no cure for asthma although symptoms may get better over time. Asthma is one the most common chronic health conditions in the United States affecting more than 8 percent of the population (Akinbami, Moorman, and Liu 2011). In 2010 1 in 12 adults (18.7 million) and 1 in 11 children (7 million) were diagnosed with asthma (Centers for Disease Control 2011). Moreover, asthma can prove fatal: approximately 9 people each day die as a result of an asthma attack. According to the Centers for Disease Control (2011), asthma costs the United States approximately $56 billion each year. Meyer (2003) estimated the average cost to treat a severe asthma attack to be $7,300.

Recent estimates suggest that the prevalence of asthma among inmate populations is high (RAND 2005). In 2002 NCCHC estimated overall rates among the inmate population to be 8.5%. A more recent 2010 examination of all inmate medical files in the Texas Department of Criminal Justice reported that more than 5 percent of the entire inmate population has been diagnosed with asthma (Harzke, Baillargeon, Pruitt, Pulvino, Parr, and Kelly 2010). A national cross-sectional study conducted by Binswanger, Krueger, and Steiner (2009) found that compared with the general population, jail and prison inmates had higher odds of, asthma. Davis 2000 estimated the difference in prevalence to be 8.5% of prisoners compared to 7.8% of the general population. Using data analyzed by Hornung, Greifinger, and Gadre (2000) this difference translates into projected baseline rate of 7.2 cases per 100 inmates. Maruschak, Berzofsky and Unangst (2016) reported self-reported prevalence of asthma as 15% among prisoners compared to 10% of the public (see Table 4-8).

Box 4-6. Complications Associated with Diabetes

- More than 60% of nontraumatic lower-limb amputations occur in people with diabetes.
- Diabetes is the leading cause of new cases of blindness among adults aged 20–74 years.
- Diabetes is the leading cause of kidney failure, accounting for 44% of all new cases of kidney failure in 2008.
- About 60% to 70% of people with diabetes have mild to severe forms of nervous system damage. The results of such damage include impaired sensation or pain in the feet or hands, slowed digestion of food in the stomach, carpal tunnel syndrome, erectile dysfunction, or other nerve problems.
- Adults aged 45 years or older with poorly controlled diabetes (A1c > 9%) were 2.9 times more likely to have severe periodontitis than those without diabetes
- People with diabetes aged 60 years or older are 2–3 times more likely to report an inability to walk one-quarter of a mile, climb stairs, or do housework compared with people without diabetes in the same age group.
- Adults with diabetes have heart disease death rates about 2 to 4 times higher than adults without diabetes.
- The risk for stroke is 2 to 4 times higher among people with diabetes.

Source: Centers for Disease Control 2011 Fact Sheet. Available at http://www.cdc.gov/diabetes/pubs/estimates11.htm#10.

Diabetes

Diabetes is an illness characterized by high than normal rate of sugar in the blood. Diabetes can cause serious health complications including heart disease, blindness, kidney failure, and lower-extremity amputations and is the seventh leading cause of death in the United States (Centers for Disease Control 2010). Symptoms of diabetes include fatigue, frequent urination, excessive thirst, extreme huger, vision changes, sores that are slow to heal, more infections than usual, and numbness in hands or feet. The long-term complications associated with diabetes involve trouble seeing, blindness, painful sores and increased susceptibility to infections, nerve damage and pain, amputations, and difficulty digesting food and eliminating waste from the body.

From 1980 through 2010, the number of U.S. adults aged 18 years or older with diagnosed diabetes has more than tripled (from 5.5 million to 20.7 million) (Centers for Disease Control 2010). The prevalence rates within institutional population (9%) is higher than rates found within the general population (6.5%) (see Table 4-8). The disorder remains extremely problematic given its presence within the smaller prison population (Davis 2002). Hornung,

Greifinger, Gadre (2002) estimated the total number of incarcerated diabetics to be 43,557. They estimate state prison rates to be approximately 2.7 per 100 inmates. Federal prisons were predicted to have the highest prevalence (3.8 per 100) rates. Moreover, these rates likely increase exponentially with age (Harzke, Baillargeon, Pruitt, Parr and Kelly 2010).

Hypertension

Hypertension is the term used for high blood pressure and affects 1 in 3 Americans (Centers for Disease Control: Vital Signs 2011). Blood pressure refers to the force of blood against your artery walls as it circulates through your body. Normal or optimal blood pressure (BP) is defined as the level above which minimal vascular damage occurs. Normal blood pressure, the pressure at which little vascular damage occurs, is defined as a systolic BP less than 120 mm Hg and diastolic BP less than 80 mm Hg. High blood pressure levels exist when readings for systolic are 140 mmHg or higher and diastolic readings are 90 mmHg or higher.

There is a large body of literature which identifies high blood pressure as a major contributing or causal factor for heart disease, stroke, kidney disease, and death (Kochanek, Xu, Murphy, Minino, and Kung (2011). High blood pressure was the primary or contributing cause of death for more than 345,000 people in the United States in 2008 (Roger, Go, Lloyd-Jones, Benjamin, Berry, Borden, et al. 2012). Medical expenses for hypertension for the nation exceed $131 billion annually (Heidenreich, Trogdon, Khavjou, Butler, Dracup, Ezekowitz, et al. 2011).

The rates of hypertension behind correctional walls are astounding given the size of the inmate population. Hornung, Greifinger, and Gadre (2000) estimated that State prisons, Federal prisons, and local jails together house more than one-quarter of a million inmates with hypertension. The institutional (18.3%) rates for hypertension are much higher than found in the general population (24.5%) (Davis 2002). Binswanger, Krueger, and Steiner (2009) when they compared the general population with jail and prison inmates found significantly higher odds of hypertension for jail (1.19) and prison (1.17). Recent data released by the Bureau of Justice Statistics indicate that prisoners are nearly three times more likely to report having ever had high blood pressure (Maruschak, Berzofsky and Unangst 2016). The prevalence of hypertension increases significantly for the incarcerated as they age (Harzke, Baillargeon, Pruitt, Pulvino, Parr, and Kelly 2010).

Heart Disease

Heart disease refers to a broad range of medical disorders that directly affect the heart and often are referred to as cardiovascular disorders. Cardiovascular disease generally refers to conditions that involve narrowed or blocked blood vessels that can lead to a heart attack, chest pain (angina) or stroke. The list of diseases falling within this category includes diseases of your blood vessels, such as coronary artery disease; heart rhythm problems (arrhythmias); heart infections; and congenital heart defects. Approximately 600,000 people die of heart disease in the United States every year (Kochanek, Xu, Murphy, Minino, and Kung 2011). Coronary heart disease is the most common type of heart disease and is associated with more than 385,000 people annually (Kochanek, Xu, Murphy, Minino, and Kung 2011). Meyer (2003) estimated that the average cost to treat a heart attack to be $25,000.

The prevalence rate for heart disease among inmates is fairly high. More than 31,000 inmates in state prisons are predicted to have heart disease (Hornung, Greifinger, and Gadre 2000). Harzke, Baillargeon, Pruitt, Pulvino, Parr, and Kelly (2010) estimate prevalence rates to be the following within institutionalized populations: ischemic heart disease 1.7%; chronic obstructive pulmonary disease 0.96%; and cerebrovascular disease 0.23%. As with other chronic illnesses these prevalence rates increase with age.

Disabilities

It is estimated that nearly 32% of prisoners and 40% of jail inmates have at least one disability (Bronson, Maruschak, and Berzofksky 2016). These numbers are far greater than what has been reported by the general public. Only 11% of the general public report having a disability (see Table 4-9). Disabilities include hearing loss, problems with vision, cognitive deficits, self-care issues, or difficulties managing daily life. We should note here that cognitive difficulties are not the same as mental health disorders. Among prisoners, cognitive deficits (20%) are the most commonly reported disabilities followed by ambulatory (10%). Support for the high rate of cognitive deficits among prisoners was confirmed by correctional officers in a recent study (Osborne Association 2014). Prisoners are "2 times more likely than persons in the general population to report independent living, ambulatory, and hearing disabilities; about 3 times more likely to report a visual disability; and 4 times more likely to report a cognitive disability" (Bronson, Maruschak, and Berzofsky 2016, p. 3).

Table 4-9. Prevalence of Disabilities among State and Federal
Prisoners and the General Population 2011–2012

| Disability | State and Federal Prisoners | | General Population |
	Percent	Standard Error	Percent
Any disability	31.6	1.4	10.9
Vision	7.1	0.69	2.1
Hearing	6.2	0.61	2.6
Ambulatory	10.1	0.76	5.1
Cognitive	19.5	1.13	4.8
Self-care	2.1	0.29	2.1
Independent living	7.5	0.71	4

Source: Bronson, J., Maruschak, L., and Berzofsky, M. (2016). Disabilities among Prison and
Jail Inmates, 2011–2012. Bureau of Justice Statistics, National Inmate Survey, 2011–12.

Disabilities are not randomly distributed across the prisoner population
(see Table 4-10). Females (40%) are more likely to report a disability than their
male (31%) counterparts (see Figure 4-1). This is especially true in the case of
cognitive difficulties (Bronson, Maruschak, and Berzofsky 2016). As with the
general public prisoners reported high rates of co-occurring chronic conditions.
For example, it would not be unusual to find that the prisoner who reported
diabetes also have vision or hearing problems. The highest rates for all disabilities are reported by prisoners aged 50 or older. Forty-four percent of prisoners
aged 50 or older reported a disability compared to 27% of prisoners ages 18–
24. Older prisoners are "6 times more likely to report having a hearing
disability, 4 to 5 times more likely to report a vision disability, and more than
twice as likely to report an independent living disability" (p. 5). Thus, older
prisoners present with significantly higher disabilities and have a greater need
for disability related assistance than their younger counterparts.

Mortality

The data detailed above all suggest that life expectancy among long-term
prisoners, geriatric prisoners and released ex-felons is not high. Still other evidence supports the notion of poorer health for those who spend time in prison

Table 4-10. Prevalence of Disabilities among State and Federal Prisoners by Demographics 2011–12

Demographic Characteristic	Any	Hearing	Vision	Ambulatory	Cognitive	Self-Care	Independent Living
All prisoners	31.6%	6.2%	7.1%	10.1%	19.5%	2.1%	7.5%
Sex							
Male	31%	6.2%	7.1%	9.9%	18.7%	2%	7.3%
Female	39.5	5.3	6.4	12.1	30.3	3.4	10.1
Age							
18–24	26.9%	2%	3.7%	1.7%	22.1%	0.8%	4.9
25–34	25.1	2.5	4.6	3.9	18.8	1	5.9
35–49	32.8	7.9	6.6	10.3	18.9	2.6	7.6
50 or older	44.2	12.1	15.3	26.8	20.3	4.1	11.9
Race/Hispanic origin							
White	37.3%	8%	6.2%	12%	22.8%	2.4%	10.5%
Black/African American	25.7	3.1	6.2	7.7	17.1	1.7	5.5
Hispanic/Latino	27.8	6.9	8.8	8.8	15.1	2.5	5.3
Two or more races	42.3	8.4	7.3	14.7	27.3	1.8	9.5
Other	37	7.9	5.5	7.5	23	1.5	15.4

Source: Bronson, J., Maruschak, L., and Berzofsky, M. (2016). Disabilities among State and Federal Prisoners by Demographics 2011–12. Bureau of Justice Statistics, National Inmate Survey, 2011–12.

Figure 4-1. Prevalence of Disabilities among State and Federal Prisoners and Jail Inmates by Sex, 2011–12

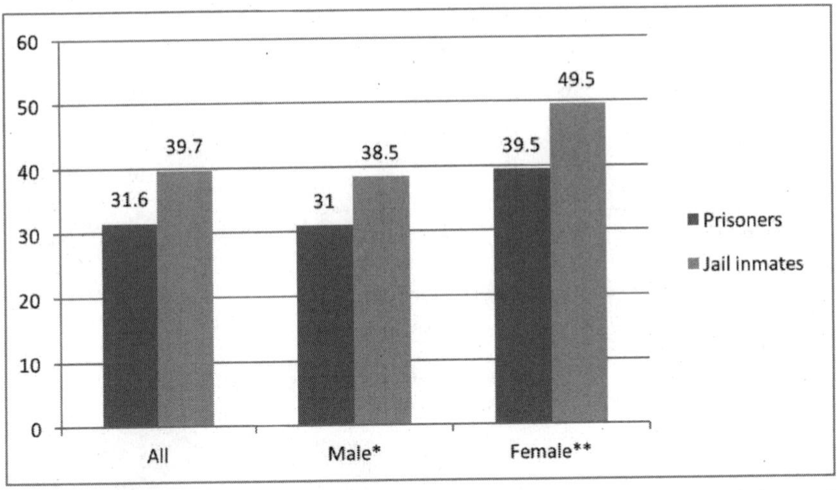

Source: Bronson, J., Maruschak, L., and Berzofsky, M. (2016). Disabilities among Prison and Jail Inmates, 2011-2012. Bureau of Justice Statistics, National Inmate Survey, 2011–12.

compared to the general population (see for example, Spaulding et al. 2011). The number of deaths in state custody has been on the rise (see Figure 4-2). In 2014 there were 3,927 inmate deaths in custody. The greatest number of prisoners who died in state custody were serving time in state prison (Noonan 2016). Consequently, 3,483 state prison inmates compared to 444 federal in-

---

Box 4-7. Differences between Cognitive Disabilities and Mental Health Disorders

- Symptoms of mental disorders may be cyclical, temporary, or episodic whereas symptoms of cognitive disabilities are permanent
- Symptoms of a mental disorder may be controlled or eliminated by medications and the person can usually live a normal life. Medication cannot fully restore, repair or alleviate cognitive limitations
- Symptoms of mental disorder may include disturbances in perceptions, emotions, and thought processes. Hallucinations and delusions are not symptoms associated with most cognitive disabilities

Source: Modified table from Bronson, J., Maruschak, L. & Berzofsky, M. (2015). *Disabilities Among Prison and Jail Inmates, 2011–2012*. U.S. Department of Justice. Bureau of Justice Statistics.

Figure 4-2. State Prison Inmate Deaths in Custody, 2001–2014

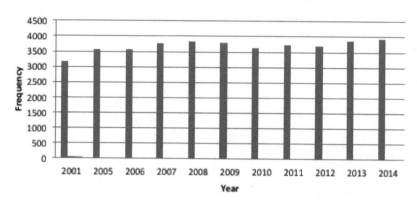

Source: Noonan, S. (2016). Deaths in Custody Reporting Program and National Prisoner Statistics, 2001–2014. Bureau of Justice Statistics.

mates died behind bars (Noonan 2016: 1). The five leading causes of death in state prisons in order of occurrence was heart disease, cancer, liver disease, AIDS related, and respiratory disease (see Table 4-11 and Table 4-12).

Mortality behind bars is not evenly distributed. White prisoners have the highest rates of mortality behind bars with a rate that is between 1.4 and 2.4 times higher than any other racial or ethnic group (Noonan 2012; 2016). Moreover, for cancer, heart disease, and liver disease, male prisoners were 2 times more likely to die than female prisoners.

An analysis of age-distributed mortality reveals significant growth in the numbers of elderly prisoners who died behind bars over the last 10 years (see Table 4-13). In 2001 34 percent (N = 971) of prisoners who died were aged 55 or older and by 2010 that figure had increased (N = 1,607) to nearly 50 percent (Noonan 2012: 15). Four years later nearly 60% of those dying behind bars were aged 55 or older (Noonan 2016). The elderly behind bars are at significant higher risk of death from chronic illnesses, unnatural deaths which include suicides, homicides, accidents, and drug or alcohol intoxication. The stark reality is that prisoners aged 55 or older have mortality rates that are 5 times higher for cancer (639 per 100,000 state prisoners) and heart disease (561 per 100,000 state prisoners) than for any other age group. The review of mortality statistics provided here provide additional evidence of the driving-forces of correctional costs in regard to elderly and aging prisoners.

Table 4-11. Mortality Rate per 100,000 State Prisoners by Cause of Death, 2001 and 2005–2014

Cause of Death	2001	2005	2006	2007	2008	2009	2010	2011	2012	2013	2014
All causes	242	253	249	256	260	258	245	260	265	273	275
Illness	216	225	218	225	229	228	217	231	234	242	240
Cancer	58	64	62	58	68	73	70	80	81	84	83
Heart disease	63	67	66	64	64	64	63	66	63	70	70
Liver disease	26	25	23	24	24	25	22	26	24	28	25
Respiratory disease	12	17	15	16	19	15	16	16	18	16	19
AIDS-related	23	12	10	9	7	7	6	4	6	4	5
All other illnesses	34	39	42	55	46	44	41	39	42	40	38
Suicide	14	17	17	16	15	15	16	14	16	15	20
Drug/alcohol intoxication	3	3	4	3	4	4	3	4	3	4	4
Accident	2	2	2	2	2	2	2	3	4	3	3
Homicide	3	4	4	4	3	4	5	5	7	7	7
Other/unknown	0	1	3	1	7	1	—	1	1	1	1

Source: Noonan, M. (2016). Mortality in State Prisons, 2001–2014 — Statistical Tables. Bureau of Justice Statistics, Deaths in Custody Reporting Program, 2001 and 2005–2014; National Prisoner Statistics, 2001 and 2005–2014.

Table 4-12. Percent of State Prisoner Deaths by Cause of Death, 2001 and 2005–2014

Cause of Death	2001	2005	2006	2007	2008	2009	2010	2011	2012	2013	2014
All causes	100%	100%	100%	100%	100%	100%	100%	100%	100%	100%	100%
Illness	89.5%	88.9%	87.5%	87.9%	87.9%	88.6%	88.7%	88.9%	88.1%	88.6%	87%
Cancer	24.1	25.4	24.9	22.8	26.2	28.5	28.7	30.7	30.5	30.6	30
Heart disease	25.9	26.4	26.4	24.8	24.5	24.7	25.7	25.5	23.9	25.8	25.6
Liver disease	10.7	10	9.4	9.3	9.2	9.7	8.9	10.1	9.1	10.2	9
Respiratory disease	5.1	6.7	6.1	6.1	7.4	5.9	6.5	6.1	6.6	5.7	6.8
AIDS-related	9.6	4.9	4.1	3.5	2.9	2.9	2.3	1.7	2.2	1.5	1.8
All other illnesses	14.1	15.5	16.7	21.4	17.8	16.9	16.7	14.8	15.8	14.8	13.8
Suicide	5.9%	6.7%	6.8%	6.3%	5.7%	5.9%	6.6%	5.5%	6.1%	5.5%	7.1%
Drug/alcohol intoxication	1.2%	1.2%	1.7%	1.2%	1.7%	1.5%	1.2%	1.7%	1%	1.6%	1.4%
Accident	0.8%	0.9%	1%	0.8%	0.8%	0.9%	1%	1.1%	1.5%	1%	1.1%
Homicide	1.4%	1.8%	1.7%	1.7%	1.2%	1.6%	2.2%	2.1%	2.5%	2.6%	2.4%
Other/unknown	0%	0.5%	1.3%	0.5%	2.8%	0.5%	0.1%	0.3%	0.4%	0.5%	0.3%

Source: Noonan, M. (2016). Mortality in State Prisons, 2001–2014 — Statistical Tables. Bureau of Justice Statistics, Deaths in Custody Reporting Program, 2001 and 2005–2014; National Prisoner Statistics, 2001 and 2005–2014.

Table 4-13. Percent of State Prisoner Deaths by Selected Decedent Characteristics, 2001 and 2005–2014

Characteristic	2001	2005	2006	2007	2008	2009	2010	2011	2012	2013	2014
Total	100%	100%	100%	100%	100%	100%	100%	100%	100%	100%	100%
Sex											
Male	96.5%	95.5%	96%	96%	95.3%	95.6%	96.4%	95.7%	96.6%	95.9%	95.6%
Female	3.5	4.5	4	4	4.7	4.4	3.6	4.3	3.4	4.1	4.4
Race/Hispanic origin											
White/a	46.7%	51.3%	50.4%	50.8%	52.8%	52.1%	52.1%	57.2%	53.4%	54.7%	55.1%
Black/African American	40.5	36.7	35.6	36.2	33.5	35.2	34.8	31.1	33.2	31.7	31.8
Hispanic/Latino	11.2	10.2	12.5	11.3	11.6	10.9	11.1	9.8	11.3	11.6	10.6
Other	1.6	1.7	1.5	1.6	2.1	1.7	1.9	1.8	2.1	2	2.5
Age											
17 or younger	0.1%	—	—	—	0.1%	0%	0.1%	0.1%	0%	0%	0.1%
18–24	3	2.5%	1.9%	2%	1.9	2	2.1	1.5	2.1	2	1.6
25–34	8.9	7.7	7.7	6.7	6.4	6.1	6.7	6	5.7	6.4	6.3
35–44	22.9	18.9	17.4	15.1	13.6	13.7	11.8	11.9	10.7	9.7	9.6
45–54	31.2	31.8	32.8	30.4	30.8	30.4	29.6	27.8	26.1	24.9	23.6
55 or older	33.9	39.1	40.2	45.7	47.2	47.7	49.7	52.8	55.5	57.1	58.8

Source: Noonan, M. (2016). Mortality in State Prisons, 2001–2014 — Statistical Tables. Bureau of Justice Statistics, Deaths in Custody Reporting Program, 2001 and 2005–2014; National Prisoner Statistics, 2001 and 2005–2014.

Effective Approaches for Reducing Costs for Medical Health Problems of Long-Term and Elderly Prisoners

Effective approaches for dealing with the medical health problems of long-term and elderly prisoners have been identified and detailed prescriptive requirements for success provided. What has been missing is the will to translate policy into practice. In an effort to reduce costs states have implemented a number of strategies (Sperber 2007: 104):

- *Inmate co-payments*—Co-payments, usually less than $5 per visit and medication, are withdrawn from the inmate's commissary fund by the department. However, co-payments are not required for emergency medical services or chronic illness treatments. While these policies are being challenged in courts as violations of cruel and unusual punishment, significant reductions in sick calls have been observed.
- *Telemedicine*—Telemedicine programs are rapidly growing in popularity among correctional jurisdictions. Often, the physical location of the institution requires medical doctors, particularly specialists, to travel significant distances in order to treat ill inmates or vice versa. Further, videoconferencing reduces the risk to doctors when treating inmates (Jones et al. 2001). Telemedicine programs allow inmates to videoconference with doctors, regardless of each individual's respective location (Jones et al. 2001; Kinsella 2004). These videoconferences usually allow doctors to visually examine the inmate and provide a diagnosis, often without any further need for attention. It is estimated that between $200 and $1000 is saved each time telemedicine is used instead of transporting the inmate (or doctor traveling to the inmate) for care.
- *Privatization*—By 2000, 34 states had some part of their correctional medical system run by private organizations and 24 state departments of corrections were completely dependent upon private groups for correctional medical care (Montague, 2003). In the early 1980s, the state of Illinois began contracting with a private company to provide health care services to inmates. Currently, Illinois has the lowest per capita inmate health care cost of any other state (Kinsella 2004).
- *Early Release for Elderly and Terminally Ill Inmates*—36 states have policies that allow for some form of compassionate release for elderly and terminally ill inmates (Aday 2003). Johnson (2003) estimates

that incarcerating an elderly inmate can cost the state approximately $70,000 each year. With the increases in age of inmates, as well as the number of elderly inmates being incarcerated, the savings for early release for terminally ill and elderly inmates could be immense. However, critics of this policy argue that justice could be compromised by allowing inmates to be released early, regardless of the reason for that release.

- *Utilization Review*—Utilization review programs ensure that medical treatments prescribed to inmates are necessary and appropriate. Typically, utilization programs entail a physician or group of professionals reviewing requests for services to determine their necessity. These programs have been credited with reducing costs by preventing unnecessary procedures or recommending a lower cost treatment alternative.

- *Reduction in Pharmaceutical Costs*—Some jurisdictions have implemented restrictions on the types of drugs that can be prescribed to inmates. Most commonly, generic, low cost drugs or only drugs on a specified list can be given to inmates. Another method for reducing the cost of pharmaceuticals is to purchase drugs at reduced or wholesale prices. Large amounts of prescriptions are purchased at one time, allowing the Department of Corrections to negotiate better prices.

- *Preferred Provider Organizations (PPOs) and Health Maintenance Organizations (HMOs)*—State departments of corrections have contracted with private providers and hospitals to provide services for standardized or discounted rates. Per capita fee disbursements are also used and require the provider to cover medical services for a specific charge for a specified number of inmates for a duration of time. Another method of utilizing PPOs and HMOs is that providers supply all medical services within a fixed budget, which places the financial burden of curtailing costs onto the provider, not the state.

- *Alternative Reimbursement for Emergency and Ambulatory Services*—For many jurisdictions, emergency and ambulatory services are major expenditures of correctional health care. There are five common ways in which emergency and ambulatory services are paid: employee model (providers are employees of the state); fee-for-service model (services are paid for as they are used); pre-negotiated, discounted fee-for-service model (payments are made for services as they are used for a predetermined specified amount, often at Medicaid pricing levels); capitated rate for specific services model (payments are made to contractors in advance of services based on the number of services provided at a preset cost, often for ambulatory or dental services); and the global capitated rates model (a fixed cost per inmate per day for all medical services). While the employee model is the most commonly used, it has been found that the global capitated rates model is the least expensive (Lamb-Mechanick and Nelson 2000).

- *Prevention versus Treatment*—Inmates often enter prison with a myriad of health issues. Further, incarceration may increase the number of health problems of inmates, particularly communicable diseases. Therefore, many jurisdictions are focusing on prevention strategies in order to offset treatment costs. Prevention activities range from screening, education, and discharge planning. While the benefits of prevention efforts are revealed in prisons, they also strive to reduce the burden of future health care costs on community providers (once the inmate is released back to the community).

Rather than speak cost reduction strategies, other policy-makers look to "best practices" for implementing quality healthcare in corrections (Anno 2001; Crosland et al. 2003; Glaser and Greifinger 1993; Vaghn and Smith 1999). Best practices are established by using the best available medical evidence to implement medical practice guidelines or protocols that will improve medical outcomes for prisoners. Such practices should begin on day one of imprisonment, follow throughout the prison term, and promote the seamless transition of medical care from prison into the free world upon release. Listed below are the commonly accepted "best practices" in medical care for providing adequate medical care to prisoners that agencies can adopt:

1. Initial screening and assessment for pre-existing medical conditions related to chronic or communicable disease, functional impairments, and cognitive impairments upon entry into prison and periodic preventative screening for chronic and communicable diseases at specified intervals for long-term and elderly prisoners (Anno 2001; Cianciolo and Zupan 2004; Williams et al. 2006)
2. Coordinated care support between medical, mental health, and security staff in correctional institutions (Cox and Lawrence 2010)
3. Improve training of prison staff and health care providers by providing training in the five areas below (Williams et al. 2012: 6)
   - common normative age-associated conditions (e.g., vision loss and hearing deficits),

- common pathological age-associated physical conditions (e.g., falls and incontinence),
- common age-related clinically diagnosed cognitive conditions (e.g., dementia and delirium),
- the challenges that all such conditions can pose in the custodial setting, and
- ways to identify patients who need rapid assessment by a health care provider.

4. Improve sick call protocol by ensuring adequate 24-hour care (Anno 2001)
5. Implement utilization review process (Anno 2001)
6. Enhance palliative care (Dubler 1998; Linder and Meyers 2007; Williams et al. 2012)
7. Discharge planning (Anno 2001; Williams et al. 2010; Williams et al. 2011; Williams et al. 2012)
   a. Establishing a transition teams and community collaborations for re-entry (Anno et al. 2004; Wang et al. 2010; Williams et al. 2010);
   b. Improve medical release policies, e.g., suspend rather than terminate Medicaid benefits for inmates (Chiu 2010; Williams et al. 2011; Williams et al. 2012)

These desired programmatic enhancements are appropriate long-term goals for correctional change. Failure to accomplish these goals will most likely result in the provision of inadequate medical care to long-term and elderly prisoners.

Conclusion

The rising cost of health care of long-term and elderly prisoners has forced states and the federal government to reconsider long-standing policies associated with incarceration. We know what should be done to provide services. Yet many correctional institutions remain ill-equipped to provide cost-effective quality care for aging prisoners. California, for example, has been under receivership since 2006 for its inability to provide a constitutional level of care to prisoners (Legislative Analyst Office 2012). States are now being forced to consider alternative cost reduction strategies. Unfortunately, the costs to care for elderly and long-term special populations are made worse as a result of the mental health deterioration that may occur as time elapses. An inescapable fact is that the approaches correctional officials use to address medical health issues has changed very little in the last decade.

Websites

For more information on mental health, visit http://www.nimh.nih.gov.
For more information on U.S. medical conditions, visit http://www.cdc.gov.
For more information on correctional healthcare, visit website: http://nicic.gov.
For more information on infectious and communicable disease from an international perspective, visit http://www.who.int/en/.

References

Abner, C. (2006). Graying prisons: States face challenges of an aging inmate population. Retrieved from http://www.csg.org/knowledgecenter/docs/sn 0611GrayingPrisons.pdf.

American Civil Liberties Union. (2008). ACLU lawsuit charges grossly inadequate medical care at state prison in Nevada. Retrieved from http://www.aclu.org/prisoners-rights/aclu-lawsuit-charges-grossly-inadequate-medical-care-state-prison-nevada.

American Civil Liberties Union. (2012). At America's expense: The mass incarceration of the elderly. Retrieved from http://www.aclu.org/files/assets/elderlyprisonreport_20120613_1.pdf.

Aday, R. (2003). *Aging prisoners: Crisis in American's prisons*. Westport, CT: Praeger Press.

Akinbami, L., Moorman, J., & Liu, X. (2011). *Asthma prevalence, health care use, and mortality: United States, 2005–2009* (Report No. 32). Retrieved from Centers for Disease Control and Prevention, National Center for Health Statistics website: http://www.cdc.gov/nchs/data/nhsr/nhsr032.pdf.

Anno, J. (Ed.). (2001). *Correctional health care: Guidelines for management of an adequate service delivery system* (Report No. 98PO2GIH4). Retrieved from U.S. Department of Justice, National Institute of Corrections website: http://www.nicic.org/pubs/2001/017521.pdf.

Baussano, I., Williams, B., Nunn, P., Beggiato, M., Fedeli, U., & Scano, F. (2010). Tuberculosis incidence in prisons: A systematic review. PLoS Med 7(12), e1000381. doi:10.1371/journal.pmed.1000381.

Beck, A. (2001). Mental Health Treatment in State Prisons, 2000. Bureau of Justice Statistics. Available at http://www.ojp.usdoj.gov/bjs/pub/pdfmhrsp00.pdf.

Bellin, E. Y., Fletcher, D. D., & Safyer, S. M. (1993). Association of tuberculosis infection with increased time in or admission to the New York City jail system. *The Journal of American Medical Association*, 269(17), 2228–2231. doi:10.1001/jama.1993.03500170058034.

Binswanger, I., Krueger, P., & Steiner, J. (2009). Prevalence of chronic medical conditions among jail and prison inmates in the USA compared with the general population. *Journal of Epidemiological Community Health, 63*(11), 912–919.

Bone, A., Aerts, A., Grzemska, M., Kimerling, M., Kluge, H., Levy, M., ... Varaine, F. (2000). *Tuberculosis control in prisons: A manual for programme managers.* Geneva: World Health Organization.

Brewer T. F., Vlahov D., Taylor E., Hall, D., Munoz, A., & Polk, B. F. (1988). Transmission of HIV-1 within a statewide prison system. *AIDS, 2*(5), 363–367.

Bronson, J., Maruschak, L., and Berzofsky, M. (2016). *Disabilities among Prison and Jail Inmates, 2011–2012.* Bureau of Justice Statistics, National Inmate Survey, 2011–12.

Centers for Disease Control and Prevention. (2003). Prevention and control of infections with hepatitis viruses in correctional settings. *Morbidity and Mortality Weekly Report, 52*(RR01), 1–33.

Centers for Disease Control and Prevention. (2005). *National diabetes fact sheet.* Retrieved from http://www.cdc.gov/diabetes/pubs/general.htm.

Centers for Disease Control and Prevention. (2006a). HIV transmission among male inmates in a state prison system—Georgia, 1992–2005. *Morbidity and Mortality Weekly Report, 55*(15), 421–426.

Centers for Disease Control and Prevention. (2006b). *Pulmonary hypertension fact sheet.* Retrieved from http://www.cdc.gov/dhdsp/library/pdfs/fs_pulmonary_hypertension.pdf.

Centers for Disease Control and Prevention. (2007a). *Men who have sex with men.* Retrieved from http://www.cdc.gov/hiv/topics/msm/resources/factsheets/msm.htm.

Centers for Disease Control and Prevention. (2007b). *Tuberculosis information for international travelers.* Retrieved from http://www.cdc.gov/tb/pubs/tbfactsheets/tbtravelinfo.htm.

Centers for Disease Control and Prevention. (2010a). *Chlamydia fact sheet.* Retrieved from http://www.cdc.gov/std/Chlamydia/STDFact-Chlamydia.htm.

Centers for Disease Control and Prevention. (2010b). *Gonorrhea fact sheet.* Retrieved from http://www.cdc.gov/std/Gonorrhea/gonorrhea.pdf.

Centers for Disease Control and Prevention. (2010c). *Hepatitis b fact sheet.* Retrieved from http://www.cdc.gov/std/hepatitis/STDFact-Hepatitis-B.htm.

Centers for Disease Control and Prevention. (2010d). *HIV basic information fact sheet.* Retrieved from http://www.cdc.gov/hiv/topics/basic/index.htm.

Centers for Disease Control and Prevention. (2010e). *Syphilis fact sheet.* Retrieved from http://www.cdc.gov/std/Syphilis/STDFact-Syphilis.htm.

Centers for Disease Control and Prevention. (2011a). *Table 1. cases of sexually transmitted diseases reported by state health departments and rates per 100,000 population, United States, 1941–2011.* Retrieved from http://www.cdc.gov/std/stats11/tables/1.htm.

Centers for Disease Control and Prevention. (2011b). Vital signs: Prevalence, treatment, and control of hypertension—United States, 1999–2002 and 2005–2008. Morbidity and Mortality Weekly Report, 60(4), 103–108.

Centers for Disease Control and Prevention. (2012a). *Asthma—You can control your asthma.* Retrieved from http://www.cdc.gov/asthma/faqs.htm.

Centers for Diseases Control and Prevention. (2012b). *Hepatitis b information for health professionals.* Retrieved from http://www.cdc.gov/hepatitis/HBV/HBVfaq.htm.

Centers for Disease Control and Prevention. (2012c). *Hepatitis c information for health professionals.* Retrieved from http://www.cdc.gov/hepatitis/HCV/index.htm.

Centers for Disease Control and Prevention. (2012d). *Living with chronic hepatitis c.* Retrieved from http://www.cdc.gov/ncidod/diseases/hepatitis/resource/PDFs/Have_C_01.pdf.

Chettiar, I., & Bunting, W. (2012). Keeping low-risk elderly prisoners behind bars is a budget buster. Retrieved from Center for American Progress website: http://www.americanprogress.org/issues/civil-liberties/news/2012/06/13/11726/keeping-low-risk-elderly-prisoners-behind-bars-is-a-budget-buster/.

Crosland, C., Poshkus, M., & Rich, J. D. (2002). Treating prisoners with HIV/AIDS: The importance of early identification, effective treatment and community follow-up. *Journal Watch HIV/AIDS Clinical Care.* Retrieved from http://aids-clinical-care.jwatch.org/cgi/content/full/2002/801/1.

Danaei, G., Ding, E. L., Mozaffarian, D., Taylor, B.; Rehm, J., Murray, C., & Ezzati, M. (2009). The preventable causes of death in the United States: Comparative risk assessment of dietary, lifestyle, and metabolic risk factors. PLOS Medicine, 6(4). Retrieved from http://www.plosmedicine.org/article/info:doi/10.1371/journal.pmed.1000058.

Dara, M., Grzemska, M., Kimerling, M. E., Reyes, H., & Zagorsky, A. (2009). *Guidelines for control of tuberculosis in prisons.* Retrieved from U.S. Agency for International Development website: http://pdf.usaid.gov/pdf_docs/PNADP462.pdf.

Davis, L. (2002). *The public health dimensions of prisoner reentry: Addressing the health needs and risks of returning prisoners and their families.* Reentry Roundtable Meeting, The Urban Institute, Los Angeles, CA. Retrieved from http://www.urban.org/uploadedpdf/410920_public_health_roundtable.pdf.

Dhami, M., Ayton, P., & Loewenstein, G. (2007). Adaptation to imprisonment: Indigenous or imported? *Criminal Justice and Behavior, 34*(8), 1085–1100.

Estelle v. Gamble, 429 U.S. 97 (1976).

Florida House of Representatives Criminal Justice and Corrections Council, & Florida Corrections Committee. (1999). *An examination of elder inmates services: An aging crisis.* Retrieved from http://www.leg.state.fl.us/Publications/1999/House/reports/corrctns.pdf.

Freedy, J. R., & Donkervoet, C. J. (1995). Traumatic stress: An overview of the field. In J.R. Freedy & S.E. Hobfoll (Eds.), Traumatic stress: From Theory to practice (pp. 1–28). New York, NY: Plenum.

Fruedenberg, N. (2001). Continuity of care from corrections to community: Jails, prisons, and the health of urban populations: A review of the impact of the correctional health [Special Feature]. *Journal of Urban Heath, Bulletin of the New York Academy of Medicine, 78*(2), 214–235.

Georgia Department of Corrections. (2000). *Executive Summary.* Retrieved from http://www.dcor.state.ga.us/pdf/agingpop.pdf.

Geisler, G. (2011). The cost of correctional health care: A correctional institution inspection committee summary of Ohio's prison health care system. Retrieved from U.S. Department of Justice, National Institute on Corrections website: http://nicic.gov/Library/024989.

Glaser, J. B., & Greifinger, R. B. (1993). Correctional health care: A public health opportunity. *Annals of Internal Medicine, 118*(2), 139–145.

Gorlick, A. (2012, November 27). Stanford researchers show a better way to curb TB in prisons. Stanford News. Retrieved from http://news.stanford.edu/news/2012/november/TB-Soviet-diagnosis-112712.html.

Hammett, T. M., Harmon, M. P., & Rhodes, W. (2002). The burden of infectious disease among inmates of and releases from U.S. correctional facilities, 1997. *American Journal of Public Health, 92*(11), 1789–1794.

Hammett, T., Harmon, P., *and* Maruschak. (1999). 1996–1997 update: HIV/AIDS, STDs, and TB in correctional facilities (Report No. NCJ 176344). Retrieved from U.S. Department of Justice, National Institute of Justice website: https://www.ncjrs.gov/pdffiles1/176344.pdf.

Hammett, T. M., Roberts, C., & Kennedy, S. (2001). Health related issues in prisoner reentry. *Crime and Delinquency, 47*(3).

Harzke, A., Baillargeon, J., Pruitt, S., Pulvino, J., Parr, D., & Kelly, M. (2010). Prevalence of chronic medical conditions among inmates in the Texas prison system. *Journal of Urban Health: Bulletin of the New York Academy of Medicine, 87*(3), 486–502. doi:10.1007/s11524-010-9448-2.

Heidenreich, P. A., Trogdon, J. G., Khavjou, O. A., Butler, J., Dracup, K, Ezekowitz, M. D., … Woo, J. Y. (2011). Forecasting the future of cardiovascular disease in the United States: A policy statement from the American Heart Association. Circulation, 123(8), 933–944. doi:10.1161/CIR.0b0 13e31820a55f5.

Hellard, M. E., & Aitken, C. K. (2004). HIV in prison: What are the risks and what can be done? Sexual Health, 1(2), 107–113.

Hensley, C., Tewksbury, R., Wright, J. (2001). Exploring the dynamics of masturbation and consensual same-sex activity within a male maximum security prison. The Journal of Men's Studies, 10(1), 59–71.

Hornung, C. A., Anno, B. J., Greifinger, R. B., & Gadre, S. (2000). Health care of soon-to-be released inmates: A survey of state prison systems (Vol. 2, Report No. 1). Retrieved from National Commission on Correctional Health Care website: http://www.ncchc.org/stbr/Volume2/Health%20Status%20(vol%202).pdf.

Hornung, C. A., Greifinger, R., & Gadre, S. (2000). A projection model of the prevalence of selected chronic diseases in the inmate population (Vol. 2, Report No. 3). Retrieved from National Commission on Correctional Health Care website: http://www.ncchc.org/stbr/Volume2/Report3_Hornung.pdf.

Horsburgh, R. C., Jarvis, Q. J., McArthur T., Ignacio, T., & Stock, P. (1990). Seroconversion to human immunodeficiency virus in prison inmates. American Journal of Public Health, 80(2), 209–210.

Hung, W., Ross, J., Boockvar, K., & Siu, A. (2011). Recent trends in chronic disease, impairment and disability among older adults in the United States. BMC Geriatrics, 11, 47 doi:10.1186/1471-2318-11-47.

Hutton, M., Cauthen, G., & Bloch, A. (1993). Results of a 29-state survey of tuberculosis in nursing homes and correctional facilities. Public Health Reports, 108(3), 305.

Jafa, K., McElroy, P., Fitzpatrick, L., Borkowf, C. B., MacGowan, R., Margolis, A., … Sullivan, P. S. (2009). HIV transmission in a state prison system, 1988–2005. PLoS ONE, 4(5), e5416. doi:10.1371/journal.pone.0005416.

John Howard Association of Illinois. (2012). Unasked questions, unintended consequences: Fifteen findings and recommendations on Illinois' prison healthcare system. Retrieved from http://thejha.org/sites/default/files/Unasked%20Questions-Unintended%20Consequences.pdf.

Jonnson, P. (2003). As prisoners age, should they go free? The Christian Science Monitor, 5. Retrieved from http://www.csmonitor.com/2003/0905/p01s01-usju.htm.

Jones, T. F., Craig, A. S., Valway, S. E., Woodley, C. L., & Schaffner, W. (1999). Transmission of tuberculosis in a jail. Ann Intern Med, 131, 557–563.

Kang, S. Y., Deren, S., Andia, J., Colon, H. M., Robles, R., & Oliver-Velez, D. (2005). HIV transmission behaviors in jail/prison among Puerto Rican drug injectors in New York and Puerto Rico. *AIDS and Behavior*, 9(3), 377–386.

Kerbs, C. P. (2002). High-risk HIV transmission behavior in prison and the prison subculture. *The Prison Journal*, 82(1), 19–49.

Kerbs, C. P. (2006). Inmate factors associated with HIV transmission in prison. *Criminology and Public Policy*, 5(1), 113–135.

Kerbs, C. P., & Simmons, M. (2002). Intraprison HIV transmission: An assessment of whether it occurs, how it occurs, and who is at risk. *AIDS Education and Prevention*, 14 (Suppl. B), 53–64.

Khan, A. J., Simard, E. P., Bower, W. A., Wurtzel, H. L., Khristova, M., Wagner, K., … Bell, B. P. (2005). Ongoing transmission of hepatitis B virus infection among inmates at a state correctional facility. *American Journal of Public Health*, 95(10), 1793–1799.

Kim, K. & Peterson, B. (2014). *Aging behind bars: Trends and implications of graying prisoners in the federal system.* Urban Institute.

Kinsella, C. (2004). *Corrections health care costs.* Retrieved from Council on State Governments website: http://www.prisonpolicy.org/scans/csg/Corrections+Health+Care+Costs+1-21-04.pdf.

Kochanek, K. D., Xu, J. Q., Murphy, S. L., Miniño, A. M., & Kung, H. C. (2011). *Deaths: Final data for 2009* (National vital statistics reports, Vol. 60, No. 3). Retrieved from Centers for Disease Control and Prevention, National Center for Health Statistics website: http://www.cdc.gov/nchs/data/nvsr/nvsr60/nvsr60_03_tables.pdf.

Koo, D. T., Baron, R. C., & Rutherford, G. W. (1997). Transmission of mycobacterium tuberculosis in a California state prison, 1991. *American Journal of Public Health*, 87, 279–282.

Kraut, J., Haddix, A. Carande-Kulis, V. and Greifinger, R. (2002). Cost-Effectiveness of Routine Screening for Sexually Transmitted Diseases Among Inmates in United States Prisons and Jails. In the health status of soon-to-be-released inmates: A report to Congress (Vol. 2, pp. 81–108). Chicago, IL: National Commission on Correctional Health Care.

Lamb-Mechanick, D., & Nelson, J. (2000). *Prison health care survey: An analysis of factors influencing per capita costs.* Retrieved from U.S. Department of Justice, National Institute of Corrections website: http://nicic.gov/Library/015999.

Legislative Analyst's Office California's Nonpartisan Fiscal and Policy Advisor. (2011). *How much does it cost to incarcerate an inmate?* (Budget Report 2008–2009). Retrieved from http://www.lao.ca.gov/laoapp/laomenus/sections/crim_justice/6_cj_inmatecost.aspx?catid=3.

Leonard, K. (2012). States efforts to outsource prison health care come under scrutiny. Retrieved from Kaiser Foundation website: http://www.kaiserhealthnews.org/Stories/2012/July/23/prison-health-care.aspx.

Loeb, S. J. & Steffensmeier, D. (2006). Older male prisoners: Health status, self-efficacy, and health-promoting behaviors. *Journal of Correctional Health Care*, 12(4), 269–278.

Macalino, G. E., Dhawan, D., & Rich, J. D. (2005). A missed opportunity: Hepatitis C screening of prisoners. *American Journal of Public Health*, 95(10), 1739–1740.

Macalino, G. E., Vlahov, D., Sanford-Colby, S., Patel, S., Sabin, K., & Rich, J. D. (2004). Prevalence and incidence of HIV, hepatitis B virus, and hepatitis C virus infections among males in Rhode Island prisons. *American Journal of Public Health*, 94(7), 1218–1223.

Macher, A., Kibble, D., & Wheeler, D. (2006). HIV transmission in correctional facility. *Emerging Infectious Diseases*, 12(4), 669–671.

MacIntyre, C. R., Kendig, N., Kummer, L., Birago, S., Graham, N. M. (1997). Impact of tuberculosis control measures and crowding on the incidence of tuberculosis infection in Maryland prisons. *Clinical Infectious Diseases*, 24, 1060–1067.

MacNeil, J. R., Lobato, M. N., & Moore, M. (2005). An unanswered health disparity: Tuberculosis among correctional inmates, 1993 through 2003. *American Journal of Public Health*, 1, 1800–1805.

Maruschak, L. (2012). *HIV in prisons, 2001–2010*. Retrieved from U.S. Department of Justice, Bureau of Justice Statistics website http://bjs.ojp.usdoj.gov/content/pub/pdf/hivp10.pdf.

Maruschak, L, Berzofsky, M. and Unangst, J. (2016). Medical Problems of State and Federal Prisoners and Jail Inmates, 2011–2012. Bureau of Justice Statistics, National Prisoner Statistics Program, 2001–2012.

Maschi, T. & Aday, R. (2014*). The social determinants of health and justice and the aging in prison crisis: A call for human rights action. International Journal of Social Work*, 1, 15–33.

Mateyoke-Schivner, A., Webster, J. M., Hiller, M. L., Staton, M. & Leukefeld, C. (2003). Criminal history, physical and mental health, substance abuse, and services among incarcerated substance abusers. *Journal of Contemporary Criminal Justice*, 19(1), 82–97.

Meyer, J. A. (2003). Improving men's health: Developing a long-term survey. *American Journal of Public Health*, 93(5), 709–711.

Milbank Memorial Fund, National Association of State Budget Officers, & Reforming States Group. (2001). *1998–1999 state health care expenditure report*. New York, NY, Washington, DC: Authors.

Montague, E. (2003). *Prison health care: Healing a sick system through private competition.* Retrieved from Washington Policy Center website: http://www.washingtonpolicy.org/publications/notes/prison-health-care-healing-sick-system-through-private-competition.

Morton, J. B. (1992). An administrative overview of the older inmate. Retrieved from U.S. Department of Justice, National Institute of Corrections website: http://www.nicic.org/pubs/1992/010937.pdf.

Mutter, R. C., Grimes, R. M., & Labarthe, D. (1994). Evidence of intraprison spread of HIV infection. *Archives of Internal Medicine,* 154(7), 793–795.

Newman v. State of Alabama, 503 F.2d 1320 (5th Cir. 1974).

Niveau, G. (2006). Prevention of infectious disease transmission in correctional settings: A review. *Public Health,* 120(1), 33–41.

Noonan, M. (2016). *Mortality in State Prisons, 2001–2014—Statistical Tables.* Bureau of Justice Statistics, Deaths in Custody Reporting Program, 2001 and 2005–2014; National Prisoner Statistics, 2001 and 2005–2014.

Okie, S. (2007). Sex, drugs, prisons, and HIV. *The New England Journal of Medicine,* 356(2), 105–108.

Osborne Association (2014). The high cost of low risk: The crisis of America's aging prison population. Retrieved from http://www.osborneny.org/images/uploads/printMedia/Osborne_Aging_WhitePaper.pdf.

Petersilia, J. (2001). Prisoner reentry: Public safety and reintegration challenges. *The Prison Journal,* 81(3), 360–375.

Petersilia, J. (2003). *When prisoners come home: Parole and reentry in the U.S.* New York, NY: Oxford University Press.

Puleo, T., & Chedekel, L. (2011). *Dollars and lives lost: The cost of prison healthcare.* Retrieved from New England Center for Investigative Reporting website: http://necir-bu.org/investigations/taxpayer-watch-series/dollars-and-lives-the-cost-of-prison-health-care-2/.

RAND. (2005). *Prisoner reentry: What are the public health challenges?* (Research Brief 6013-PSJ). Retrieved from http://www.rand.org/content/dam/rand/pubs/research_briefs/2005/RB6013.pdf.

Restum, Z. G. (2005). Public health implications of substandard correctional health care. *American Journal of Public Health,* 95(10), 1689–1691.

Roberts, C. (2012). Elderly inmates—The cost of dealing with an elderly prison population. Universal Senior Living. Retrieved from http://www.universalseniorliving.com/article/elderly-inmates-cost-dealing-elderly-prison-population.

Robillard, A. G., Gallito-Zaparaniuk, P., Arriola, K. J., Kennedy, S., Hammett, T., & Braithwaite, R. L. (2003). Partners and processes in HIV services for inmates and ex-offenders: Facilitating collaboration and service delivery. *Evaluation Review*, 27(5), 535–562.

Roger, V. L., Go, A. S., Lloyd-Jones, D. M., Benjamin, E. J., Berry, J. D., Borden, W. B., ... American Heart Association Statistics Committee and Stroke Statistics Subcommittee. (2012). Heart disease and stroke statistics—2012 update: a report from the American Heart Association. Circulation, 125(1) e2–e220. doi:10.1161/CIR.0b013e31823ac046.

Rudolph, J. (2012, June 13). Elderly inmate population soared 1300 percent since 1980. *Huffington Post*. Retrieved from http://www.huffingtonpost.com/2012/06/13/elderly-inmate-population-soars_n_1594793.html.

Sabin, K. M., Frey, R. L., Horsley, R. & Greby, S. M. (2001). Characteristics and trends of newly identified HIV infections among incarcerated populations: CDC HIV voluntary counseling, testing, and referral system, 1992–1998. *Journal of Urban Health: Bulletin of the New York Academy of Medicine*, 78(2), 241–255.

Sampson, R. & Lauritsen, J. (1990). Deviant lifestyles, proximity to crime, and the offender-victim link in personal violence. *Journal of Research in Crime and Delinquency*, 27(2), 110–139.

Seal, D. W., Belcher, L., Morrow, K., Eldridge, G., Binson, D., Kacanek, D., Project START Study Group. (2004). A qualitative study of substance use and sexual behavior among 18 to 29-year-old men while incarcerated in the United States. *Health Education and Behavior*, 31(6), 775–789. DOI: 10.1177/1090198104264134.

Seal, D. W., Margolis, A. D., Morrow, K. M., Belcher, L., Sosman, J., Askew, J., & Project START Substudy Group. (2008). Substance use and sexual behavior during incarceration among 18 to 29-year old men: Prevalence and correlates. *AIDS and Behavior*, 12(1), 27–40.

Shaffer, J. (2004). *The victim-offender overlap: Specifying the role of peer groups* (Unpublished thesis). Retrieved from National Crime Justice Reference Service website: https://www.ncjrs.gov/pdffiles1/nij/grants/205126.pdf\.

Shuter, J. (2002). Communicable diseases in inmates: Public health opportunities. In the health status of soon-to-be-released inmates: A report to Congress (Vol. 2, pp. 167–202).Chicago, IL: National Commission on Correctional Health Care.

Sieck, C. & Demba, A. (2011). Results of a pilot study of pre-release STD testing and inmates' risk behaviors in an Ohio prison. *Journal of Urban Health.* 88(4), 690–699.

Solomon, L., Flynn, C., Muck, K., & Vertefeuille, J. (2004). Prevalence of HIV, syphilis, hepatitis B, and hepatitis C among entrants to Maryland correctional facilities. *Journal of Urban Health: Bulletin of the New York Academy of Medicine,* 81(1), 25–37.

Spaulding, A., Stephenson, B., Macalino, G., Ruby, W., Clarke, J. G., & Fanigan, T. (2002). Human immunodeficiency virus in correctional facilities: A review. *Clinical Infectious Diseases,* 35(3), 305–312.

Stead, W. W. (1978). Undetected tuberculosis in prison: source of infection for community at large. *JAMA,* 240, 2544–2547.

Stephan, J. (2004). *State Prison Expenditures, 2001.* Retrieved from U.S. Department of Justice, Bureau of Justice Statistics website: http://www.ojp.usdoj.gov/bjs/pub/pdf/spe01.pdf.

The Pew Charitable Trusts & the John D. and Catherine T. MacAuthur Foundation (2014). *State prison health care spending: An examination.* The Pew Charitable Trust and the John D. and Catherine T. MacAuthur Foundation.

Thomas, C. (1977). Theoretical perspectives on prisonization: A comparison of the importation and deprivation models. *The Journal of Criminal Law and Criminology,* 689(1), 135–145.

Thomas, J. C., Levandowski, B. A., Isler, M. R., Torrone, E., & Wilson, G. (2007). Incarceration and sexually transmitted infections: A neighborhood perspective. *Journal of Urban Health: Bulletin of the New York Academy of Medicine,* 85(1), 90–99.

Travis, J., & Visher, C. (2005). *Prisoner reentry and crime in America.* Cambridge, MA: Cambridge University Press.

Unger, C., & Buchanan, R. (1985). Managing long term offenders: A guide for the correctional administrator. Retrieved from U.S. Department of Justice, National Institute of Corrections website: http://www.nicic.org/pubs/pre/004022.pdf.

Useem, B., & Kimball, P. (1989). *States of siege: U.S. prison riots, 1971–1986.* Cambridge, MA: Sage Publications, Oxford University Press.

U.S. Department of Justice, National Commission on Correctional Health Care. (2002). Health status of soon-to-be-released inmates, Volume 1. Retrieved from https://www.ncjrs.gov/pdffiles1/nij/grants/189735.pdf.

U.S. Department of Health and Human Services, National Institutes of Health, National Institute of Mental Health. (2006). *Depression.* Retrieved from http://www.nimh.nih.gov/health/publications/depression/complete-index.shtml.

U.S. Department of Mental Health, National Institute of Mental Health. (2006). Anxiety Disorders. Retrieved from http://www.nimh.nih.gov/health/publications/anxiety-disorders/complete-index.shtml.

U.S. Department of Mental Health and Human Services, National Institute of Mental Health. (2007). *Bipolar Disorder. Retrieved from:* http://www.nimh.nih.gov/health/publications/bipolar-disorder/nimh-bipolar-adults.pdf.

U.S. Department of National Institute of Mental Health. (2007). *Schizophrenia*. Retrieved from http://www.nimh.nih.gov/health/publications/schizophrenia/complete-index.shtml.

Varghese, B., & Peterman, T. A. (2001). Cost-effectiveness of HIV counseling and testing in U.S. prisons. *Journal of Urban Health: Bulletin of the New York Academy of Medicine*, 78(2), 304–312.

Vaughn, M. S., & Smith, L. G. (1999). Practicing penal harm medicine in the United States: Prisoners' voices from jail. *Justice Quarterly*, 16(1), 175–231.

Vito, G. F. & Wilson, D. G. (1985). Forgotten people: Elderly inmates. *Federal Probation*, 49, 18–24.

Vlahov, D., & Putnam, S. (2006). From corrections to communities as an HIV priority. *Journal of Urban Health: Bulletin of the New York Academy of Medicine*, 83(3), 339–348.

Webster, J. M., Leukfeld, C. G., Staton-Tindall, M., Hiller, M. L., Garrity, T. F., & Narevic, E. (2005). Lifetime health services use by male drug-abusing offenders. *Prison Journal*, 85(1), 50–64.

White, M. C., Tulsky, J. P., Portillo, C. J., Menendez, E., Cruz, E., & Goldenson, J. (2001). Tuberculosis prevalence in an urban jail: 1994 and 1998. *International Journal of Tuberculosis and Lung Disease*, 5, 400–404.

Winter, S. J. (2012). A comparison of acuity and treatment measures of inmate and noninmate hospital patients with a diagnosis of either heart disease or chest pain. *Journal National Medicine Association*, 103(2), 109–115.

Wolfe, M. I., Xu, F., Patel, P., O'Cain, M., Schillinger, J. A., St. Louis, M. E., & Finelli, L. (2001). An outbreak of syphilis in Alabama prisons: Correctional health policy and communicable disease control. *American Journal of Public Health*, 91(8), 1220–1225.

Chapter 5

Mental Health Needs

Doing time in prison is hard for everyone. Prisoners struggle to maintain their self-respect and emotional equilibrium in facilities that are typically tense, overcrowded, fraught with the potential for violence, cut off from families and communities, and devoid of opportunities for meaningful education, work, or other productive activities. But life in prison is particularly difficult for prisoners with mental illnesses that impair their thinking, emotional responses, and ability to cope (Human Rights Watch 2003: 2).

Prisons are known to be inhabited by a fairly large number of offenders who suffer from mental health disorders (Freudenberg 2001). Haney (2001) suggested that upwards of 20 percent of prisoners suffer from some psychological disorder or developmental delay. As a result of the deinstitutionalization of the state mental health system, people with mental disorders have been increasingly incarcerated during the past three decades. There are three times as many mentally ill in U.S. prisons as in the country's mental health hospitals (Fellnar and Abramasky 2004). There is also some evidence supporting the perception that mentally ill prisoners serve longer sentences (Edwards 1985). The United States is not alone in grappling with significant increases in prisoners diagnosed with mental illnesses. A meta-analytic review conducted by Anasseril (2007) across 12 Western countries revealed that a significant percentage of male prisoners throughout all countries reported psychotic illnesses, major depression, and personality disorders. Women in this study primarily experienced psychosis, major depression, and personality disorders. As the long term and elderly prisoner population continues to grow, it is important to evaluate what we know about the trends in mental health? What are the mental health disorders experienced by this population? Are the mental health challenges increasing significantly as prisoners' age or are incarcerated for long periods of time? Are

> **Box 5-1. Why Focus on Mental Health Issues?**
>
> - The prison environment as designed fosters the development of mental disorders rather than mental health.
> - Correctional institutions have become de facto state hospitals.
> - The stigma and discrimination experienced by the mentally disordered are reproduced in correctional environments.
> - The presence of a mental illness may create additional institutional problems for elderly and long-term prisoners.
> - The majority of mentally disordered prisoners will be released back into the community.
>
> Source: World Health Organization (2007).

prison systems providing an adequate level of care? This chapter deals with the prevalence and incidence of mental health issues among the long-term and elderly inmate population.

Why Focus on the Mental Health Needs of Long-Term and Elderly Inmates?

Owing to the fact that aging prisoners often experience higher rates of mental illness, a lack of understanding of their mental health needs represents a unique challenge for correctional administrators. There are five principal reasons why greater attention is needed (see Box 5-1). First, the prison environment itself as designed is not conducive to mental health stability. There are a plethora of environmental factors such as the lack of privacy, overcrowding, social isolation experienced, and violence that seem to have a negative effect on mental health (World Health Organization 2007). According to the Forensic Taskforce of the NAMI Board of Directors (2008: 3), "The correctional facility's overriding need to maintain order and security, as well as its mandate to implement society's priorities of punishment and social control, greatly restrict the facility's ability to establish a therapeutic milieu and provide all the necessary interventions to treat mental illness successfully." Prisons are not designed to provide treatment; they are designed to punish, and, as such, may exacerbate mental health problems (Lamb and Weinberger 1998).

Second, "correctional institutions have become the de facto state hospitals, and there are more seriously and persistently mentally ill in prisons than in all state hospitals in the United States" (Anassenl 2007: 406). In 1955, the United States embraced a policy referred to as deinstitutionalization. This policy moved severely mentally ill people out of state run mental health facilities, which were later shuttered, and placed them back into the community (Torrey 1997). The net result of this policy was that 90% of the people who would have been living in public psychiatric hospitals in 1955 were not living there in 1994 (Torrey 1997). We have long known that moving the mentally disordered from state run mental health facilities to prison is not effective. To quote a jail official from Ohio, "Deinstitutionalization doesn't work. We just switched places. Instead of being in hospitals the people are in jail. The whole system is topsy-turvy and the last person served is the mentally ill person" (Torrey et al. 1992). Consequently, the mentally ill offender may serve longer periods of incarceration than what he or she would have spent in a state run mental health facility. Churgin (1980) reported the transfer of a prison inmate to a mental health facility could in some states result in a long-term stay, deny the inmate an opportunity for good-time credit, delay parole consideration, and stigmatize the inmate by the label *mentally ill.*

Third, the stigma and discrimination experienced by the mentally disordered are reproduced in correctional environments (World Health Organization 2007). The treatment of the mentally ill in prison often exacerbates the problem. As Torrey (1995) states, the "bad" and the "mad" don't mix. The experience of incarceration for mentally ill prisoners is often characterized by periods of social isolation and victimization (Edwards 1988; Edwards 1999; Stone and Hirliman 1982; Torrey 1995). Even correctional officers, whose responsibility it is to ensure the safety and security of all inmates, sometimes treat mentally disordered prisoners with a level of disdain because such prisoners are perceived to be more dangerous and unpredictable (Fellner 2006a; 2006b). Mentally disordered prisoners may find themselves placed in the most restrictive correctional settings and ineligible for early release (Forensic Taskforce of the NAMI Board of Directors 2008; Miller and Metzner 1994). There is also a corresponding double stigma that occurs upon release back into the community (Forensic Taskforce of the NAMI Board of Directors 2008).

Moreover, mental health disorders may create an additional institutional burden. Prisons are orderly places, and, as such, require strict adherence to routine, and negative consequences are visited against those that are unable to follow the rules. Prisoners with mental disorders may be unable to follow the strict regime required within correctional contexts as a result of loss of short-term or long term memory, impairments in cognitive functioning, impairments in visual and/or auditory processing, deficits in reasoning abilities, and so forth (Maschi et al. 2012). For example, Maschi et al. (2012: 444) report "Behavior typical of early to late stages of dementia, such as not being able to follow directions, pacing about a cell, or aggressive behavior may cause disruptions in the general population prison movement or in congregate living quarters." The net result is that these behaviors place the prisoner at enhanced risk of punitive consequences from correctional officials. Ultimately, as detailed later in this chapter, such prisoners often find themselves subject to the harshest aspect of prison life, characterized by isolation, severe restrictions on movement, and visitation limitations. Additional evidence suggests that older prisoners and those with mental health disorders are at particular risk for violent victimization which can worsen rather than improve mental health (Cox and Lawrence 2010; Maschi et al. 2012).

Finally, the majority of mentally disordered prisoners will be released back into the community. At least 95 percent of state prisoners will be released back into the community and this figure includes a significant percentage of prisoners who suffer from mental illnesses (Hughes and Wilson 2002). During 2011, this translated into 688,384 sentenced prisoners returning to the community (Carson and Sabol 2011). Moreover, given that the incidence of mental illness is two to four times higher among correctional populations than in the general public, the number of mentally ill returning inmates is quite high (Hammett, Roberts, and Kennedy 2001). Because of inadequate release mechanisms, ineffectual treatment and rehabilitation programs in the community, at least 50 percent of mentally ill released offenders will return to prison within 3 years of release (Anserrill 2007; Binswanger et al. 2007).

Characteristics of Mentally Disordered Prisoners

There are a limited number of large scale studies in the U.S. that have included specific information on the mental health status of prisoners. A Bureau of Justice Statistics Special Report (2006) estimated that 705,600 mentally ill adults were incarcerated in State prisons, 78,800 in Federal prisons and 479,900 in local jails (James and Glaze 2006). This data represents more than half of state prison inmates (56%) and 46 percent of federal prison inmates who self-reported having a mental health problem (see Table 5-1 and Table 5-2). In 2004, an estimated one in six prisoners in the United States was mentally ill (Fellnar and Abramsky 2004). A significant percentage, 8 to 19 percent, of prisoners had mental health disorders that resulted in functional disabilities, and another 15 to 20 percent would require psychiatric intervention while incarcerated (Human Rights Watch 2012: 1).

The most recent data on the prevalence of mental health problems comes from data collected as part of the PREA (Beck, Berzofsky, and Kerbs 2013).

Table 5-1. Recent History and Symptoms of Mental Health Problems among Prison and Jail Inmates

Mental Health Problem	Percent Inmates in		
	State Prison	Federal Prison	Local Jail
Any mental health problem	56.2	44.8	64.2
Recent history of mental health problems	24.3	13.8	20.6
Told had disorder by mental health professional	9.4	5.4	10.9
Had overnight hospital stay	5.4	2.1	4.9
Used prescribed medications	18	10.3	14.4
Had professional mental health therapy	15.1	8.3	10.3
Symptoms of mental health disorders	49.2	39.8	60.5
Major depressive disorder	23.5	16	29.7
Mania disorder	43.2	35.1	54.5
Psychotic disorder	15.4	35.1	23.9

Source: James, D. and Glaze, L. (2006). Mental Health Problems of Prison and Jail Inmates. Bureau of Justice Statistics.

An estimated 36% of prisoners reported having a history of mental health problems (manic depression, bipolar disorder, depressive disorder, schizophrenia, other psychotic disorder, PTSD, anxiety disorder or other personality disorder) and were told of this problem by a mental health professional (see Table 5-3). More than a third of prisoners stated that they had received some counseling or therapy and 15% reported taking prescription medication. While the PREA data indicate that 254,900 prisoners reported currently having an anxiety-mood disorder or being in serious psychological distress, the number is most likely larger.

There have been some consistent findings regarding the nature of mentally ill prisoners. The majority of mentally ill prisoners had prior arrest records (Forensic Taskforce of the NAMI Board of Directors 2008; James and Glaze 2006), had prior arrests for violent crimes (Forensic Taskforce of the NAMI Board of Directors 2008; Lamb et al. 2007), had a history of substance abuse (Forensic Taskforce of the NAMI Board of Directors 2008; James and Glaze 2006; Lamb et al. 2007), and had a history of prior mental health problems

Table 5-2. Prevalence of Mental Health Problems among Prison and Jail Inmates

Mental Health Problem	State Prison Inmates		Federal Prison Inmates		Local Jail Inmates	
	Number	%	Number	%	Number	%
Any mental health problem	705,600	56.2	70,200	44.8	479,900	64.2
History and symptoms	219,700	17.5	13,900	8.9	127,800	17.1
History only	85,400	6.8	7,500	4.8	26,200	3.5
Symptoms only	396,700	31.6	48,100	30.7	322,900	43.2
No mental health problem	549,900	43.8	86,500	55.2	267,600	35.8

Source: James, D. and Glaze, L. (2006). Mental Health Problems of Prison and Jail Inmates.

(Forensic Taskforce of the NAMI Board of Directors 2008; James and Glaze 2006). Other common factors include being homeless in the year prior to incarceration, and a history of physical and sexual abuse (James and Glaze 2006).

Age and Prisoner Mental Health Problems

With regard to the relationship between age and mental illness, the United States Department of Health and Human Services (1999) estimated that at least 20 percent of people aged 55 and older experience mental disorders that are not part of normal aging. James and Glaze (2006) found that 51 percent of state inmates aged 45 to 54 and 39.6 percent of state prison inmates 55 and older had mental health problems (see Table 5-3). The most common mental illnesses among inmates are reviewed (see Box 5-2).

Most Common Mental Illnesses among Inmates Aged 55 and Up

Late Onset Schizophrenia

Schizophrenia is a severe disabling brain disorder that affects approximately 1 percent of the U.S. population (Regier et al. 1993). People diagnosed with this disorder may have difficulty distinguishing what is real and not real, find

Table 5-3. Mental Health Status and History of Mental Health Problems among Inmates, 2011–12

Mental Health Status	Adult Prison Inmates	
	Number	Percent
Current mental health status		
No mental illness	926,800	67.1
Anxiety-mood disorder	251,700	18.2
Serious psychological distress	203,200	14.7
History of mental health problems		
Ever told by mental health professional had disorder		
Yes	505,600	36.6
No	875,500	63.4
Had overnight stay in hospital in year before current admission		
Yes	122,800	8.9
No	1,257,700	91.1
Used prescription medications at time of current offense		
Yes	211,800	15.4
No	1,165,000	84.6
Ever received professional mental health therapy		
Yes	492,000	35.8
No	884,000	64.2

Source: Bureau of Justice Statistics, National Inmate Survey, 2011–12.

Box 5-2. Most Common Mental Illnesses among Inmates Aged 55 and Up

- Late Onset Schizophrenia
- Depression
- Dementia/Alzheimer's
- Anxiety

Source: United States Department of Health and Human Services (1999).

it difficult to act normally in social situations, may have problems thinking clearly, and may not be able to exhibit normal emotional responses. With regard to incarcerated populations, the concern is that as prisoners age the rates of late onset schizophrenia will increase. Such individuals functioned well at earlier ages and stages of their incarceration but begin to exhibit signs of schizophrenia as they age.

The development of the late onset schizophrenia is likely to have followed a period of severe stress or physical illness (Kansas State University Department on Aging 1999). While there is disagreement about the age at which late onset schizophrenia begins, most studies use age 40 to 65 as the cutoff for late onset and age 65 or older to establish very late onset schizophrenia (Jeste, Paulsen, and Harris 1995). (See Table 5-4 for a comparison of late onset with very late onset.) This subtype of schizophrenia often manifests with the following positive symptoms: bizarre delusions, auditory hallucinations, and thought disorder. These individuals are more likely to experience persecutory delusions and hallucinations related to sight, smell, or taste (http://www.schizophrenic.com/articles/schizophrenia/late-onset-schizophrenia). Negative symptoms reflect problems relating to others and can include lack of emotional expression, a reduced amount of speech or speech that has no obvious content, social withdrawal, lack of interest or slowing down, and difficulty concentrating or performing tasks. While late onset schizophrenia is presumed to have a hereditary component, very late onset schizophrenia is not hereditary (Wetherell and Veste 2003).

Older adults with schizophrenia experience various functioning problems. Approximately 20 percent of older adults with late onset schizophrenia experience worsening symptoms, but it is not uncommon for late onset patients to experience remission or improvement with the correct course of treatment (Wetherell and Veste 2003). A major challenge facing older adults diagnosed with schizophrenia is impairment in their ability to learn new information and perform executive functions. However, older adults with lower educational levels and poor quality backgrounds seem to experience the most decline cognitively and functionally (Wetherell and Veste 2003). The treatment for late onset schizophrenia requires long term maintenance on antipsychotic medicine, cognitive behavioral therapy, and social skills training (Csernansky 2002; Kansas State University Department on Aging 1999).

Older adults with schizophrenia are at increased risk of developing other physical illnesses. Such adults often experience higher rates of diabetes and heart diseases (Csernansky 2002). This finding may be a result of the fact that antipsychotic medications are associated with weight gain, increased levels of sugar in the blood, and elevated lipid levels (Allison et al. 1999). Older adults

Table 5-4. Prison and Jail Inmates Who Had Mental Health Problems by Gender, Race, and Age

Characteristic	Percent of Inmates in		
	State Prison	Federal Prison	Local Jail
All inmates	56.2	44.8	64.2
Gender			
Male	55	43.6	62.8
Female	73.1	61.2	75.4
Race			
White	62.2	49.6	71.2
Black	54.7	45.9	63.4
Hispanic	46.3	36.8	50.7
Other	61.9	50.3	69.5
Age			
24 or younger	62.6	57.8	70.3
25–34	57.9	48.2	64.8
35–44	55.9	40.1	62
45–54	51.3	41.6	52.5
55 or older	39.6	36.1	52.4

Source: James, D. and Glaze, L. (2006). Mental Health Problems of Prison and Jail Inmates. Bureau of Justice Statistics.

with schizophrenia may also develop dementia which can worsen problems. Moreover, because of the nature of the disorder this population may miss the warning signs of other treatable physical illnesses such as cancer and heart disease, and not receive care for these until the diseases have progressed to a point where treatment is problematical (Csernansky 2002; Goldman 1999).

Prevalence of Schizophrenia in Correctional Settings

Schizophrenia is more common among the incarcerated population (2.3% to 3.9%) than in the general population (NCCHC 2002: 24). On any given

Table 5-5. Characteristics of Late Onset and Very Late Onset Schizophrenia

Characteristic	Late Onset	Very Late Onset
Age at Onset	Age 40–65	Late life (Older Than 65)
Paranoid	Very common	Common
Negative symptoms	Present	Absent
Thought disorder	Present	Absent
Minor physical anomalies	Present	Absent
Brain structure abnormalities (strokes, tumors)	Absent	Marked
Neuropsychological impairment: Learning Retention	Present Absent	Probably marked Probably marked
Progressive cognitive deterioration	Absent	Probably marked
Family history schizophrenia	Present	Absent
Early childhood maladjustment	Present	Absent

Source: Adapted from Wetherell, J. L. and Jeste. D. V. (2003). Older Adults With Schizophrenia Patients are living longer and gaining researchers' attention. Elder Care 3(2): 8–11. Available at http://www.stanford.edu/group/usvh/stanford/misc/Schizophrenia%202.pdf.

day, 2 to 4 percent of state prisoners and up to 3 percent of Federal prisoners were estimated to have schizophrenia or other psychotic disorders (Veysey and Bichler-Robertson 2002). A 2006 study revealed much higher rates. Approximately 15 percent of State prisoners and 10 percent of Federal prisoners reported at least one symptom of psychotic disorder (James and Glaze 2006). The disorder frequently occurs among prisoners aged 55 and over (Cox and Lawrence 2010; James and Glaze 2006).

Depression

Depression is a mood disorder characterized by feeling of sadness, miserableness, and unhappiness which interferes with an individual's ability to function normally. While major depressive disorder can develop at any age, the median age at onset is 32 (Kessler et al. 2005). According to the National Alliance on Mental Health (2009), depression affects more than 6.5 million of

---

Box 5-3. Symptoms of Depression in Older Adults

- memory problems
- confusion
- social withdrawal
- loss of appetite
- weight loss
- vague complaints of pain
- inability to sleep
- irritability
- delusions (fixed false beliefs)
- hallucinations

Source: National Alliance on Mental Illness (2009). Depression in Older Adults Fact Sheet. Available at http://www.nami.org/Template.cfm?Section=Depression&Template=/ContentManagement/ContentDisplay.cfm&ContentID=88876.

---

the 35 million Americans aged 65 or older. The symptoms of depression for older adults differ from the symptoms of other populations (see Box 5-3).

Depression often goes untreated among the elderly. Many people assume that depression is a natural state of affairs as a person ages and are not aware that it is not a normal part of aging. Others fail to recognize the signs of depression because the symptoms for the elderly are similar to other illnesses such as dementia, Alzheimer's, and heart disease. Because of the stigma associated with depression, some older Americans fail to seek help out of fear of being teased or humiliated (Centers for Disease Control 2012).

Older adults who suffer from depression are at increased risk for other medical problems. Untreated depression can be fatal. "Depression is the single most significant risk factor for suicide in the elderly population" (National Alliance on Mental Illness 2009). Depression can slow recovery from heart attack, stroke, hip fracture or macular degeneration, and surgical procedures such as bypass surgery (National Alliance on Mental Illness 2009).

Prevalence of Depression in Correctional Settings

The diagnosis of major depression among prisoners, especially older inmates, is a significant problem (Cox and Lawrence 2010). Approximately 18.1% of the general population suffers from major depression, while an estimated 13.1–18.6% of inmates present this illness (Veysey and Bichler-Robertson 2002: 24). A Bureau of Justice Special Report in 2006 found that 23 percent of state prisoners and 16 percent of federal prisoners reported a recent history of symptoms associated with major depressive disorder (James and Glaze

---

Box 5-4. Dementia Defined

"Dementia is the loss of cognitive functioning — thinking, remembering, and reasoning — and behavioral abilities, to such an extent that it interferes with a person's daily life and activities. Dementia ranges in severity from the mildest stage, when it is just beginning to affect a person's functioning, to the most severe stage, when the person must depend completely on others for basic activities of daily living."

Source: National Institute on Aging. Available at http://www.nia.nih.gov/alzheimers/publication/alzheimers-disease-fact-sheet.

2006). Given that 50 percent of elderly inmates sent to prison when they were 60 or older are first-time inmates, it is not surprising that for this population depression rates are high. Elderly first-time prisoners experience incarceration as a psychological trauma (Cox and Lawrence 2010) and, consequently, experience high levels of depression (Adday 1994a; Adday 1994b).

Dementia/Alzheimer's

Dementia is the loss of cognitive functioning (National Institute on Aging). Alzheimer's is the most common form of dementia, accounting for 60 to 80 percent of dementia cases; the condition represents a growing concern for correctional administrators as the prison population ages (Belluck 2012; Cox and Lawrence 2010). It is a progressive, degenerative disease, meaning that symptoms worsen over time. The disease attacks the brain's nerve cells resulting in loss of memory, language skills, and behavioral changes over time (see Box 5-5 for warning signs). Alzheimer's is not considered a normal part of aging. There are two categories of symptoms: cognitive and intellectual. Cognitive symptoms include amnesia (loss of memory or inability to remember facts), aphasia (inability to communicate effectively), apraxia (inability to do motor tasks such as brushing teeth and dressing); and agnosia (inability to correctly interpret signals from the five senses) (Alzheimer's Foundation of America 2012). Psychotic symptoms include hallucinations and delusions. The early symptoms of the disease may be mild. In the late stage Alzheimer's, individuals lose their ability to speak, respond to environmental stimuli, and care for themselves. Early onset of Alzheimer's occurs in the 40s and 50s. Alzheimer's is the sixth leading cause of death in the U.S. and is the only disease in the top 10 which currently does not have a cure (Elder Authority 2012).

An estimated 5.4 million U.S. citizens have Alzheimer's disease (Hebert et al. 2003). According to the Alzheimer's Association (2011) one in eight people aged 65 and older (13 percent), and nearly half of people aged 85 and older

---

Box 5-5. Warning Signs of Alzheimer's

- Memory loss that disrupts daily life
- Challenges in planning or solving problems
- Difficulty completing familiar tasks at home, at work or at leisure
- Confusion with time or place
- Trouble understanding visual images and spatial relationships
- New problems with words in speaking or writing
- Misplacing things and losing the ability to retrace steps
- Decreased or poor judgment
- Withdrawal from work or social activities
- Changes in mood and personality

Source: Alzheimer's Association (2012). Ten Early Signs and Symptoms of Alzheimer. Available at http://www.alz.org/alzheimers_disease_10_signs_of_alzheimers.asp.

(43 percent) have Alzheimer's disease. The Alzheimer Foundation of America (2012) reports that the prevalence of Alzheimer's disease doubles every five years beyond the age of 65.

The complications from Alzheimer's can range from the mild to the severe. The more severe forms of the disease can create complications such as immobility, swallowing disorders, and malnutrition (Alzheimer's Association 2012). Such complications have been associated with the development of pneumonia and can lead to death. "Regardless of the cause of death, 61 percent of people with Alzheimer's at age 70 are expected to die before age 80 compared with 30 percent of people at age 70 without Alzheimer's" (Alzheimer's Association 2012).

Prevalence of Alzheimer's in Correctional Settings

The prevalence of Alzheimer's in correctional settings is high. Wilson and Barboza (2010) estimate the number of prisoners with dementia in 2010 to be 125,220, a figure that they believe will double in 2030 (n = 211,020) and triple in 2050 (n = 381,391). Maschi et al. (2012) reported the estimated prevalence rate ranges for dementia in correctional settings at between 1 percent and 44 percent, depending on the nature and size of the correctional setting.

What has driven the rate of Alzheimer's up in correctional settings? The answer to this question depends on whom you ask. Some researchers refer to an overabundance of biological risk factors among prisoners, such as neuron degeneration, frontal lobe degeneration, metabolic imbalances, such as thyroid, kidney, and liver disorders, and mental disorders as the primary cause of the high rate of Alzheimer's (Cox, 2007; Maschi et al. 2012). The accelerated aging process experienced by the incarcerated is frequently blamed for the increase in dementia cases behind bars (Wilson and Barboza 2010). Others allude to pre-prison lifestyles characterized by limited education, chronic substance abuse, poor nutrition, limited health care, and brain injuries associated with fighting as a primary contributors (Belluck 2012; Maschi et al. 2011; Maschi et al. 2012). It seems that the prison environment itself might have a multiplicative effect on Alzheimer's rates. The exposure to violence, the poor physical and mental health status of prisoners, and the lack of adequate geriatric services in all likelihood increases the odds that an older adult will develop Alzheimer's (Maschi et al. 2012).

Anxiety Disorders

Anxiety disorders refer to a group of mental health disorders characterized by excessive, irrational fear and dread, and these impact approximately 40 million American adults age 18 years and older (about 18 percent) in a given year (Kessler et al. 2005). Box 5-6 provides a description of several anxiety disorders. The focus of the anxiety is on some future threat, whether real or imagined, which results in avoidance behaviors. According to the National Alliance on Mental Illness (2012), anxiety disorders affect approximately 20 percent of the population at any given moment. Moreover, anxiety disorders are as common among older adults as among the young (Anxiety and Depression Association of America 2012). Between 3 and 14 percent of older adults experience anxiety in any given year (National Institute Health-Senior Health 2012). At least one study reported 11 percent as the prevalence rate for the total U.S. population aged 55 and older (Flint 1994). In older adults, anxiety disorders often occur at the same time as other medical and mental health problems such as depression, heart disease, and diabetes (Kessler et al. 2005; National Institute Health-Senior Health 2012). The anxiety disorders include panic disorder, which affects 6 million U.S. adults each year, obsessive-compulsive disorder (OCD), which affects 2.2 million, post-traumatic stress disorder (PTSD), which affects 7.7 million, phobias, generalized anxiety disorder (GAD), which affects 6.8 million, and social anxiety disorder, which affects 5 million (Anxiety and Depression Association of America 2012).

Prevalence of Anxiety Disorders in Correctional Settings

While approximately 11 percent of the U.S. population over age 55 presents with anxiety disorders, up to 30 percent of the jail population, 12 percent of the state prison population, and 23 percent of federal prisoners on any given day are predicted to have an anxiety disorder (Flint 1994; Veysey and Bichler-

---

Box 5-6. Anxiety Disorders

- Panic Disorder — Characterized by "panic attacks," panic disorder results in sudden feelings of terror that can strike repeatedly and sometimes without warning. Physical symptoms of a panic attack include chest pain, heart palpitations, upset stomach, feelings of being disconnected, and fear of dying.

- Obsessive-Compulsive Disorder (OCD) — OCD is characterized by repetitive, intrusive, irrational and unwanted thoughts (obsessions) and/or rituals that seem impossible to control (compulsions). Some people with OCD have specific compulsions (e.g., counting, arranging, cleaning) that they "must perform" multiple times each day in order to momentarily release their anxiety that something bad might happen to themselves or to someone they love.

- Posttraumatic Stress Disorder (PTSD) — When people experience or witness a traumatic event such as abuse, a natural disaster, or extreme violence, it is normal to be distressed and to feel "on edge" for some time after this experience. Some people who experience traumatic events have severe symptoms such as nightmares, flashbacks, being very easily startled or scared, or feeling numb/angry/irritable, that last for weeks or even months after the event and are so severe that they make it difficult for a person to work, have loving relationships, or "return to normal."

- Phobias — A phobia is a disabling and irrational fear of something that really poses little or no actual danger for most people. This fear can be very disabling when it leads to avoidance of objects or situations that may cause extreme feelings of terror, dread and panic.

- Generalized Anxiety Disorder (GAD) — A severe, chronic, exaggerated worrying about everyday events is the most common symptom in people with GAD. This is a worrying that lasts for at least six months, makes it difficult to concentrate and to carry out routine activities, and happens for many hours each day in some people.

- Social Anxiety Disorder — An intense fear of social situations that leads to difficulties with personal relationships and at the workplace or in school is most common in people with social anxiety disorder. Individuals with social anxiety disorder often have an irrational fear of being humiliated in public for "saying something stupid," or "not knowing what to say."

Source: National Alliance on Mental Illness (2012). Anxiety Fact Sheet. pp. 1–2. Available at http://www.nami.org/factsheets/anxietydisorders_factsheet.pdf.

Robertson 2000). The prevalence estimates are worse for PTSD. Upwards of 40 percent of state prisoners, 46 percent of jail prisoners and 7 percent of federal prisoners are estimated to have PTSD on any given day. Given the increase in the numbers of veterans entering prisons, the rates of PTSD are assumed to be much higher than predicted (Cox and Lawrence 2010; Veysey and Bichler-Robertson 2000).

Box 5-7. Definitions of Self-Directed Violence

Suicide

Death caused by self-directed injurious behavior with any intent to die as a result of the behavior.

Suicide attempt

A non-fatal self-directed potentially injurious behavior with any intent to die as a result of the behavior. A suicide attempt may or may not result in injury.

Suicidal ideation

Thinking about, considering, or planning for suicide.

Source: Centers for Disease Control (2012). Definitions of Self-Directed Violence. Available at http://www.cdc.gov/ViolencePrevention/suicide/definitions.html.

Suicide

Suicide is a major problem in the U.S. See Box 5-7 for basic definitions of types of self-directed violence. In 2010 on average there 105 deaths per day as a result of suicide, and more than 487,700 people with self-inflicted injuries were treated in emergency departments in 2011 (Centers for Disease Control 2012). More than 90 percent of people who kill themselves have a diagnosable mental disorder (Connel and Brent 1995). Suicide is the 8th leading cause of death in the general population for those aged 55 to 64. Men are four times more likely than women to die from suicide (see Table 5-6); but larger numbers of women have suicidal ideations (Centers for Disease Control 2012; Kochanek et al. 2004). Suicide is a problem throughout the life-course. A 2004 study suggested that the highest rates of suicide in the U.S. were found in white men over age 85 (Kochanek et al. 2004).

Prevalence of Suicide in Correctional Environments

The suicide rate among prison inmates is more than twice that of the general population (Jenkins et al. 2005; Kupers 1999: Snow et al. 2001). Still other researchers report rates from three to nine times higher in correctional environments than in the general public (Hall and Gabor 2004; Tartaro and Lester 2005). The fact that inmates have higher suicide rates than the general population remains true despite reductions in the number of people incarcerated (Fruehwald and Frottier 2005). Suicide is a leading cause of death in U.S. prisons (Gater and Hayes, 2005; Metzner 2002). More than 200 prison suicides occur in the U.S. each year (Suto and Amaut 2010). For the past three decades,

Table 5-6. Suicide Rates* among Persons Ages 65 Years and Older by Race/Ethnicity and Sex, United States, 2005–2009

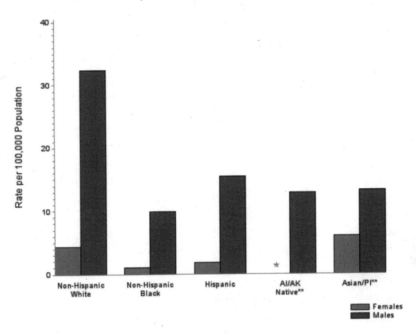

Source: Centers for Disease Control (2012). National Suicide Statistics at a Glance. Available at http://www.cdc.gov/ViolencePrevention/suicide/statistics/rates05.html.

the prison suicide rate ranged from 18 to 40 per 100,000 (Annasseril 2006). Between 2001 and 2004, the Deaths in Custody Program recorded 12,129 state prisoner deaths and approximately one in ten of those deaths were a result of prisoner suicide (Mumola 2007). In state prisons, the rate of suicide for state prisoners aged 55 and older was 13 suicides per 100,000 prisoners (Cox and Lawrence 2010).

The true rate of suicide in correctional environments may be much higher (Suto et al. 2010). Suicides may be categorized incorrectly by correctional officials as accidents, or not recorded because the actual death occurred at a hospital rather than at a prison (Daniel, 2006; Hayes 1989; Suto et al. 2010). Kupers (1999) also referred to the fact that inmates who wish to take their lives may seek ways to end their life by creating conflict between themselves and other inmates or staff. For example, an inmate may choose not to pay a debt in prison, or attempt an escape with the hope that the associated violence will end with death. Kupers (1999) referred to such actions as "invisible suicides" which would not be categorized as part of official suicide records by prison officials.

There are some common characteristics among prisoners who commit suicide. The majority of prisoner suicides occur in maximum security facilities, where inmates experience the greatest deprivations (Daniel and Fleming 2006; Salive, Smith, and Brewer 1989; Way et al. 2005). According to the World Health Organization (2007), prisoners who commit suicide are typically older and have committed violent crimes. The fact that inmates convicted of violent crimes in prison are at a higher risk for suicide than nonviolent offenders was confirmed in a study conducted by Way et al. (2005). Furthermore, a large number (45 to 63 percent) of inmates who successfully commit suicide attempted to do so previously (Annasseril 2006). The most common methods used by prisoners to commit suicide are hanging, overdose on psychotropic drugs, anti-hypertensive medicine, or over-the-counter medicine (Annasseril, Lester, and Danto 2006; Cox, 2003; Tatarelli et al. 1999; White and Schimmel 1995). There was some variation across race. African-American prisoners are less likely to commit suicide compared to white prisoners (Way et al. 2005; White and Schimmel 1995).

Causes of Higher Suicide Rates in Correctional Contexts

While it can be argued that prisoners import into prison characteristics and behaviors that make them more vulnerable to suicide, much of the literature has focused on the nature of institutional life. Close to half of the prisoners who commit suicide do so at a time where they are experiencing the chronic or acute stressors associated with institutionalized life (Annasseril 2006; He et al. 2001; White, Schimmel, and Frickey 2002). Stressors include long terms of incarceration characterized by isolation (Metzner and Hayes 2006), lack of social support by family (Annasseril 2006; Lester and Danto 2006), fear of victimization and the future (World Health Organization 2007), complications from co-existing medical and mental problems (Annasseril 2006; Hurley 1997; Lester and Danto 2006; World Health Organization 2007); and inadequate services (Anno 1995; Jones 1996; Lester and Danto 2006). Over time such stressors may exceed the coping abilities of the average inmate resulting in a suicide attempt. The causes of higher suicide rates (see Box 5-8) are discussed in the next section.

Long-Term Incarceration

The suicide rate increases with length of stay in institutional settings (Frottier et al. 2002). A World Health Organization (2007) report on prison suicide sug-

---

Box 5-8. Causes of Higher Suicide Rates in Correctional Contexts

- Long-term incarceration
- Isolation and the lack of social support from family
- Interpersonal conflict with other inmates
- Institutional conflict
- Fear of victimization
- Co-existing medical and mental health problems
- Inadequate institutional programs and services

---

gests that rates increase significantly after spending four or five years in prison. Lifers seem to be at particularly high risk for suicide (Borrill 2002; Liebling 2006). Hayes in a 1995 study found that federal prisoners sentenced to 20 years or more accounted for 28 percent of suicides, but comprised only 12 percent of the federal prison population. That inmates with longer prison sentences experience heightened risk of suicide is not surprising. We have known since the mid-1980s that inmates with longer imposed sentences were at greater risk for suicide (Lester 1987). A study conducted by Correia in 2000 concluded that an inmate's sentence length and feelings about this sentence were important determinants of suicide risk. The highest rate of suicide is associated with death row inmates at rate of 146.5 per 100,000 (Daniel 2006; Lester and Danto 1993).

According to Annasseril (2006), there are two types of prisoners who commit suicide. Using Durkheim's typology of suicide, Annasseril (2006: 18) suggests that prisoners either commit egoistic or fatalistic suicide. "Egoistic suicide occurs when an individual has a low level of integration into society, while fatalistic suicide occurs in a highly regulated, social environment where the individual sees no possible way to improve his or her life." It is argued that the majority of prisoners who commit suicide are egoistic, and that such suicides are a result primarily of social isolation that prison perpetuates. Death row inmates, he argues, may commit suicide for egoistic or fatalistic reasons. Thus, the importance of assessing suicide risk among long-term inmates is of critical importance.

Lack of Social Support

The lack of social support from families outside prison walls precipitates suicide (Annasseril 2006). Durkheim (1952), in his classic work, examined the impact of family on suicide, and concluded that the higher and better social integration the less likely suicide rates were to increase. Social support refers to the various types of support that people receive from others and is often classified into three major categories: emotional support (empathy, caring, love, trust, esteem, concern); instrumental support (providing aid, time, direct help); informational support (providing advice, providing information to help with coping with life's stressors) (Cooke et al. 1988). A significant body of literature identifies social support as having a positive impact on psychological well-being among the general population (George et al. 1989). Moreover, social support has been linked with the incidence of major diseases such as stroke and cancer (Seeman 1996). Evidence also suggests that emotional support is a protective factor associated with better physical and cognitive health at older ages (Seeman, 1996; Seeman et al. Albert 2001; Fratiglioni, Paillard-Borg, and Winblad 2004). The absence of social support or poor quality social support is a risk factor associated with negative outcomes such as poor health, the development of mental health problems, disease; and suicide (Moak and Agrawal 2010). For example, perceived lower levels of social support among the general population is associated with suicidal ideation among older adults (Rowe et al. 2006).

The impact of poor social support on suicide rates is magnified among the prisoner population (Jenkins et al. 2005). Familial social support from outside prison walls is associated with help seeking behaviors and improved coping among prisoners (Correia 2000). Because of their long prison sentences and their age, prisoners are at risk of losing social support as a result of death, divorce and distance. The longer a prisoner is incarcerated the greater the chance that family members will die or move on with their lives and minimize contact (Lester and Danto 2006). As a result long-term and elderly prisoners gradually lose what support, if any, once existed outside prison walls. The loss of emotional and instrumental support creates a coping vacuum. The prisoner has fewer social mechanisms for dealing with the stressors of prison life and may spiral into hopelessness and depression. According to Hall, Platt, and Hall (1999), prisoners who have recently experience, the loss of a significant person from their lives due to death or divorce are a particular risk for suicide. Similar results were found if family conflict was present, and resulted in a loss of support (World Health Organization 2007). For example, a prisoner in the Suto and Arnaut study (2010: 299) reported

I was having a lot of problems with my mom, like fights with my mom.... My mom comes to see me once every two months and we usually don't fight when she comes but that month had been particularly hard. So I call her once a week. And we'd fight over the phone a little bit more than we would when she came to see me in person. And, it was more about money and just about me asking her for things and being needy, because I was. You need things in here and you don't really have anybody to ask except for her. Then it just kind of just escalated to the point where she was yelling at me about it and I just really got under the weather.

It was at this point that the prisoner considered suicide as an option.

Prisoners also receive a great deal of support from one another. The longer a prisoner is incarcerated, and the older he or she becomes, the odds of losing a close friend to death or release increases. The loss of this friendship is often stressful and can lead to depression.

Interpersonal Conflict with Other Inmates

Interpersonal conflict with other inmates is a chronic stressor in prison (Annasseril 2007; Suto and Arnaut 2010) and increases the potential for self-harm (World Health Organization 2007; Way et al. 2005). According to a World Health Organization (2007) report, prisoners who fear physical or sexual violence are at increased risk of suicide. Still other researchers have found a significant relationship between inmate-to-inmate conflict and suicide (Suto and Arnaut 2010; Way et al. 2005). Wright and Schimmel (1995) found in their sample of prisoners who completed suicide that 23 percent of the suicides were triggered by inmate-related conflicts. Suicidal inmates often experience bullying by others in prison (Blaauw, Winkel, and Kerkhof 2001). Several participants in the Suto and Arnaut (2010) study attempted suicide after receiving threats from other prisoners. As one participant in the study stated "One group of people at the institution, who made it clear that they would prefer to see me in a form of a corpse.... I felt like if I remained in that environment my life would be terminated by them" (Suto and Arnaut 2010: 300).

High Rate of Medical and Mental Health Problems

Suicidal prisoners exhibit elevated rates of mental health problems (Annasseril 2006; Cox 2003; Jenkins et al. 2005; Tatarelli et al. 1999; White, Schimmel, and Frickey 2002). In a 1985 study, Anno found that 68 percent of suicide victims had a history of mental illness. The rates are much higher today. Inmates with a psychiatric history are eight times more likely to consider or attempt suicide (Ivanoff, Jang, and Smyth 1996). One of the more consistent findings in the literature is the presence of depression (Annasseril 2006; Hurley 1989; Palmer and Connelly 2005; White, Schimmel, and Frickey 2002), anxiety (Annasseril 2006), and hopelessness (Annasseril 2006; Palmer and Connelly 2005; World Health Organization 2007). A diagnosis of depression is the best predictor of suicide (Rowan and Hayes 1988; Sutto et al., 2010). Many such prisoners experience suicidal ideations and prior suicide attempts (Moscicki 1997; Palmer and Connelly 2005; Way et al. 2005). The presence of other personality and mood disorders has also been associated with increased risk (Jenkins et al. 2005; Marzano et al. 2011; Tatarelli et al. 1999; Way et al. 2005).

The presence of other medical problems is also associated with the elevated suicide rates among prisoners (Lester and Danto 2006; World Health Organization 2007). Prisoners with chronic, painful diseases, or who are positive for HIV, are more likely to consider suicide (Lester and Danto 2006; Salive, Smith and Brewer 1990). Prisoners with a history of alcohol or substance abuse are at increased risk for suicide (Rowan and Hayes 1995; Way et al. 2005). Prisons, particularly those designed for long-term inmates, are well known as places where prisoners can obtain illegal drugs, goods, and services (Lankenau 2001). Prisoners with money are able to obtain marijuana, cocaine, opiates, and other illicit substances (Feucht and Keyser 1999), and thereby have access to the means for taking their own lives should they wish to do so.

Institutional Contextual Problems

Research suggests the institutional context as a major contributor to prisoner suicide. The relationship between prison disciplinary practices and suicide is well established (Annasseril 2007; World Health Organization 2007; Metzner and Hayes 2006). The isolation experienced as a result of a prison housing assignment to a single-occupancy cell or segregation unit is a major risk factor (Anno 1985; Marzano et al. 2011; Metzner and Hayes 2006; World Health Organization 2007; Way et al. 2005). Prisons with dominant single-cell style housing experience higher suicide rates than those with more dormitory style facilities (Huey and McNulty 2005). In the 1985 study conducted by Anno, 97 percent of inmates who committed suicide were single-celled. Daniel and Fleming (2006) determined that 60 percent of prisoners who committed suicide were single-celled, and nearly half of those resided in an administrative segregation unit or institutional punishment oriented cells. Reviews of Federal prisoner suicides also support the relationship between punitive housing (e.g., segregation, administrative detention, and psychiatric seclusion units) and suicide (White, Schimmel, and Frickey 2002; White and Schimmel 1995). Haney (2001) reported that long-term solitary-like confinement's negative impacts include "... an impaired sense of identity; hypersensitivity to stimuli; cognitive dysfunction (confusion, memory loss, ruminations); irritability, anger, aggression, and/or rage; other-directed violence, such as stabbings, attacks on staff, property destruction, and collective violence; lethargy, helplessness and hopelessness; chronic depression; self-mutilation and/or suicidal ideation, impulses, and behavior; anxiety and panic attacks; emotional breakdowns; and/

or loss of control; hallucinations, psychosis and/or paranoia; overall deterioration of mental and physical health." Such housing may be even more problematic for long-term and elderly inmates who may already be deprived of social support and who may suffer from mental illnesses.

Prison overcrowding has also been associated with higher rates of suicide. Several studies in the 1980s indicated that as the prison population increased, the number of suicides within a correctional institution escalated (Cox, Paulus, and McCain 1984; Innes 1987). Cox, Paulus, and McCain (1984) reported amplified suicide rates which were three times greater as the prison population increased. Such corresponding increases in population and suicide rates occur regardless of institutional type. Huey and McNulty (2005) report that even minimum security facilities experience higher suicide rates as the prison becomes overcrowded.

Another major institutional problem has been the lack of effective assessment programs, and services for prisoners. "In some settings, there may be no formal policies and procedures to identify and manage suicidal inmates. In particular, even where screening for high-risk indicators is undertaken, there is often inadequate monitoring of prisoners' distress levels and hence there is little chance of detecting acute risk. Even if appropriate policies and procedures exist, overworked or untrained correctional, health care, and mental health personnel may miss the early warning signs of a suicide risk" (World Health Organization 2007: 4). Supporting evidence of these problems was revealed in a Texas Department of Corrections review of suicide cases. The Texas study reported situations consistent with mishandling of cases to include prisoners telling staff they were considering suicide, staff then noting prisoners withdrawn, depressed behavior, but not taking steps to prevent the suicide (Anno 1985; Hayes et al. 1995).

Effective Approaches for Dealing with the Mental Health Problems of Long-Term and Elderly Prisoners

The realization that an effective approach to mental health is required for correctional systems has not gone unnoticed. Several scholars have identified the steps that correctional systems should take to address the mental health needs of long-term and elderly prisoners. Their work is summarized below.

1. Implement effective screening processes for medical and mental health problems at intake and at regularly spaced intervals for long-term and elderly prisoners (Cox and Lawrence 2010; Maschi et al. 2012);
2. Implement a post-detection disclosure protocol (Maschi et al. 2012);

3. Provide adequate mental health treatment to include
   a. specific mental health disorder treatments for long-term and geriatric prisoners, e.g., depression, personality disorders, schizophrenia, Alzheimer's, etc. (Cox and Lawrence 2010);
   b. more substance abuse programs (Cox and Lawrence 2010);
   c. more suicide prevention program (Cox and Lawrence 2010);
   d. coping strategies programming, particularly for elderly first-time incarcerated population (Cox and Lawrence 2010);
   e. bereavement services (Cox and Lawrence 2010);
   f. addressing co-existing mental and physical health problems to include coordination of medical and mental health services (Cox and Lawrence 2010);
4. Increase staff competencies and training (Cox and Lawrence 2010; Maschi et al. 2012);
5. Modify prison dress, design, and policies to include the unique mental health challenges associated with aging and long-term incarceration (Maschi et al. 2012); and
6. Address reentry challenges (Cox and Lawrence 2010).

Conclusion

The fact that American prisoners are sentenced to spend more time in prison than their counterparts in other Western industrialized parts of the world has culminated in an incarcerated population that not only is aging, but one that is experiencing an unprecedented rise in mental health problems. It is certainly undeniable that the framers of lengthy prison terms did not anticipate this unintended consequence. Regardless of aims, the current system for dealing with the mental illnesses of long-term and elderly inmates requires modification.

Websites

For more information on Alzheimer's, visit http://www.alz.org.
For more information on mental health, visit http://www.nimh.nih.gov.
For more information on mental health disorder, visit http://www.nami.org.
For more information on correctional healthcare and mental disorder, visit http://nicic.gov.
For more information on mental health conditions of prisoners, visit https://www.bjs.gov/.

For more information on mental health from an international perspective, visit http://www.who.int/en/.

References

Allison, D., Mentore, J., Heo, M., Chandler, L., Cappelleri, J., Infante, M., & Weiden, P. (1999). Antipsychotic-induced weight gain: A comprehensive research synthesis. *American Journal Psychiatry*, 156(11), 1686–1696.

Alzheimer's Association. (2011). 2011 Alzheimer's disease facts and figures. *Alzheimer's & Dementia*, 7(2), 1–68. Retrieved from http://www.alz.org/downloads/facts_figures_2011.pdf.

Alzheimer's Association. (2006). Early-onset dementia: A national challenge, a future crisis. Washington, DC: Author.

Anasseril, D. E. (2006). Preventing suicide in prison: A collaborative responsibility of administrative, custodial, and clinical staff. *Journal of American Academy Psychiatry Law*, 34, 165–175.

Anxiety and Depression Association of America. (2012). Facts & Statistics. Retrieved from http://www.adaa.org/about-adaa/press-room/facts-statistics.

Beck, A., Berzofsky, M & Kerbs, C. (2013). *Sexual victimization in prisons and jails reported by inmates 2011–2012*. Washington, DC: US Department of Justice, Office of Justice Programs, Bureau of Justice Statistics.

Belluck, P. (2012, February 25). The vanishing mind: *Time's toll behind bars*. *The New York Times*. Retrieved from http://www.nytimes.com/2012/02/26/health/dealing-with-dementia-among-aging-criminals.html?_r=0.

Blaauw, E., Winkel, F. W., & Kerkhof, A. J. F. M. (2001). Bullying and suicidal behaviour in jails. *Criminal Justice and Behaviour*, 28(3), 279–299.

Borrill, J. (2002). Self-inflicted deaths of prisoners serving life sentences 1988–2001. *British Journal of Forensic Practice*, 4(4), 30–38.

Carson, E. A., & Sabol, W. (2011). *Prisoners in 2011* (NCJ 239808). Washington, DC: US Department of Justice, Office of Justice Programs, Bureau of Justice Statistics. Retrieved from bjs.gov/content/pub/pdf/p11.pdf.

Centers for Disease Control and Prevention. (2012). *Understanding Suicide*. Retrieved from http://www.cdc.gov/ViolencePrevention/pdf/Suicide_Fact Sheet_2012-a.pdf.

Churgin, M. J. (1980). Mental health services and the inmate: Problems and considerations. In I. P. Robbins (Ed.), *Prisoners' rights handbook: Theory-litigation-practice* (pp. 295–316). New York, NY: Clark Boardman.

Conwell, Y., & Brent, D. (1995). Suicide and aging: Patterns of psychiatric diagnosis. *International Psychogeriatrics*, 7(2), 149–64.

Cooke, B., Rossmann, M., McCubbin, H., & Patterson, J. (1988). Examining the definition and assessment of social support: A resource for individuals and families. *Family Relations*, 37(2), 211–216.

Correia, K. (2000) Suicide assessment in a prison environment: A proposed protocol. *Criminal Justice and Behavior*, 27, 5581–5599.

Cox, G. (2003). Screening inmates for suicide using static risk factors. *The Behavior Therapist*, 26, 212–214.

Cox, J. F., & Lawrence, J. E. (2010). Planning services for elderly inmates with mental illness. *Corrections Today*, 72(3), 52–57.

Cox, V., Paulus, P., & McCain, G. (1984). Prison crowding research: The relevance for prison housing standards and a general approach regarding crowding phenomenon. American Psychologist, 38(1), 1148–1160.

Daniel. A. E. (2006). Preventing suicide in prison: A collaborative responsibility of administrative, custodial, and clinical staff. Journal *of the American Academy of Psychiatry and the Law*, 34, 165–175.

Duckworth, K., & Freedman, J. L. (2012). [Review of the Fact Sheet *Anxiety Disorders*, National Alliance on Mental Illness]. Retrieved from http://www.nami.org/factsheets/anxietydisorders_factsheet.pdf.

Downey, D. (2012). Alzheimer's behind bars. Retrieved from http://www.elder authority.com/alzheimers-behind-bars.

Edwards, K. A. (1985). *Mental illness in prison: A study of inmates transferred to a mental hospital* (Unpublished manuscript). Oklahoma State Penitentiary, McAlester, OK.

Edwards, K. A. (1988). Some characteristics of inmates transferred from prison to a state mental hospital. *Behavioral Sciences and the Law*, 6(1), 131–137.

Fellner, J. (2006a). A conundrum for corrections, a tragedy for prisoners: Prisons as facilities for the mentally ill. *Journal of Law and Policy*, 22(135), 135–144.

Fellner, J. (2006b). A corrections quandary: Mental illness and prison rules. *Harvard Civil Rights-Civil Liberties Law Review*, 41, 391–412.

Fellner, J., & Abramsky, S. (2004). Ill-equipped: U.S. prisons and offenders with mental illness. Retrieved from Human Rights Watch website: http://www.hrw.org/reports/2003/usa1003/usa1003.pdf.

Feucht, T., & Keyser, A. (1999). Reducing drug use in prisons: Pennsylvania's approach. *National Institute of Justice Journal*, 241, 10–15. Retrieved from https://www.ncjrs.gov/pdffiles1/jr000241c.pdf.

Flint, A. (1994). Epidemiology and comorbidity of anxiety disorders in the elderly. *American Journal of Psychiatry*, 151, 640–649.

Fratiglioni, L., Paillard-Borg, S., & Winblad, B. (2004). An active and socially integrated lifestyle in late life might protect against dementia. *Lancet Neurology*, 3(6), 343–353.

Fruehwald, S., & Frottier, P. (2005). Suicide in prison. *Lancet, 366,* 1242–1244.

Frottier, P., Fruehwald, S., Ritter, K., Eher, R., Schwaerzler, J., & Bauer, P. (2002). Jailhouse blues revisited. *Social Psychiatry and Psychiatric Epidemiology, 37,* 68–73.

George, L., Blazer, D., Hughes, D., & Fowler, N. (1989). Social support and the outcome of major depression. *The British Journal of Psychiatry, 154,* 478–485 doi:10.1192/bjp.154.4.478.

Glaze, L., Parks, E. (2012). *Correctional populations in the United States, 2011* (NCJ 239972). Washington, DC: US Department of Justice, Office of Justice Programs, Bureau of Justice Statistics.

Goldman, L. (1999). Medical illness in patients with schizophrenia. *Journal of Clinical Psychiatry, 60*(Suppl 21), 10–15.

Hall, B., & Gabor, P. (2004) Peer suicide prevention in a prison. *Journal of Crisis Intervention and Suicide Prevention, 25,* 19–26.

Hall, R. C., Platt, D. E., & Hall, R. W. (1999) Suicide risk assessment: A review of risk factors for suicide in 100 patients who made several suicide attempts: Evaluation of suicide risk in a time of managed care. *Psychosomatics, 40,* 18–27.

Hammett, T., Roberts, C., & Kennedy, S. (2001). Health-related issues in prisoner reentry. *Crime and Delinquency, 47*(3), 390–409.

Hayes, L. M. (1989). National study of jail suicides: Seven years later. *Psychiatric Quarterly, 60,* 7–29.

Hayes, L. M. (1995). *Prison suicide: An overview and guide to prevention.* Washington, DC: U.S. Department of Justice, National Institute of Corrections.

Hayes, L. M. (1999). Suicide in adult correctional facilities: Key ingredients to prevention and overcoming the obstacles. *Journal of Law, Medicine and Ethics, 27,* 260–268.

Hayes, L. M. & Hunter, S. M., Moore, J.E., & Thigpen, M. L. (1995). *Prison suicide: An overview and guide to prevention* (pp, 2–3, 11–12, 34–38, & 41). Retrieved from U.S. Department of Justice, The National Institute of Corrections website: http://www.nicic.org/pubs/1995/012475.pdf.

He, X.Y., Felthous, A. R., Holzer, C., Nathan, P., & Veasey, S. (2001). Factors in prison suicide: One year study in Texas. *Journal Forensic Science, 46,* 896–901.

Hebert, L. E., Scherr, P. A., Bienias, J. L., Bennett, D. A., Evans, D. A. (2003). Alzheimer's disease in the U.S. population: Prevalence estimates using the 2000 census. *Archives of Neurology, 60*(8), 1119–1122.

Huey, M., & McNulty, T. (2005). Institutional conditions and prison suicide: Conditional effects of deprivation and overcrowding. *The Prison Journal, 85*(4), 477–491.

Hughes, T., & Wilson, D. (2002). *Reentry Trends in the United States*. Retrieved from U.S. Department of Justice, Office of Justice Programs, Bureau of Justice Statistics website: bjs.ojp.usdoj.gov/content/pub/pdf/reentry.pdf.

Hurley, W. (1989). Suicides by prisoners. Medical Journal of Australia, 151, 188–90.

Innes, C. (1987). The effects of prison density on prisoners. Criminal *Justice Archive and Information Network*, 1, 3.

Ivanoff, A., Jang, S. J., & Smyth, N. J. (1996). Clinical risk factors associated with para suicide in prison. *International Journal of Offender Therapy and Comparative Criminology*, 40, 135–146.

Kansas State University Department on Aging. (1999). *Schizophrenia in older adults* (USVH Disease of the Week No. 4). Retrieved from University of Stanford, United Students of Veterans Health website: http://www.stanford.edu/group/usvh/stanford/misc/Schizophrenia%201.pdf.

Jenkins, R., Bhugra, D., Meltzer, H., Singleton, N., Bebbington, P., Brugha, T., ... Paton, J. (2005). Psychiatric and social aspects of suicidal behavior in prisons. *Psychology of Medicine*, 35(2), 257–269.

Kessler, R. C., Berglund, P. A., Demler, O., Jin, R., Walters, E. E. (2005). Lifetime prevalence and age-of-onset distributions of DSM-IV disorders in the National Comorbidity Survey Replication (NCS-R). *Archives of General Psychiatry*, 62(6), 593–602.

Kessler, R. C., Chiu, W. T., Demler, O., & Walters, E. E. (2005) Prevalence, severity, and comorbidity of twelve-month DSM-IV disorders in the National Comorbidity Survey Replication (NCS-R). *Archives of General Psychiatry*, 62(6), 617–27.

Kochanek, K. D., Murphy, S. L., Anderson, R. N., & Scott, C. Deaths: Final data for 2002. (2004). *National Vital Statistics Reports*, 53(5), 1–115.

Kupers, T. (1999). *Prison madness: The mental health crisis behind bars and what we must do about it*. San Francisco, CA: Jossey-Bass.

Lamb, H. R., & Weinberger, L. E. (2005). The shift of psychiatric inpatient care from hospitals to jails and prisons. *Journal of the American Academy of Psychiatry and Law*, 33, 529–534.

Lankenau, S. (2001). Smoke 'em if you got 'em: Cigarette black markets in U.S. prisons and jails. *Prison Journal*, 81(2), 142–161.

Lester, D. (1987). *The death penalty: Issues and answers*. Springfield, IL: Charles C. Thomas.

Lester, D., & Danto, B. (1993). Suicide behind bars: Prediction and prevention. Philadelphia, PA: The Charles Press.

Lester, D., & Danto, B. (2006). *Suicide behind bars: Prediction and prevention* (pp. 18–21). Philadelphia, PA: The Charles Press.

Liebling, A. (2006). The role of the prison environment in prison suicide and prisoner distress. In G. E. Dear (Ed). *Preventing suicide and other self-harm in prison* (pp. 16–28). Basingstoke, UK: Palgrave-Macmillan.

Marzano, L., Hawton, K., Rivlin, A., & Fazel, S. (2011). Psychosocial influences on prisoner suicide: A case-control study of near-lethal self-harm in women prisoners. *Social Science & Medicine, 72*(6), 874–883.

Metzner, J. L. (2002). Class action litigation in correctional psychiatry. *Journal of American Academy Psychiatry Law,* 30, 19–29.

Metzner, J., & Hayes, L. (2006). Suicide prevention in jails and prisons. In R. Simon & R. Hales (Eds), *Textbook of Suicide Assessment and Management* (pp. 139–155). Washington, DC: American Psychiatric Publishing, Inc.

Miller, R., & Metzner, J. (1994). Psychiatric stigma in correctional facilities. *Journal of American Academy Psychiatry Law,* 22(4), 621–628.

Moak, Z., & Agrawal, A. (2010). The association between perceived interpersonal social support and physical and mental health: Results from the National Epidemiological Survey on Alcohol and Related Conditions. *Journal of Public Health, 32*(2), 191–201.

Mumola, C. (2007). *Medical causes of death in state prison, 2001–2004* (NCJ 216340). Retrieved from U.S. Department of Justice, Office of Justice Programs, Bureau of Justice Statistics website: http://www.ojp.usdoj.gov/bjs/pub/pdf/mcdsp04.pdf.

Palmer, E. J., & Connelly, R. (2005). Depression, hopelessness and suicide ideation among vulnerable prisoners. *Criminal Behaviour and Mental Health,* 15, 164–170.

Regier, D. A., Narrow, W. E., Rae, D. S., Manderscheid, R. W., Locke, B. Z., & Goodwin, F. K. (1993). The de facto US mental and addictive disorders service system: Epidemiologic catchment area prospective 1-year prevalence rates of disorders and services. *Archives of General Psychiatry,* 50(2), 85–94.

Rowe, Conwell, Schulberg, & Berg. (2006). Social support and suicidal ideation in older adults using home healthcare services. *American Journal of Geriatric Psychiatry,* (9), 758–766.

Rowan, J. R., & Hayes, L. M. (1988). Training curriculum on suicide detection and prevention in jails and lockups. Mansfield, MA: U.S. Department of Justice, National Center on Institutions and Corrections.

Salive, M., Smith G., & Brewer, T. (1990). Death in prison: Changing mortality patterns among male prisoners in Maryland, 1979–87. *American Journal of Public* Health, 80, 1479–80.

Seeman, T. E. (1996). Social ties and health: The benefits of social integration. *Ann Epidemiol,* 6(5), 442–451.

Seeman, T. E., Lusignolo, T., Berkman, L., Albert, M. (2001). Social environment characteristics and patterns of cognitive aging: MacArthur studies of successful aging. *Health Psychology*, 20, 243–255.

Shaw, J., Appleby, L., & Baker, D. (2003, May 1). *Safer Prisons: A national study of prison suicides 1999–2000 by the national confidential inquiry into suicides and homicides by people with mental illness* (pp. 4–7). [Publication]. The UK Government web archives for the Department of Health. Retrieved from http://webarchive.nationalarchives.gov.uk/+/www.dh.gov.uk/en/Publicationsandstatistics/Publications/PublicationsPolicy AndGuidance/DH_4130857.

Snow, L., Paton, J., Oram, C., & Teers, R. (2002). Self-inflicted deaths during 2001: An analysis of trends. *The British Journal of Forensic Practice*, 4(4), 3–17.

State Plan for Alzheimer's Disease in Oregon Task Force. (2012). Report of the SPADO Task Force on *Alzheimer's and Related Dementias*. Retrieved from http://www.alz.org/oregon/documents/spado_report.pdf.

Stone, W. G., & Hirliman, I. (1982). The hate factory. Agoura, CA: Paisano.

Suto, I., & Arnaut, G. L. (2010). Suicide in prison: A qualitative study. *The Prison Journal*, 90(3), 288–312.

Tartaro, C., & Lester, D. (2005). An application of Durkheim's theory of suicide to prison suicide rates in the United States. *Death Studies*, 29, 413–422.

Tatarelli, R., Mancinelli, I., Taggi, F., & Polidori, G. (1999). Suicide in Italian prisons in 1996 and 1997: A descriptive epidemiological study. *International Journal of Offender Therapy and Comparative Criminology*, 43, 438–447.

Torrey, E. F. (1995). Editorial: Jails and prisons America's new mental hospitals. *American Journal of Public Health*, 85(12), 1611–1613.

Torrey, E. F., Stieber, J., Ezekiel, J., Wolfe, S. M., Sharfstein, J., Noble, J. H., & Flynn, L. M. (1992). *Criminalizing the seriously mentally ill* (p. 43). Washington, DC: National Alliance for the Mentally Ill and Public Citizen Health Research Group.

U.S. Department of Health and Human Services. (1999). *Mental health: A report of the surgeon general-Executive summary*. Rockville, MD: U.S. Department of Health and Human Services, Substance Abuse and Mental Health Services Administration, Center for Mental Health Services, National Institutes of Health, National Institute of Mental Health.

U.S. Department of Health and Human Services, National Institute of Health, National Library of Medicine, & U.S. Department of Health and Human Services, National Institute of Health, National Institute on Aging. (2012). *Anxiety Disorders*. Retrieved from http://nihseniorhealth.gov/anxietydisorders/aboutanxietydisorders/01.html.

Veysey, B., & Bichler-Robertson (2003). Prevalence estimates of psychiatric disorders in correctional settings. In *Health status of soon-to-be released inmates: A report to Congress* (Vol. 2, pp. 157–165).

Way, B. B., Miraglia, R., Sawyer, D. A., Beer, R., & Eddy, J. (2005) Factors related to suicide in New York State prisons. *International Journal of Law and Psychiatry*, 28, 207–221.

Weissman, M. M., Bland, R. C., Canino, G. J., Greenwald, H. G., Joyce, E. G., Karam, C.K., ... Yeh, E. K. (1999). Prevalence of suicide ideation and suicide attempts in nine countries. *Psychological Medicine*, 29(1), 9–17.

Wetherell, J. L., & Jeste, D. V. (2003). Older adults with schizophrenia patients are living longer and gaining researchers' attention. *Elder Care*, 3(2), 8–11. Retrieved from http://www.stanford.edu/group/usvh/stanford/misc/Schizophrenia%202.pdf.

White, T. W., & Schimmel, D. J. (1995). Suicide prevention in federal prisons: A successful five-step program. In L. M. Hayer (Ed.), *Prison suicide: An overview and guide to prevention* (pp. 46–57). Mansfield, MA: National Center on Institutions are Alternatives.

White, T., Schimmel, D., & Frickey, R. (2002). A comprehensive analysis of suicide in federal prisons: A fifteen-year review. *Journal of Correctional Health Care*, 9, 321–345.

World Health Organization. (2007). *Mental health and prisons*. Retrieved from Department of Mental Health & Substance Abuse, WHO Geneva, The WHO MIND Project: Mental Improvement for Nations Development website: http://www.who.int/mental_health/policy/development/MH&PrisonsFactsheet.pdf.

World Health Organization, Department of Mental Health and Substance Abuse. (2007). *Preventing suicide in jails and prisons*. Retrieved from http://www.who.int/mental_health/prevention/suicide/resource_jails_prisons.pdf.

Chapter 6

Victimization

Prisons are volatile and violent places where victimization is common and where the impact of being a victim can for some last a lifetime (Bottoms 1999; Irwin 1980; Toch 1977). Since the passage of The Prison Rape Elimination Act of 2003 (PREA), we now know a great deal about general rates of victimization in prison. Unfortunately, the researchers who received PREA grant funds to study victimization often neglected analyses of rates for special populations such as the elderly in prison (see for example, Fleisher and Kreinert 2006; Zweig et al. 2007). To say that victimization and incarceration are linked for every person who is incarcerated does not dismiss the unique adverse complications faced by geriatric prisoners. A full understanding of the prevalence, incidence, and distinct challenges faced by geriatric prisoners necessarily presupposes an understanding of victimization within the general population of prisoners. Moreover, the psychological trauma associated with being a victim whether the victimization occurred inside prison walls or prior to incarceration is associated with deterioration of mental and physical health among prisoners (Morrissey et al. 2012). Such problems are often magnified among older adult prisoners. In the United States today it is estimated that there are more than 124,000 prisoners who are aged 55 or older (Human Rights Watch 2012). Consequently, violence against aging inmates has become such a concern that many state agencies segregate their older prisoners in separate units or blocks away from their younger counterparts (Aday 1994; Aday 2003). Because the aging prisoner population is growing at a rapid pace, research on elderly prisoners' victimization experiences and the corresponding adjustment problems deserves more attention.

Given the dearth of literature centered on victimization among geriatric prisoners, it is important that readers be informed about the basic nature of victimization behind prison walls. Discussions of victimization in prison are complicated as a result of non-uniformity in definitions of victimization and concerns about the accuracy of reporting. With this in mind the first section reviews some of the basic challenges faced when drawing conclusions about the scope of victimization in prison. Then a brief review of victimization rates for all types of prisoners is provided. That victimization differences between younger and older prisoners exist should not be surprising, explanations for why this is the case are examined. Special attention is given to sexual victimization in prison.

Victimization Research Is Complicated

The study of prisoner victimization is complicated. The research is considered unreliable by some due to lack of a common definition of victimization, low response rates from the prisoner victims, and an inability to verify that the victimization actually occurred (Kaufman 2008; Struckman-Johnson and Struckman-Johnson 2000a, 2000b). Still others suggest victimization data suffers from underreporting as a result of a prison culture where there is a natural reluctance of prisoners and staff to report victimization as a result of the "code of silence," concerns about retaliation, or perceptions about the nature of victims (Fleisher and Krienert 2006; Kaufman 2008; Parsell 2007; Smith and Batuik 1989; Smith and Yarussi 2007). Despite these challenges some prisoners do report their own personal victimization and that of fellow prisoners (Fleisher and Krienert 2006; Tewksbury and Mahoney 2009).

Defining Prisoner Victimization

The definition of victimization among institutionalized populations varies depending on the intention of the definition. Yet, defining what is meant by victimization is an essential first step toward understanding and ultimately ameliorating the problem. Prisoner victimization falls within one of two categories: personal or property victimization (see Box 6-1). Property victimization refers to the taking or theft of the personal property of another prisoner. Personal victimization most often refers to a physical attack on a prisoner. A physical assault occurs when an individual or group of prisoners attacks another prisoner physically, with or without the use of a weapon or threatens to harm. Examples of prisoner physical assault analyzed in the literature include hitting, biting, kicking, choking, beating up, threatening to

---

Box 6-1. Types of Prisoner Victimization

A. Personal Victimization

Physical Assault: Occurs when an individual or group of prisoners attacks another prisoner physically, with or without the use of a weapon or threatens to harm.

Sexual Abuse/Assault: The use of debt, threats of physical harm, peer pressure, deceit, personal favors, or positional authority to force or cajole sexual favors from a person, including sexually abusive contacts, sexually abusive penetration, and/or sexual harassment.

Sexually Abusive Contact: Non-penetrative touching by an inmate (either directly or through the clothing) of the genitalia, anus, groin, breast, inner thigh, or buttocks without penetration of another inmate without the latter's consent, or of an inmate who is coerced into sexual contact by threats of violence, or of an inmate who is unable to consent or refuse.

Sexual Abusive Penetration: Penetration by an inmate of another inmate without the latter's consent, or of an inmate who is coerced into sexually abusive penetration by threats of violence, or of an inmate who is unable to consent or refuse.

Staff-on-Inmate Sexual Abuse: Encompasses all occurrences of staff-on-inmate sexually abusive contact, penetration, indecent exposure, voyeurism and harassment. A staff solicitation of inmates to engage in sexual contact or penetration encompasses attempted staff-on-inmate sexual abuse.

B. Property Victimization — Theft

State of Vermont PREA Definitions of Sexual Abuse. Available at http://www.doc.state. vt.us/about/policies/rpd/for-comment/prison-rape-elimination-act-prea-staff-sexual-misconduct-2013-vermont-facilities.

---

harm another prisoner with a knife or shank (Tewksbury and Mahoney 2009; Wolff, Shi, and Siegel 2009; Wolff and Shi 2009; Wolff, Blitz, Shi, Siegel, and Bachman 2007).

The Prisoner Rape Elimination Act (PREA) of 2003 is most often used to define prisoner sexual abuse. Sexual abuse refers to the use of debt, threats of physical harm, peer pressure, deceit, personal favors, or positional authority to force or cajole sexual favors from a person, including sexually abusive contacts, sexually abusive penetration, and/or sexual harassment. The definition includes nonconsensual penetration and sexually abusive contact (see Box 6-2). PREA also encompasses staff on inmate sexual abuse which includes all occurrences of staff-on-inmate sexually abusive contact, penetration, indecent exposure, voyeurism and harassment.

> **Box 6-2. Prison Rape Definition**
>
> In the Prison Rape Elimination Act of 2003, "rape" is defined as "carnal knowledge" (contact between the penis and the vulva or penis and the anus, including penetration of any sort, however slight), "oral sodomy" (contact between the mouth and the penis, the mouth and the vulva, or the mouth and the anus), sexual assault with an object, or sexual fondling of a person:
>
> - Forcibly or against that person's will.
> - Not forcibly or against the person's will, where the victim is incapable of giving consent because of his or her youth or temporary or permanent mental or physical incapacity.
> - Achieved through the exploitation of the fear or threat of physical violence or bodily injury (Kaufman 2008: 25).

Prevalence and Incidence of Victimization in Prison

Personal and property victimization are much higher within correctional institutions than in the general population (Teplin et al. 2005). The assault rate for people in poor communities, for example, is more than thirteen times lower than the six-month rate for male inmates inside prison (Wolff, Shi and Siegel 2009). While property victimization is more common than personal victimization (Wooldrege 1998), most of the literature on prisoner victimization has focused on physical victimization—assaults and sexual abuse. Exposure to physical victimization is widespread in prison. A national study conducted by the Bureau of Justice Statistics found that one in ten prisoners is charged with physical assault or injured in a fight. The number charged and injured doubles for prisoners with mental health problems (James and Glaze 2006). Wolff et al. (2009) define personal victimization as physical and sexual abuse. The most common type of physical victimization is non-lethal physical assault (Wolff, Shi, and Siegel 2009). In their study one in five prisoners reported some form of inmate-on-inmate personal victimization. In contrast, one in five prisoners experienced staff-on-inmate victimization. Regardless of the type of victimization few offenses resulted in death.

The rate of victimization across groups of prisoners varies significantly. According to Wolff and Shi (2009) rates of physical victimization are lower for women than men. But the rate of sexual victimization is higher for women than men. Vulnerable populations, such as the elderly and mentally ill, within prison settings also report greater victimization of all types of victimization (Austin, Fabelo, Gunter, and McGinnis 2008; Blitz, Wolff, and Shi 2008; Bureau of Justice Statistics 2010; Wolff, Blitz, and Shi 2007). Many academics assert that the reason for increased victimization for these latter groups is related to their increased vulnerability (Blitz et al. 2008; Edgar and O'Donnell 1998; Kerbs and Jolley 2007; Morrison 1991; Wolff, Blitz, and Shi 2007; Wolff and Shi 2009).

Less clear is whether there are significant differences across racial or ethnic groups. Here the research findings are mixed. Studies from the 1980s indicate that while victimization is a common occurrence African-American prisoners tend to victimize Whites inmates (Bowker 1980; Irwin 1980). In more recent research, however, findings are inconsistent, with some studies concluding inter-racial acts are more common while race is not a significant predictor of physical and sexual victimization in others (Wooldredge 1994; Wooldredge 1998; Wolff, Shi, and Blitz 2008).

Special Circumstance — Sexual Victimization

Far more is known about the sexual victimization than any other type of physical assault that occurs in prison (Fleisher and Kreinert 2006; Kaufman 2008; PREA Data Collection Activities 2012; Wolff, Shi, and Siegel 2009; Wolff and Shi 2009; Wolff, Blitz, Shi, Siegel, and Bachman 2007; Zweig and Blackmore 2008; Zweig et al. 2007). Prior to PREA prison sexual abuse was an undisclosed problem with limited information on prevalence, incidence, impact and cause (Hensley 2002; Lehrer 2001; Tewksbury and West 2000). While it was widely understood that sexual assaults occurred in prison, many researchers were initially hesitant to take up the challenge of exploring the prevalence and nature of this offense.

Sexual Victimization through the Ages

In the 1980s only a few states and the Bureau of Prisons provided rough estimates of sexual victimization and pressure to engage in sexual acts behind bars. A California study conducted by Wooden and Parker (1982) revealed that 14% of their prison sample reported being sexually victimized. The percentage of prisoners reporting being a target of sexual abuse in New York was even greater where Lockwood (1980) indicated that nearly a third of male prisoners recounted experiences with sexual abuse. Whether forced or consensual the literature showed fairly high self-reported rates of sexual acts taking placing behind bars and significant pressure being placed on prisoners to engage in such acts (Hensley 2002; Nacci and Kane 1983; Tewksbury 1989; Wooden and Parker 1982) By the end of the 1990s, it was fairly common to find research indicating victimization rates approaching 20 percent across various types of correctional settings (Saum,

Surratt, Inciardi, and Bennett 1995; Struckman-Johnson, Rucker, Bumby, and Donaldson 1996; Struckman-Johnson and Struckman-Johnson 2000a, 2002).

In a 2007 a Bureau of Justice study found that nearly five percent of inmates in state and federal prison reported sexual victimized in the previous year (Beck and Harrison 2007). Not surprisingly, this translates into just over 165,000 incidents of sexual victimization among those prisoners who reported being a victim of at least one incident of sexual victimization.

Tewksbury and Mahoney (2009) analyzed correspondence written by prisoners informing government officials of physical and sexual victimization. The results indicated that 42 percent of the letters were related to staff victimizing prisoners and 18 percent reflected prisoner-to-prisoner violence. Moreover, 33 percent of the inmates reporting victimization by staff and prisoners specifically reported physical victimization and 1.7 percent reported some act of sexual victimization. One hundred percent of the prisoners who reported victimization by other prisoners reported acts of sexual victimization.

More recent studies continue to indicate that sexual victimization is taking place. According to Beck, Berzofsky and Kerbs (2013) there were more than 57,000 incidents of sexual victimization in prisons in the U.S. (see Table 6-1). Prisoners reported 29,300 inmate-on-inmate incidents of sexual victimization and more than 34,000 staff sexual misconduct. The majority of these inmate-on-inmate acts were nonconsensual (15,400). Beck, Berzofsky, and Kerbs (2013:10) note that reports by inmates of "willing" sexual activity declined from 2007 to 2011. Eleven male facilities were considered high rate institutions and one female prison (Mabel Bassett Correctional Center in Oklahoma) was considered to have a high rate of victimization.

There is significant variation in terms of who is victimized behind prison walls. 1.3 million male inmates reported some sort of inmate-on-inmate victimization or staff sexual misconduct. Female inmates were far more likely to report inmate-on-inmate victimization than their male counterparts (see Table 6-2). African-American (507,900 reporting) prisoners were also more likely to report sexual victimization than White (430,000 reporting) or Hispanic (330,800 reporting) prisoners (Beck, Berzofsky, and Kerbs 2013).

How Does Sexual Victimization Differ in Prison from the Community?

Sexual victimization in prison diverges in unique ways from victimization among the general population. The literature indicates that the victims of sexual

Table 6-1. Adult Prisoners Reporting Sexual Victimization by Incident, National Inmate Survey, 2011–12

Type of Incident	Number of Victims Prisons	Percent of Inmates Prisons
Total	57,900	4
Inmate-on-inmate	29,300	2
Nonconsensual sexual acts	15,400	1.1
Abusive sexual contacts only	13,900	1
Staff sexual misconduct	34,100	2
Unwilling activity	21,500	1.5
Excluding touching	15,400	1.1
Touching only	5,600	0.4
Willing activity	19,700	1.4
Excluding touching	17,000	1.2
Touching only	2,700	0.2

Source: Beck, A., Berzofsky, M. & Krebs, C. (2013). Sexual victimization in Prisons and Jails Reported by Inmates, 2011–2012. U.S. Department of Justice, Office of Justice Programs, Bureau of Justice Statistics.

abuse tend to be White and the perpetrators African-American (Carroll 1977; Moss, Hosford, and Anderson 1979; Wolff et al. 2006). Another major trend in prisons is the fact that the majority of victimizations are a result of sexually abusive contact rather than penetration (Wolff et al. 2006). A comparison of differences between male and female institutions indicates that male facilities have higher rates of sexual abuse which includes staff whereas in female institutions there are a larger number of inmate-on-inmate assaults (Wolff et al. 2006).

Consequences of Victimization

The negative effects of nonconsensual sexual activities in prison are legion. According to Dumond and Dumond (2002: 69) "sexual victimization causes a psychological disequilibrium from a situation that cannot be avoided and for

Table 6-2. Prevalence of Sexual Victimization by Incident and Inmate Characteristics, National Inmate Survey, 2011–12

Characteristic	Inmates Sexual Victimization		
	Number of Inmates	Inmate-on-Inmate	Staff Sexual Misconduct
Sex			
Male	1,345,200	1.70%	2.40%
Female	96,600	6.9	2.3
Race/Hispanic origin			
White	430,000	2.9	1.6
Black	507,900	1.3	2.6
Hispanic	339,800	1.6	2.2
Other	38,200	1.7	2.6
Two or more races	108,300	4	3.9
Age			
18–19	18,500	1.6	2.4
20–24	162,500	2.2	3.5
25–34	457,100	2.3	2.9
35–44	398,200	2	2.3
45–54	281,400	2	1.7
55 or older	124,000	1.1	0.8
Education			
Less than high school	813,300	1.9	2.4
High school graduate	293,900	1.7	2.3
Some college	231,100	2.7	1.8
College degree or more	98,700	2.7	2.4
Marital status			
Married	265,600	1.4	1.9
Widowed, divorced, or separated	390,500	1.9	1.6
Never married	741,200	2.1	2.5

Source: Beck, A., Berzofsky, M. & Krebs, C. (2013). Sexual victimization in Prisons and Jails Reported by Inmates, 2011–2012. U.S. Department of Justice, Office of Justice Programs, Bureau of Justice Statistics.

which a person cannot use their normal problem-solving resources." The victims in prison experience physical, cognitive, psychological, and social problems (Cotton and Groth 1982; Donaldson 1995; Lockwood 1980a; McCorkle 1993; Struckman-Johnson and Struckman-Johnson 1999, 2000a). A common finding in the literature is that the assault often results in increased fear (Dumond 1992; Dumond and Dumond 2002). Victims fear a loss of masculinity (Cotton and Groth 1982; Scacco 1982; Sykes 1958), future targeting (Dumond and Dumond 2002), retaliation should they report (Fleisher and Krienert 2006; Kaufman 2008; Parsell, 2007; Smith and Batuik, 1989; Smith and Yarussi 2007); and suffer from PTSD as the trauma is relived (Dumond and Dumond 2002). One study found that even the report of a rape can increase feelings of fear (Jones and Schmid 1989). Because of the level of fear and inability to cope, some inmates become suicidal in the aftermath of victimization (Dumond and Dumond 2002; Struckman-Johnson and Struckman-Johnson 1999, 2000).

In addition to the emotional and psychological toll that occurs with victimization, problems are compounded because the assault could lead to more violence and harm. For example, victims who fight back may be injured or sought out for continued victimization (Hensley 2002). Ultimately, some victims may find themselves becoming sexual slaves (Mariner 2001; Dumond and Dumond 2002).

Moreover, sexual abuse in prison also carries with it increased risks of negative health consequences. As detailed in Chapter 5, prisoners are at significant risk for transmitting communicable diseases, particularly TB, hepatitis and HIV. The possibility of having such diseases be transferred to the victim is enhanced as a result of the exchange of body fluids during the sexual assault. In addition to sexually transmitted diseases, the stress associated with victimization has been associated with increase rates of other diseases such as asthma, ulcers, colitis, and hypertension (McCorkle 1993a; 1993b).

What Does All This Mean for Elderly Prisoners?

Nearly two million Americans age 65 or older have been injured, exploited, or otherwise mistreated by someone on whom they depended for care or protection (Bonnie and Wallace 2003). While the possibility of abuse is great within the community, risk of abuse or neglect is heightened for elderly prisoners. As shown in Table 6-3 the longer a prisoner spends in prison sexual victimization remains a possibility. "Older prisoners become 'easy prey' for prison 'wolves', 'gorillas', and 'rip offs'" (Bowker 1980: 159). Not surprisingly, they report

Table 6-3. Prevalence of Sexual Victimization by Type of Incident and Inmate Criminal Justice Status and History, National Inmate Survey, 2011–12

Criminal Justice Status and History	Inmates Reporting Sexual Victimization		
	Number of Prison Inmates	Inmate-on-Inmate	Staff Sexual Misconduct
Most serious offense			
Violent sexual offense	211,300	3.70%	2.10%
Other violent	440,900	2.3	3.4
Property	244,100	2.4	2.6
Drug	310,300	0.7	1.1
Other	162,900	1.7	2.1
Sentence length			
Less than 1 year	53,400	1.5	1.6
1–4 years	350,400	1.8	1.3
5–9 years	311,100	1.6	2.2
10–19 years	296,900	1.8	2.3
20 years or more	239,300	2.2	2.5
Life/death	139,600	2.7	3.2
Time in a correctional facility prior to current facility			
None	296,400	1.8	1.5
Less than 6 months	161,400	2.3	1.7
6–11 months	131,200	1.7	2.1
1–4 years	384,900	1.6	1.8
5 years or more	423,500	2.2	3
Number of times arrested			
1 time	217,600	2	1.7
2–3	427,200	2	2.2
4–10	495,400	1.8	2
11 or more	253,200	2	2.8

Time since admission			
Less than 1 month	79,600	1.4	0.8
1–5 months	367,500	1.6	1.7
6–11 months	263,200	2.2	2.6
1–4 years	558,100	2.1	2.5
5 years or more	172,400	2.9	3.4

Source: Beck, A., Berzofsky, M. & Krebs, C. (2013). Sexual victimization in Prisons and Jails Reported by Inmates, 2011–2012. U.S. Department of Justice, Office of Justice Programs, Bureau of Justice Statistics.

feeling vulnerable to attack, fearful and express a preference for living with inmates their own age (Adday 1994; Aday and Krabill 2013; Kerbs and Jolley 2009; Krajick 1979; McCorkle 1993; Vito and Wilson 1985; Walsh 1989). Evidence suggests that geriatric prisoners may be justified in their concerns. Table 6-4 reveals that in 2011–2012 National Inmate Survey more than 124,000 inmates aged 55 or older reported some form of sexual victimization (Beck, Berzofsky, and Kerbs 2013).

Table 6-4. Prevalence of Sexual Victimization by Type of Incident and Age of Inmate, National Inmate Survey, 2011–12

Age	Prison Inmates		
	Number	Inmate-on-Inmate	Staff Sexual Misconduct
16–17	1,700	1.8%	2.8%
18–19	18,550	1.6	2.4
20–24	162,520	2.2	3.5
25–34	457,060	2.3	2.9
35–44	398,230	2	2.3
45–54	281,390	2	1.7
55 or older	124,050	1.1	0.8

Source: Beck, A., Berzofsky, M. & Krebs, C. (2013). Sexual victimization in Prisons and Jails Reported by Inmates, 2011–2012. U.S. Department of Justice, Office of Justice Programs, Bureau of Justice Statistics.

Why Does Victimization Matter?

The victimization experiences of older prisoners matter for several reasons. There are more geriatric prisoners incapacitated for longer periods of time today than at any other point in history. Moreover, geriatric prisoners enter prison having experienced greater trauma and perhaps extensive personal victimization. Prior victimization, regardless of whether the incident(s) occurred prior to incarceration or during incarceration, increases the odds that an individual will become a victim behind prison walls and have problems coping with institutional life. As the number of geriatric prisoners increase, the inmate cultural adaptations to prison make the aging prisoner more susceptible to victimization (Carroll 1977; Clemmer 1958; Hensley 2002; Messerschimdt 1993; 2000; Tewksbury and West 2000; Toch 1997; Sykes 1958). Moreover, given the state's obligation to provide adequate care, failing to address victimization among this population may have lasting legal ramifications. Last but not least, victimization has a direct effect on institutional costs, costs that will be assumed by society for the provision of care and protection for elderly prisoners within state and federal institutions.

Pre-Prison Trauma

When examining the impact of victimization on institutional behavior and prisoner well-being, it is important to review the literature on pre-prison victimization. Older prisoners enter prison having experienced more traumatic life events than any other population (Morrissey, Courtney, and Maschi 2012). Recent research indicates that nearly 80 percent of older male prisoners had documented histories of abuse (Haugebrook et al. 2010). The picture is not that much brighter for female prisoners where 70 percent of female prisoners report histories of rape (McDaniels-Wilson and Belknap 2008).

This history of prior victimization is associated with subsequent victimization and negative institutional adjustment (Morrissey, Courtney, and Maschi 2012). Abuse, whether physical, sexual or emotional can have lasting effects, such as PTSD, personality disorders, stress, depression, acting-out and other forms of psychological and physical distress (American Friends Society 2013; Dehart 2005; Maschi et al. 2011; Petersilia 2001). Such problems may be exacerbated by the nature of institutional life where having been a victim once is associated with subsequent victimization (Maschi et al. 2011; Struckman-Johnson et al. 1996). Approximately two-thirds of prisoners who reported physical victimization in the prior 6 months of incarceration also reported experiencing childhood physical abuse (Wolff, Shi, and Siegel 2008). This connection between past history of abuse and victimization in prison among older inmates was recently confirmed in a study conducted by Morrissey et al. (2012). Given the already extensive histories of trauma prior to incarceration, we should not be surprised to find that victimization among older prisoners is continued during incarceration.

Inmate Subculture and Adaptation

As a result of the deprivations experienced by prisoners and the inmate subculture, violence directed toward the vulnerable is a common mode of adaptation placing aging prisoners at heightened risk. Inmates are deprived of heterosexual relationships but still experience the drive for sex. Without access to willing heterosexual partners, some inmates force weaker and more vulnerable prisoners to engage in sexual activity. Inmates also experience deprivation of goods and services. With limited funds to purchase necessary items, some inmates increasing resort to theft and use of force to obtain food, basic items necessary for grooming, and other types of contraband. Consequently, as prisoners begin to experience the negative effects of aging and are housed with younger and stronger prisoners, the older and weaker prisoners become vulnerable to attack (Kozlov 2008; Wolff, Shi, and Siegel 2009).

Extant literature on the male inmate subculture also suggests that the victimization of weaker prisoners reflects the limited means that male prisoners have for "doing gender" (Bowker 1980, 1982; 1998; Walklate 1995). Characteristics of masculinity in prison include to be tough, to be physically and mentally dominant; and to be willing to resort to violence to handle interpersonal disputes (Bowker 1998; Sykes 1956; 1958). For male prisoners violent situations enhance masculinity regardless of whether such incidents occur through traditional (e.g., athletic activities) or alternative displays such as property, physical or sexual victimization (Messerschimdt 1993; Cavendar 1999). Thus, male prisoners may be "doing masculinity" by victimizing weaker institutional populations. "Doing masculinity" provides status and relief from deprivations among the males in prison (Bowker 1998; Hensley 2002; Lockwood 2000; Reed and Nelson 1977). The expectation that causing harm as a way to do masculinity becomes a shared understanding of what it means to be an ideal man in prison and reproduced across situational contexts (Polk 1997). As suggested by the literature (Messerschmidt 2000), once institutionalized males identify causing harm to vulnerable populations as a mechanisms for asserting masculinity, they become predisposed to using violence, theft, and intimidation as a source for maintaining a masculine identify behind prison walls placing the vulnerable elderly prisoner at risk.

Age-Related Mental and Physical Decline

The longer an individual is incarcerated the greater the chance that he or she will experience personal victimization. As Wolff, Shi and Siegel (2009) suggest, we expect victimization rates for younger prisoners to be high. Unfortunately, because of the impact of aging on prisoners, we should have also foreseen enhanced victimization problems as a result of age-related changes for the elderly in prison. As detailed in Chapter 5, a significant number of aging prisoners exhibit cognitive impairments as a result of dementia, depression, anxiety and a host of other mental health problems (Belluck 2012; Cox and Lawrence 2010; Maschi, Kwak, Ko, Morrissey 2012; Veysey and Bichler-Robertson 2000). The reduction in cognitive functioning among older prisoners may make them more vulnerable to scams or having their property taken as a result of not being able to distinguish when younger inmates are engaging in "the con" (Wolff, Shi, and Siegel 2009). In addition to scams, younger prisoners may use their physical strength to assault and take property (Kerbs and Jolley 2007).

Nature of Offense

Kerbs and Jolley (2007) also speculate that the higher rate of victimization among older prisoners in their study is a result of the nature of geriatric prisoners' committal offenses. Nearly a third of all older prisoners are sex offenders. Existing literature indicates that child molesters, for example, get continuously harassed and abused by other inmates behind institutional walls (Bowker 1982; McGrath 1982). This combination of increased susceptibility to violence coupled with their offense related stigma make elderly inmates a vulnerable population.

Victimization Is Under-Reported

Much of the abuse experienced by older inmates is undetected or unreported (see sexual victimization anecdote in Box 6-3). Despite a predominate fear of victimization among older prisoners, current estimates likely underreport the true amount of physical, sexual, and property victimization among elderly prisoners. The most commonly given justification for failing to report victimization is fear of reprisal (Alarid 2000; Beck and Hughes 2005; Kerbs and Jolley 2007;

Box 6-3. Visitor Voices: Older Prisoner Reports

Property Victimization

"I had my house [cell] broken into and [they] took everything I had out of my foot locker.... I had the lock on there, but it wasn't [locked].... see because I have a hard time opening that combination ..." (Kerbs and Jolly: 205).

Physical Victimization

"It was in the shower ... and that's when I had my walker here ... and I have to take my walker in the shower with me so I can stand up. And the guy, he didn't like it, because my walker was too close. And he shoved the walker into me and the floor is kind of slick, because of the paint that they got on it ..." (Kerbs and Jolley: 207).

Sexual Victimization

"[A few years ago], I was put in a room with two younger prisoners.... They had found out what had happened to me a long time ago [i.e., being raped in prison] and when they started asking me about it, I told them, 'No, no, no.' And then one night I was laying in bed sleeping and both of them just grabbed me and stuck a knife up to my throat and told me to turn over. I turned over and they both raped me ... And they told me that if I told, I would be killed, so I never said anything ..." (Kerbs and Jolley: 2007).

Miller 2007). Even inmates who are not directly involved in assaults are reluctant to come forward as witnesses out of fear of retaliation (Banbury 2004; Miller 2007). Miller (2007) reported fear of harassment to be one of the most salient explanations for failure to report among older prisoners. Some prisoners fail to report victimization out of a concern that they will not be believed. There may be an element of truth in this assumption; recent studies indicate that the majority reported of sexual victimization cases in prison were ultimately determined to be unsubstantiated or unfounded (Beck, Harrison and Adams 2007). Older inmates more so than their younger counterparts are also more likely to adhere to the inmate code which stresses 'doing your own time', 'don't be a rat', and 'handling your own business' (Clemmer 1958). More recent models of the inmate code indicate that older prisoners are more likely to have been socialized into an inmate code which emphasizes violence, power, and masculinity (Miller 2007). Regardless of which code is identified with, the net result is an older prisoner who is less likely to officially report his/her victimization.

What Is the Extent of Victimization?

Academics, advocates, and policy makers now recognize geriatric prisoners as a special population; yet little is known about geriatric prisoner victimization characteristics, causes, or consequences. Kerbs and Jolley (2007) have conducted one of the most extensive studies of victimization as it relates to older prisoners. They interviewed 65 older male prisoners in the North Carolina Department of Corrections about their psychological, property, physical and sexual victimization. Close to one third of the prisoners reported being victims of property crime. Ten percent or less reported some sort of physical victimization such as being punched, kicked, pushed, robbed, mugged, or attacked with a weapon. With regard to sexual victimization, 10.8 percent reported sexual harassment, 1.5 percent reported having been forced to have sex in order to repay a debt, and 1.5 percent reported sexual assault. By far the victimization reported most by the group was psychological in nature. Psychological victimization includes verbal insults, verbal threats, and threats in the form of fake punches. Perhaps as a result of their victimization, 3 out of 4 would prefer to live in an age-segregated facility. Box 6-3 presents a few of the qualitative responses made by participants.

Consequences of Victimization

Prisoners who experience victimization suffer from a multitude of consequences. There is a significant body of evidence which indicates that victims exhibit higher rates of depression (Biggam & Power 1999; Wooldredge 1999), anxiety (Biggam & Power 1999; Wooldredge, 1999), stress (Biggam & Power 1999; Wooldredge 1999), anger (Biggam & Power 1999; Wolff and Shi 2009; Wooldredge, 1999) and hopelessness (Biggam & Power 1999; Wooldredge, 1999). Prisoners who have been victimized also are known to become hyper vigilant and fearful (Dumond and Dumond 2002; McCorkle, 1993). Repeat victimization has been associated with mental and physical deterioration (Wolff and Shi 2009). There is some evidence that some victims become self-destructive taking their anger and frustration out on others (Fleisher 1989; Wolff and Shi 2009). In the case sexual abuse with penetration, prisoners are at significant risk of exposure to sexually transmitted diseases (Dumond and Dumond 2002; Tewksbury and West 2000). Additionally, existing literature indicates greater suicidal ideation and self-harm as consequences of victimization (Dumond and Dumond 2002). To sum up, the result is greater harm to the older prisoner's psychological and physical well-being.

Conclusion

Despite the small number of studies which specifically examine prison victimization among the elderly and challenges to validity, several conclusions can be drawn from the literature. First, the aging prisoner population poses unique challenges for correctional administrators because they exhibit some of the highest rates of pre-prison trauma (Morrissey et al. 2012). In one study more than 80 percent of older male prisoners had documented histories of trauma (Haugebrook et al. 2010). Second, extant literature suggests that older prisoners are at heightened risk for property, sexual, physically assaultive, and other types of victimization while incarcerated (Dawes 2009; Hoscstetler et al. 2004; Maschi et al. 2011; Struckman-Johnson et al. 1996). Consequently, older prisoners may experience greater rates of psychological distress resulting in institutional behavioral problems and administrative concern about the ability of the correctional system to protect older prisoners from harm (Morrissey et al. 2012).

Solutions to address the problem of victimization for older prisoners typically focus on segregating them from potential abusers. Unfortunately, while this may appear to alleviate some of the pressures for victimization, not enough is known about the prevalence and incidence of victimization for us to disentangle long-term impacts. The victimization of older prisoners, in particular has largely been ignored (Morrissey et al. 2012). A result which is puzzling to many given that older prisoners have more extensive trauma histories, can experience reactivation of trauma associated with PTSD symptoms, and because prior victimization experiences predict revictimization in prison (Hochstetler, Murphy, and Simons 2004; Morrissey et al. 2012). The state has an obligation to protect older prisoners. Failing to assess the prevalence of victimization and to consider the impact of such victimization on offender well-being could prove costly. It is well within reason to expect that advocates for the elderly, prisoner families, and perhaps federal court judges might view such failings as 'deliberate indifference' and unconstitutional resulting in even greater costs to an overburdened system.

Websites

For more information on PREA statistics, visit https://www.bjs.gov.

References

Aday, R. (2003). *Aging Prisoners: Crisis in American corrections*. Connecticut: Praeger.

Aday, R. (1994). Golden years behind bars: Special programs and facilities for older inmates. *Federal Probation*, 58(2), 47–54.

Aday, R. & Krabill, J. (2013). Older and geriatric offenders: Critical issues for the 21st century. In Lior Gideon (Ed) *Special Needs Offenders in Correctional Settings*, (pp. 203–232). Thousand Oaks: Sage.

Alarid, L. (2000). Sexual perspectives of incarcerated bisexual and gay men: The county jail protective custody experience. *The Prison Journal*, 80(1), 80–95.

American Friends Society (2013). *Lifetime Lockdown: How Isolation Conditions Impact Reentry*. Retrieved from http://afsc.org/sites/afsc.civicactions.net/files/documents/AFSC-Lifetime-Lockdown-Report_0.pdf.

Austin, J., T. Fabelo, A. Gunter, & McGinnis, K. (2006). *Sexual violence in the Texas prison system*. National Institute of Justice, September 2006 (NCJ 215774).

Beck, A. J., Harrison, P. M., & Adams, D. (2007). *Sexual violence reported by correctional authorities, 2006*. Washington, DC: U.S. Department of Justice, Bureau of Justice Statistics.

Beck, A. J. & Hughes, T. (2006). *Sexual violence reported by correctional authorities, 2005*. Washington, DC: U.S. Department of Justice, Bureau of Justice Statistics.

Beck, A., Berzofsky, M. & Kerbs, C. (2013). Sexual victimization in Prisons and Jails Reported by Inmates, 2011–2012. U.S. Department of Justice, Office of Justice Programs, Bureau of Justice Statistics.

Belluck, P. (2012). The Vanishing Mind Time's Toll Behind Bars. *The New York Times February 25, 2012. Retrieved from* http://www.nytimes.com/2012/02/26/health/dealing-with-dementia-among-aging-criminals.html?_r=0.

Bottoms, A.E. (1999). Interpersonal violence and social order in prisons. In M. Tonry & J. Petersilia (Eds.), *Prisons* (pp. 205–281). Chicago: University of Chicago Press.

Bowker, L. (1980). *Prison victimization*. New York: Elsevier North Holland.

Bowker, L. (1982). Victimizers and victims in American correctional institutions. In R, Johnson & H. Toch (Eds.), *The Pains of Imprisonment* (pp. 63–76). Beverly Hills: Sage.

Bowker, L. (1998). *Masculinities and Violence*. Thousand Oaks, CA: Sage Publications, Inc.

Blitz, C. L., Wolff, N., & Shi, J. (2008). Physical victimization in prison: the role of mental illness. *International Journal of Law and Psychiatry, 31*, 385–393.

Cavender, G. (1999). Detecting masculinity. In *Making Trouble: cultural constructions of crime, deviance and control*, edited by J. Ferrell and N. Websdale: Aldine de Gruyter.

Clemmer, D. (1958). *The prison community*. New York: Holt, Rinehart, and Wilson.

Dawes J. (2009). Ageing Prisoners: Issues for social work. *Australian Social Work*, 62(2), 258–271.

Dumond, R. & Dumond, D. (2002). "The treatment of sexual assault victims." In *Prison Sex Practice and Policy*, pp. 67–87.

Caes, C. C., & Goldberg, A. L. (2004). *Prison rape: A critical review of the literature.* Washington, D.C. United States Department of Justice, National Institute of Justice.

Cox, J. F. & Lawrence, J. E. (2010). Planning services for elderly inmates with mental illness. *Corrections Today*, 72(3), 52–57.

Dehart, D. (2005). Pathways to Prison: Impact of Victimization in the Lives of Incarcerated Women. Retrieved from https://www.ncjrs.gov/pdffiles1/nij/grants/208383.pdf.

Edgar, K., & O'Donnell, I. (1998). Assault in prison: The 'victim's' contribution. *The British Journal of Criminology*, 38, 635–651.

Fleisher, M. & Krienert, J. (2006). *The Culture of Prison Sexual Violence.* NCJ 216515. 2006. Washington, D.C. United States Department of Justice, National Institute of Justice.

Fleisher M. (1989). *Warehousing Violence.* Newbury Park, California: Sage Publications.

Gaes, G. & Goldberg A. (2004). *Prison Rape: A Critical Review of the Literature.* Washington, District of Columbia: National Institute of Justice.

Hensley, C. & Tewksbury, R. (2005). Warden's perceptions of prison sex. *The Prison Journal*, 85, 186–197.

Hensley, C. (2002). Introduction: Life and sex in prison. In (eds.) Christopher Hensley, *Prison Sex Practice & Policy*, pp. 1–13. Lynne Rienner Publishers: London.

Irwin, J. (1980). *Prisons in turmoil.* Boston, MA: Little, Brown.

James, D. J., & Glaze, L. E. (2006). *Mental health problems of prison and jail inmates* (NCJ 213600). Washington, DC: Bureau of Justice Statistics, US Department of Justice.

Kaufman, P. (2008). *Prison Rape: Research Explores Prevalence, Prevention,* National Institute of Justice (March 2008). Retrieved from http://www.nij.gov/journals/259/prison-rape.htm.

Kerbs, J., & Jolley, J. (2007). Inmate-on-inmate victimization among older male prisoners. *Crime & Delinquency*, 53, 187–217.

Krajick, K. 91979). Growing old in prison. *Corrections Magazine*, 5(1), 32–46.

Lehrer, E. (2001). Hell behind bars: The crime that dares not speak its name. *National Review*, 53(2), 24–26.

Maschi, T., Kwak, J., Ko, E.J., & Morrissey, M. (2012). Forget me not: Dementia in prisons. *The Gerontologist.* doi: 10.1093/geront/gnr131.

McGrath, G. M. (1982). Prions society and offence stigma: Some doubts. *Australian and New Zealand Journal of Criminology*, 15, 235–244.

McCorkle, R. (1993). Fear of victimization and symptoms of psychopathology among prison inmates. *Journal of Offender Rehabilitation*, 19(2), 27–41.

Messerschmidt, J. (1993). *Masculinities and Crime: Critique and Reconceptualization of Theory*: Rowan & Littlefield Publishers, Inc.

Messerschmidt, J. (1997). *Crime as structured action: gender, race, class and crime in the making*: Sage Publications.

Messerschmidt, J. (2000). *Nine Lives: Adolescent Masculinities, the Body, and Violence*: Westview Press.

Miller, K. (2007). The darkest figure of crime: Perceptions of reasons for male inmates to not report sexual assault. *Justice Quarterly*, 27(5), 692–712.

Morrissey, M., Courtney, D. and Maschi, T. (2012). Sexual Abuse Histories Among Incarcerated Older Adult Offenders: A Descriptive Study, Sexual Abuse — Breaking the Silence, Dr. Ersi Abaci Kalfoglu (Ed.), ISBN: 978-953-51-0425-4, InTech. Retrieved from http://www.intechopen.com/books/sexual-abuse-breakingthe-silence/sexual-abuse-histories-among-incarcerated-older-adults-a-descriptive-study.

Morrison, E. (1991). Victimization in prison: Implications for the mentally ill inmate and for health professionals. *Archives of Psychiatric Nursing*, 5, 17–24.

Parsell, T. J. (2006). *Fish.* New York: Carroll & Graf Publishers.

Petersilia, J. (2001). When prisoners return to communities. *Federal Probation*, 65(1), 3–8.

Polk, K. (1999). Males, honor contests and violence. Homicide Studies, 3 (1), 6–9.

PREA Data Collection Activities, 2012. (2012). Bureau of Justice Statistics. Retrieved from http://bjs.ojp.usdoj.gov/content/pub/pdf/pdca12.pdf.

Prison Rape Elimination Act of 2003, Public Law 108–79, 1.

Saum, C., Surratt, H., Inciardi, J., & Bennett, R. (1995). Sex in prison: Explaining the myths and realities. *The Prison Journal*, 75(4), 413–430.

Smith, B. V., & Yarussi, J. M. (2007). *Breaking the Code of Silence: Correction officers' Handbook on Identifying and Addressing Sexual Misconduct.* National Institute of Corrections. The NIC/WCL Project on addressing prison rape, Washington D.C.

Smith, N. & Batiuk, M. E. (1989). Sexual victimization and inmate social interaction. *The Prison Journal*, 69, 29–38.

Struckman-Johnson C., Struckman-Johnson D. (2000). Sexual coercion rates in seven mid-western prison facilities. Prison Journal, 80, 379–390.

Struckman-Johnson C., Struckman-Johnson D., Rucker L., Bumby K., Donaldson S. (1999). Sexual coercion reported by men and women in prison. *Journal Sex Research*, 33, 67–76.

Struckman-Johnson C., & Struckman-Johnson D. (2002). Sexual coercion reported by women in three Midwestern prisons. *Journal Sex Research* 39, 217–227.

Struckman-Johnson, C. and Struckman-Johnson, D. (2000a). Sexual coercion rates in seven Midwestern prison facilities for men. *The Prison Journal*, 80(4), 379–390.

Sykes, G. (1958). *The Society of Captives*. Princeton NJ, Princeton University Press.

Sykes, G. (1995). The structural-functional perspective on imprisonment. In T. Blomberg and S. Cohen (eds.) *Punishment and Social Control: Essays in Honor of Sheldon L. Messinger*. New York: Aldine de Gruyter.

Teplin, L., McClelland, G., Abram, K., & Weiner, D. (2005). Crime victimization in adults with severe mental illness: Comparison with the national crime victimization survey. Archives of General Psychiatry, 62, 911–921.

Tewksbury, R. & Mahoney, M. (2009). Sexual victimization and requests for assistance in inmates' letters to the national prison rape elimination commission. *Federal Probation*, 73(3), 57–61.

Tewksbury, R. & West, A. (2000). Research on sex in prison during the late 1980s and early 1990s. *The Prison Journal*, 80(4), 368–378.

Toch, H. (1977). Living in prison: The ecology of survival. New York: Free Press.

Toch, Hans. (1997). *Corrections: A humanistic approach*. Guilderland, NY: Harrow and Heston.

Veysey, B. M. & Bichler-Robertson, G. (2002). Prevalence estimates of psychiatric disorders in correctional settings, *in Health Status of Soon-to-be Released Inmates. Report to Congress. Vol. 2.* Chicago: National Commission on Correctional Health Care.

Vito, G. F. & Wilson, D. G. (1982). Forgotten people: Elderly inmates. *Federal Probation*, 49(1), 18–23.

Walklate, S. (1995). *Gender and Crime*: Prentice Hall.

Walsh, E. E. (1989). The older and long term inmate growing old in the new Jersey prison system. In S. Chaneles & C. Barnett (Eds.), *Old prisoners: Current trends*. New York: Haworth.

Wolff, N. and Shi, J. (2009). Victimization and feelings of safety among male and female inmates with behavioral health problems. *The Journal of Forensic Psychiatry & Psychology*, 20(1), 56–S77.

Wolff, N., Shi, J. & Siegel, J. (2009). Understanding physical victimization inside prisons: factors that predict risk. *Justice Quarterly*, 26(3), 445–474.

Wolff, N., Blitz, C., Shi, J. Bachman, R., & Siegel, J. (2006). Sexual violence inside prisons: Rates of victimization. *Journal Urban Health, 83(5)*, 835–848.

Wooldredge, J. (1998). Inmate lifestyles and opportunities for victimization. *Journal of Research in Crime and Delinquency*, (35), 480–502.

Wooldredge, J. (1999). Inmate experiences and psychological well-being. *Criminal Justice and Behavior*, (26), 235–250.

Zweig, J. and Blackmore, J. (2008*). Strategies to prevent prison rape by changing the correctional culture. National Institute of Justice.* Retrieved from https://www.ncjrs.gov/pdffiles1/nij/222843.pdf.

Zweig, J. M., R. L. Naser, R. L. Blackmore, J. & Schaffer, M. (2007). *Addressing Sexual Violence in Prisons: A National Snapshot of Approaches and Highlights of Innovative Strategies.* Washington, DC: U.S. Department of Justice, National Institute of Justice, NCJ 216856.

Chapter 7

Programs and Sentencing Options

> This hesitation to release high cost prisoners who are more profoundly incapacitated by their health than by prison walls tells us something. The extreme caution with which compassionate release is approached suggests that even the terminally ill, much more so the relatively healthy elderly prisoner, if convicted of a violent crime, are understood by corrections authorities and the political class as an object of public apathy. The same antipathy may put obstacles in the path of cost-efficient humane prison elder care because it resembles, as it must, elder care for the 'deserving' elderly in the free world (Rapaport 2013: 8–9).

As states face a burgeoning elderly prison population concerns about relief mechanisms have become paramount. Quantifying the costs associated with long-term and elderly prisoners without addressing corresponding relief mechanisms as many do seems to trivialize the importance of expanding options. Certainly states grappling with these issues would pursue options with more fervor if they thought the American public would support such practices. The reality is that despite an extensive body of literature which identifies appropriate and effective geriatric release mechanisms few states have enacted provisions for early release. And those jurisdictions with such provisions rarely use them. According to Chiu (2010, p. 3) states such as Alabama, North Carolina, and Washington sanctioned policies that would allow certain elderly prisoners to serve the remainder of their sentence in the community; yet some of these states have never released a single older prisoner or released an insignificant number of eligible prisoners. Washington State, for example, released only 22 prisoners in the first five years of its program which authorized early release only for those inmates who were physically incapacitated due to age or medical condition (Chiu 2010;

Washington State Engrossed House Bill Report, HB 2194 2009). This chapter reviews current sentencing strategies designed to reduce the number of elderly prisoners and describes current geriatric prison initiatives.

Driving Forces of the Shift in Sentencing

The shift towards considering practices and sentencing strategies which temper the state's desire to keep elderly inmates behind bars is driven by three factors. First, the number of state and federal prisoners age 55 and over quadrupled between 1995 and 2010 (Human Rights Watch 2012). Second, older prisoners are also two to five times more expensive than their younger counterparts (Human Rights Watch 2012; Lee 2011; Williams and Abraldes 2007). Box 7-1 provides a list of average expenditures for several states. "A recent effort to assess the impact of age on healthcare costs nationally concluded that the average annual cost per prisoner was $5,482, but that for prisoners age 55 to 59, the amount was $11,000, and the figure steadily increased with age cohorts, reaching $40,000 for prisoners age 80 or over" (Human Rights Watch 2012: 75). According to McCarthy (2013) states on average spend $70,000 a year to incarcerate someone aged 50 or older.

Moreover, there has long been consensus among academics that elderly inmates pose little risk to society upon release (Laub and Sampson 2003; Steffensmeier et al. 1989; Williams and Abraldes 2007). According to the life-course perspective criminals age out of crime. Consequently, older prisoners are less likely to commit additional crimes upon release (Steffensmeier et al. 1989). Two national recidivism studies found that released elderly prisoners are four to five times less likely to return to prison within two years of release (Chiu 2010). As discussed by Miller (2009: 36), "whether because of health or other reasons, elderly offenders have the lowest rate of recidivism of all types of offenders; in fact, only about one percent of elderly offenders ever face a second conviction." Less than two percent of elderly inmates ultimately recidivate (Corwin 2001). Politicians and correctional administrators have only just begun to take this literature seriously and to consider releasing some elderly prisoners early because they pose little threat to free citizens.

Solutions to the Elderly Prisoner Problem

While there is wide variation in how states and the federal government address and implement solutions to the elderly prisoner problem, there can be

---

Box 7-1. Average Expenditures for Elderly Prisoners in Several States

- In Georgia average annual expenditure inmate 65 and older $8,565
- In Michigan average annual expenditure inmate 55 or older ranges $11,000 to $40,000
- In Nevada average annual expenditure inmate over 60 $4,000–$5,000
- In North Carolina average annual expenditure inmate over 50 $5,970
- In Texas average annual expenditure inmate over 55 $4,853
- In Virginia average annual expenditure inmate over 50 $5,400

Source: Summarized from Human Rights Watch (2012). Old Behind Bars: The Aging Prison Population in the United States. Available at http://www.hrw.org/sites/default/files/reports/usprisons0112webwcover_0.pdf.

---

no doubt that the ultimate aim of such programs is to reduce the number of elderly behind bars and to reduce costs. Responses across states fall into three categories: do nothing and allow nature to take its course behind bars, implement early release programs, or develop alternative living environments for this special population of inmates (see Box 7-2).

The Do Nothing Argument

There is a case to be made that we should do nothing to push geriatric inmates out of the institutional setting prior to the expiration of their prison terms. Prisons by definition are places of punishment where those who are sentenced experience the pains of incarceration. For this reason alone, it is to be expected that geriatric prisoners will not fare as well as older citizens in the free world. Those who support non-differential treatment argue that the perception that older prisoners suffer more than their younger counterparts is false (Miller 2009). This position has been supported by federal courts where justices viewed the notion that the elderly suffered more as "an untested conclusion, unsupported by any psychological and sociological analysis" (Miller 2009: 37).

From a retributivist perspective those who age in prison are deserving of lengthy prison terms which could perhaps result in death. To alter the punish-

---

Box 7-2. Solutions to the Elderly Prisoner Problem

- The Do Nothing Argument—Make no age-based allowances
- Release the Elderly From Prison Early
- Provide Alternative Living Arrangements During Incarceration

---

ment experience by reducing prison sentences based on age violates the principle of just deserts which requires the punishment to be proportioned to the unfair advantage the offender gained by lawbreaking. This fact is especially salient for the elderly in prison who for the most part committed violent preda- tory crimes or sex offenses to earn their prison time (Human Rights Watch 2012). "Arguing for cost savings reforms from which this population would benefit is much less easily buttressed with soothing claims about enhancing public safety. Even if, and it big if, exaggerated fear of predation were success- fully addressed, the advocate of cost cutting reform cannot address demands for retribution within the discourse of the 'tough on crime' era" (Rapaport 2013: 5). Still others argue that releasing the elderly from prison will not result in huge cost savings (See for example the General Accounting Office 2012 Report on the BOP Elderly Offender Pilot). Instead, early release results in a simple transfer of societal expense from the correctional system to state or fed- eral welfare rolls. Thus, elderly offenders might best be served by staying where they are and having the system make no age-based allowances for early release.

Finally, there is an argument to be made that we should not allow the cost of incarcerating the elderly and long-term prisoner to compel us towards leniency. The costs incurred may well be worth the expense for three reasons. First expense alone is an insufficient reason to reduce the sentence of an offender who otherwise is culpable and deserving of a particular sentence. Second, and perhaps more persuasive, is the argument that the cost of elderly offenders to the system does not represent any additional burden on either state or federal government. This could be so because should elderly offenders receive shorter sentences or alternative sentences that enable them to return to their home com- munities, they will still require services and care that may nonetheless remain largely taxpayer-funded, either through Medicare, Medicaid, Social Security, or other government resources. It is only a matter of where the care is being provided. (Miller 2009: 38). This sentiment is shared by others who argue that the "sickest and oldest prisoners are beyond second chances" (see for example Rapaport's 2013 discussion of the challenges to reducing the elderly prisoner population). Rapaport points out that correctional authorities and politicians are very reluctant to release even terminally ill prisoners.

Early Release

From a jurisprudence perspective there is no constitutional prohibition against incorporating leniency in sentencing elderly offenders or releasing elderly prisoners early from prison. Federal case law holds that age could rightfully be considered as a mitigating factor (*United States v. Carey; United States v. Harrison, United States v. Tolson*). Additionally, several states allow age as a mitigating factor in sentencing (Chiu 2010). The Project for Older Prisoners (POPS) managed within several law schools around the country has long been advocating early release as a legitimate practice for older prisoners. This program reviews the case files of eligible prisoners, those deemed low risk for reoffending, and uses the legal system to help gain their release. The POPS legal programs have obtained early release for more than 500 prisoners (Aday and Krabill 2013).

Parole Prisoners as Normal

Parole refers to the process of releasing an inmate prior to the expiration of his or her full sentence. Parole guidelines mandate automatic release consideration after an inmate has served a specific portion of his or her sentence. Discretionary parole refers to the decision by a paroling authority to release back into the community an inmate from prison whose sentence has not expired under supervision and monitoring by a parole agent who ensures that the ex-offender engages in lawful behavior. The discretionary parole decision often reflects the need to balance punishment, the perception of the inmate's ability to successfully reintegrate back into society, and the needs of the victim and society. The factors that are considered to determine whether an inmate should be released early on supervision include the nature of the crime, the inmate's criminal history, behavior while incarcerated, the victim's statement of crime impact and risk posed to the community should the offender be released. Offenders deemed too dangerous to be released will remain behind bars; but those who pose little threat to society and who are deemed ready for reintegration earn the privilege of a shortened prison term.

The process of release under discretionary parole is one that is based on a rational calculation of the offender's odds of success upon release back into the community. The assumption is that the parole board will examine the totality of the inmate's pre-prison behavior and institutional behavior and use their discretion to release only those inmates who have exhibited good behavior during incarceration and use their discretion to release the best prospects for successful reintegration early while keeping offenders who are not motivated to change in prison longer.

Discretionary parole does not require that consideration be given directly to the age of the offender. A decision to release an inmate early under supervision is made on the basis of the totality of circumstances for a particular inmate. Thus, if an elderly inmate has a long history of institutional misbehavior, continues to espouse attitudes, values and beliefs supportive of crime and is deemed a risk to society, then that particular inmate would remain imprisoned regardless of age.

Elderly prisoners experience significant challenges upon release. According to a report published by the Osborne Association (2014:9) older released prisoners' experience:

- Greater rates of homelessness
- High unemployment rates
- Increased anxiety
- Poor community and family connections
- Released with a limited supply of medicine and may experience difficulty obtaining benefits upon release which exacerbates existing medical conditions

As a result of these challenges, their outcomes upon release are not optimal.

Geriatric Release—
Considering Age and Disability

A few states offer early parole based on age or disability. Such programs are referred to as compassionate release for those who are dying or general geriatric release for more chronic medical conditions. Compassionate release refers to the courts authorization of the release of a prisoner prior to the expiration of a sentence based on "extraordinary and compelling" reasons. This practice is most often associated with early release for terminal illnesses or diseases. Compassionate release as an option was mandated by Congress in federal statute 18 U.S.C. §3582(c)(1)(A)(i). Since then several states have codified various forms of compassionate release, however in some states the code refers specifically to age-based geriatric release while others adhere to a combination of early release based on age and medical condition (Chiu 2010). As of 2011 only 5 states failed to include some sort of release mechanism for dying prisoners (Williams et al. 2011).

A number of reports have been released in the last couple of years which suggest that states and the federal government could witness significant cost-savings by implementing compassionate and geriatric release parole programs for elderly inmates (Bunting 2012; Chiu 2010; Miller 2009). Bunting (2012) estimates that taxpayers could save an estimated $28,362 per year by releasing aging state prisoners who pose little threat to the community.

Box 7-3. List of States with Geriatric Release Policies

Alabama	Missouri	Virginia
Colorado	North Carolina	Washington
Connecticut	New Mexico	Wisconsin
District of Columbia	Oklahoma	Wyoming
Louisiana	Oregon	
Maryland	Texas	

Source: Chiu, T. (2009). It's About Time: Aging Prisoners, Increasing Costs, and Geriatric Release. New York: Vera Institute of Justice.

Eligibility for geriatric release programs vary by state. The majority of states with such policies have minimum age and minimum time served requirements. Some restrict eligibility on the basis of conviction offense and prior criminal record. For example, Oklahoma requires that eligible applicants have committed their crime before 7/1/1998, be 60 years of age, and have served at least half of a sentence imposed under applicable truth-in-sentencing guidelines (Chiu 2010: 7). In contrast, the state of Maryland requires that the applicant be 65 and have served at least 15 years of a sentence for a crime of violence. Still others states such as Alabama, Colorado, the District of Columbia, and Washington incorporate age criteria with a requirement that the elderly prisoner have a medical disorder which incapacitates the prisoner to such an extent that he or she is incapable of taking care of themselves and posing a risk to society.

Unfortunately, few eligible applicants receive the privilege of early release by these measures. The eligibility criteria discussed above often preclude older inmates from participation. A 2008 Virginia Department of Corrections report revealed that the nature of offense committed by geriatric inmates and concerns for public safety were given as the most common reason by Parole Board members for not releasing geriatric prisoners (Virginia Department of Corrections 2008). Four factors are responsible for limiting the use of geriatric release:

- Political considerations and public opinion which inhibit implementation on the grounds that costs savings will not accrue or punishment is diminished (Chiu 2010);
- Eligibility criteria which exclude prisoners convicted of violent and sex offenses. Both are populations of inmates most likely to receive life sentences and the death penalty. Eligibility numbers are further reduced by criteria which require that the prisoner be so incapacitated that he or she poses no threat to public safety (Chiu 2010; Williams et al. 2011);

- Application procedures which severely limits the pool of potential applicants (Chiu 2010; Williams et al. 2011). Prisoners may not even know that early release programs exist; and
- Referral and review processes which are laborious or require extensive time to process; time which elderly and dying prisoners may not have. Many prisoners die during the review process (Chiu 2010; Williams et al. 2011).

A recent report commissioned by the Office of Inspector General (2015) was highly critical of the Federal Bureau of Prisons handling of aging and elderly prisoners.

> … Over a year ago, the Department concluded that aging inmates are generally less of a public safety threat and the BOP announced an expanded compassionate release policy to include them as part of the Attorney General's 'Smart on Crime' initiative. However, the Department significantly limited the number of inmates eligible for this expanded release policy by imposing several eligibility requirements, including that inmates be at least age 65, and we found that only two inmates had been released under this new provision (p. iii).

Thus, not much progress has been made even at the federal level.

Williams et al. (2011) argues that a primary barrier to the use of compassionate release is related to problems associated with flaws in the medical eligibility criteria. To meet most guidelines, prisoners must have a predictable terminal prognosis, be expected to die quickly, or have health or functional status that considerably undermine the justification for incarceration (p. 123). Williams argues that predicting life expectancy is difficult for certain life-threatening and terminal diseases such advanced liver, heart, and lung disease. Functional decline also proves problematic for certain terminal illnesses such as cancer where trajectories vary and are unpredictable. The net result is that requiring prediction of life expectancy of 6 months or less excludes prisoners with "… severe, but not end-stage dementia; in persistent vegetative state; or with end-stage organ disease (such oxygen-dependent chronic obstructive pulmonary disease)" (p. 123).

Fear also plays a role in limiting the utilization of geriatric release. There may as Rapaport (2013) suggests be a class of elderly prisoners who are deemed "too frightening" for the public to consider releasing early. Only two of Charles Manson's followers have been released from prison. The most recent Manson follower, Bruce Davis, who is 70 years old, was denied release by the Governor of California in February of 2013 despite the fact that he had served more than 40 years in prison and the parole board approved of his release (Associated Press 2013).

Box 7-4. BOP Elderly Offender Home Detention Program Eligibility

- Prisoner incarcerated in a federal prison for federal offense
- Must be 65 years old
- No prior history of violent crime
- Not serving a life sentence
- Served at least 10 years in prison
- Served at least 75% of entire sentence
- Not been convicted of an act of terrorism
- No history of escape or escape attempt

Home Detention

The Federal Bureau of Prisons has a program where elderly prisoners can be placed on home confinement until the end of their prison term. Home detention refers to confinement and supervision that restricts the prisoner to his or her residence continuously, except for authorized absences for work or medical care, religious services participation and education or training activities. The Elderly Offender Home Detention Pilot program was established a pilot as part of the Second Chance Act in 2008 and was implemented at every federal Bureau of Prison facility. As detailed in Box 7-4, BOP has narrowly defined eligibility criteria. The program allows elderly inmates who can provide for their own food, housing, and medical care to be released on home confinement while remaining in federal custody. Prisoners may also be subject to a home confinement fee. The prisoners are subject to increased surveillance, may wear electronic monitoring devices which notify authorities when the offender leaves a defined geographic area, and may be subject to curfews. The conditions for supervision via the Elderly Offender Home Detention program are clearly specified and failure of the prisoner to comply with terms can result in a return to prison.

Alternative Living Environments within the Institution

Rather than focusing on options which release elderly and infirm prisoners early from prison, another viable option is to expand the utilization of alternative housing options of elderly prisoners. Prisons are designed for the young and able and until recently only limited attention was given toward whether and how prisons might accommodate the needs of the elderly. The problem is so severe that Crawley and Starks (2005) coined the phrase institutional thoughtlessness to depict correctional organizational indifference to the needs of elderly prisoners. Structural examples of institutional thoughtlessness include the use of stairs, use of bunk beds, not allowing sufficient time for elderly inmates to finish activities or to get to places, being denied additional clothing or bedding in cold weather, showering in slippery stalls with no handrails or mats, having to stand in line for long periods of time to get their medications, and having to sit in hard chairs to watch television or attend classes (Crawley 2005; Sperber 2007).

To meet the needs of the elderly in prison will require that states find ways to implement cost-effective geriatric programs. The elderly in prison may require the use of chronic care clinics (Aday and Kabrill 2013; Florida Corrections Commission 2009) and health-related education programs (see Aday and Kabrill 2013: 220 and Rikard and Thompson 2007: 104). Additional security and support staff may be necessary to prevent victimization and to provide help performing routine tasks (Rikard and Thompson 2007). More recent efforts on behalf of correctional agencies to address such needs have focused on determining where within correctional settings elderly prisoners should be housed.

There is a great deal of debate over whether elderly prisoners should be segregated in specialized housing or merged with the general population or prisoners in meaningful ways (Rikard and Thompson 2007). The argument for segregating elderly prisoners rests on the belief that older and younger prisoners have different medical and mental health needs and that older inmates are safer when housed together (Aday 2003; Doron and Love 2013; Yates and Gillespie 2000; Rosefield 1993). Correctional administrators report greater confidence in shared living environments where older inmates can have a calming influence, have access to geriatric and non-geriatric services, and can build social supports (Doren and Love 2013; Rikard and Thompson 2007). The reviews on which perspective is best indicate that it depends on whose work is read. For example, a study by Marquart, Merianos, and Doucet (2000) revealed that elderly inmates experienced greater boredom, depression and isolation when placed in segregated housing.

A fairly robust literature base supports calls for specialized medical and non-medical housing units for elderly prisoners (Aday 2003; Council of State Governments 1998; Flynn 1982; Mara 2002; Morton 2001; Rikard and Rosenberg 2007). The primary requirement is that the unit or facility address the mobility issues of aging prisoners by offering handicap accessible bathrooms and wheelchair ramps, provide access to special work assignments and geriatric programming, and making available 24-hour access to nursing care. At least 15 states have implemented some form of specialized care for geriatric inmates (Chiu 2010; Gavin 2009). Such living environments often include additional pharmacy services, special diets, and supportive programming to address the mental, severe medical, nutritional, and other special needs problems often associated with the elderly and dying (Flynn 1992; LaMere et al. 1996). A Council of State Government report in 1998 recognized that there was a dearth of available facilities, services and adequately trained staff to address the needs of geriatric prisoners.

There are several models that could be deployed here. The most common option is to simply modify existing portions of prisons to create specialized geriatric units. Since nearly one third of elderly inmates will die in prison, it is not unusual to find end-of-life, hospice units attached to correctional medical facilities (Thomas et al. 2005). A second option utilized by a limited number of states has been the creation of a centralized, separate geriatric prison. Those states utilizing a central facility typically only have one and rarely two prisons dedicated to geriatric prisoners. Still others have privatized care via a competitive bidding process from vendors who manage the care of severely disabled and dying elderly prisoners within privately run nursing homes. A few states have privatized the delivery of services and care for their elderly and infirm prison population. The state of California, for example, contracts with private providers for the operation of skilled nursing facilities. Skilled nursing care facilities provide help to those prisoners who require help getting into and out of bed, and provide help those persons who require assistance with daily tasks such as feeding, bathing, and dressing. These facilities provide nursing care 24-hours a day.

Sample of U.S. Prison Programs

A vast body of literature indicates that modest investments in prison programs reduce serious and less serious institutional misconduct (French and Gendreau 2006; Serin 2005), improve prisoners' ability to cope with institutional life (Camp, Daggett, Kwon and Klein-Saffran 2008; Johnson, Larson and Pitts 1997; Winterfield, Coggeshall, Burke-Storer, Correa and Tidd 2007), and lead to more positive health outcomes (Harrison 2006; Harrison and Benedetti Whitney 2009; Loeb et al. 2006). These benefits are shared by male and female prisoners alike. Institutional security and personal safety for both staff and inmates is enhanced. Consequently, levels of violence and victimization are reduced and there is the potential to save millions in dollars in taxes as health care costs are reduced (Gendreau and Keyes 2001; Lovell and

Jemelka 1996). The benefits of enhanced programs are magnified among the elderly behind bars. The implementation of specialized programs has been associated with reductions in the number of infirmary visits and reductions in the amount of psychotropic and psychoactive medications (Harrison 2006).

True Grit Geriatric Unit in Northern Nevada Correctional Center (NNCC)

The True Grit program was established in Nevada in 2004 at the Northern Correctional Center (NNCC) which is home to the Department of Corrections Regional Medical Facility. The program was designed to be a structured living unit to motivate geriatric inmates to become active and improve their health. Structured living is defined as "a comprehensive program of structured physical, mental, psychological and spiritual programs, which have asset routing and within which the inmate is required to participate, to the best of his abilities, on a regular and on-going basis" (Harrison and Benedetti 2009: 1). The majority of offenders in the True Grit program are in their seventies.

Program Description:

1. Designed to house 120 men.
2. Admission Criteria: a) 60 years or older; b) referred by a caseworker; c) have a positive history of institutional adjustment; and d) be willing to abide by and comply with program rules.
3. Staff: Psychologist who oversees the program.
4. Activities designed to focus on cognitive functioning and physical life skills (e.g. music; wheelchair softball, tennis, basketball; pet therapy; victim awareness programs; sex offender treatment; anger management; relationship skills; and substance abuse).
5. Funding for Activities: The program is supported primarily by volunteers and donations from the community.
    a. More than half of the men in the True Grit program are veterans—University Veterans Coalition at the University of Nevada Reno, Vietnam Veterans of America, and Vet-to-Vet.
    b. End of life volunteers from faith-based organization.

Florida Programs

The state of Florida has opted to provide geriatric care in specialized housing units within existing prisons. The Department of Corrections reports that there were more than 17,000 elderly prisoners as of June 20, 2011. The units housing elderly prisoners include the south unit at the Central Florida Reception Center and the F-Dorm at the South Florida Reception Center. These reception center units afford specifically designed palliative care and provide step down care for inmates who have been released from the hospital but who are not yet ready to return to infirmary level care. Zephyrhills Correctional Institution has two dorms specifically designed to address the medical needs of elderly prisoners. To be eligible for the Zephyrhills dorms prisoners must be at least aged 59 with mental health problems. Florida also has a work camp for elderly prisoners who are in good health and able to work. The work camp at River Junction serves inmates aged 50 and over who do not have an escape history, do not have a history of violence and who are within ten years of parole.

The State of Louisiana Hospice Program at Angola

Angola prison in Louisiana houses one of the state's largest elderly prison populations. Recent estimates suggest that 85 percent of Angola's prison population will die there. The hospice program at Angola is managed by inmate volunteers who provide support and care within the prison infirmary. The program does not cost additional money. Inmates with terminal illness qualify for the program which the prognosis deems that the prisoner has only about six months to live. Each hospice patient is assigned 6 volunteers to oversee care.

The Maryland Hospice Program

The Maryland Department of Corrections established a hospice program in early 2000. The program is designed to provide hospice care to prisoners who have 6 months or less to live, have a signed do-not-resuscitate (DNR) order on file, and have given consent to participation (Boyle 2002). The program provides medical care, social work, pastoral care, mental health services to the prisoners. Bereavement services are also provided for families and inmate friends left behind. The program makes extensive use of community volunteers.

Laurel Highlands in Pennsylvania

The SCI Laurel Highlands institution houses a long-term care unit for geriatric inmates. The prison houses more than 400 prisoners who are over the age of 50 (McCarthy 2013). The prison has two skilled care units that house about 100 inmates. In addition to the skilled care units, the facility maintains a four-bed hospice that offers nutrition and chaplain services. During their stay on the unit, inmates may receive a variety of services. These include life skills programs, education, and employment for inmates who are able to work. Inmates with substance abuse problems may also receive a range of substance abuse treatment services. These services incorporate issues specific to a geriatric population, such as identifying addiction in the elderly, generational attitudes, physical changes in the elderly, and limited interpersonal skills. Psychological services often focus on such issues as depression, grief, death and dying, Alzheimer's, stress, and family issues. Recreation activities also incorporate the special needs of this population through such things as large print books and puzzles and physical exercise modified for an elderly population. The cost per inmate for Laurel Highlands is nearly 30 percent higher than for a typical prison.

The Virginia Special Needs Facility

The Virginia Department of Corrections houses geriatric inmates across a number of facilities; but has had a dedicated assisted living program at Deerfield Correctional Center since 1998. In addition to the assisted living program, a skilled-nursing medical unit was established in 2006. The Deerfield facility is a one-story, handicap accessible facility. Deerfield provides geriatric work (horticulture), mental health (cognitive skill training, large print books, computer programs, and medical programs (e.g. dementia and Alzheimer's). Age-based leisure activities such as arts, crafts, and music are also promoted. Deerfield's 2008 operating per capita was $25,395 (Virginia Department of Corrections 2008).

Conclusion

Our options for handling elderly and infirm prisoners remain much the same as in the past. We can do nothing and pretend that the problem does not exist. If we continue this trend we are essentially allowing the total number of elderly behind bars to continue to creep. An alternative approach would be to take advantage of the early release tools currently at hand and release back into the community those elderly prisoners who pose little risk to society. The release decision is not an easy one. Public fears about elderly prisoners must be alleviated. This task will require significant public service awareness campaigns to convince the public that their risk from an aging population of prisoners is minimal.

The early release decision includes other unique challenges. While the elderly might represent low risk of harm to society from new crime commission, there are significant adjustment problems which occur upon release. The elderly are slow to adapt to the outside world upon release where family support and social support networks may be minimal (Rikard and Thompson 2007). Moreover, given the significant medical and mental health problems finding housing, employment, and quality medical care may prove difficult. Elderly prisoners do not qualify for many welfare-based programs and public housing programs. Consequently, the elderly ex-offender may quickly find himself or herself homeless and once again dependent on the state for care. Attention must be given to the implementation of a more holistic approach to reentry for elderly prisoners.

Websites

For more information on the Osborne White Paper, visit http://www.osborn-eny.org/.

For more information on correctional programs for aging prisoners, visit at https://www.aca.org.

For more information on aging in prisons and programs, visit http://www.urban.org.

For more information on elderly prisoners, visit http://nicic.gov/.

References

Aday, R. (2003). *Aging prisoners, crisis in American corrections.* Westport, CT: Praeger Publishers.

Associated Press (2013). *California governor denies parole to Charles Manson Follower.* Retrieved from http://www.foxnews.com/us/2013/03/01/california-governor-denies-parole-to-former-charles-manson-follower/#ixzz2SmF7IIJ1.

Auerhahn, K. (2006). Selective incapacitation, three strikes, and the problem of aging prison populations: Using simulation modeling to see the future. *Criminology & Public Policy,* 1 (3), 353–388.

Boyle, B. (2002). The Maryland division of correction hospice program. *Journal of Palliative Medicine,* 5(5), 671–674.

Bunting, W. (2012). *A more cost effective way to deal with the elderly prisoner boom.* Retrieved from http://www.aclu.org/blog/prisoners-rights-criminal-law-reform/more-cost-effective-way-deal-elderly-prisoner-boom.

Chiu, T. (2010). *It's about time: Aging prisoners, increasing costs, and geriatric release.* New York: Vera Institute of Justice.

Corwin, P. (2001). Senioritis: Why elderly federal inmates are literally dying to get out of prison. *Journal of Contemporary Health Law Policy*, 17(2), 687–714.

Doron, I. & Love, H. (2013). Aging prisoners: A brief report of key legal and policy dilemmas. *International Journal of Criminology and Sociology*, 2, 322–327.

Florida Corrections Commission. (2008–2009). *State of Florida Correctional Medical Authority.* Annual Report. Available at www.doh.stte.fl.us.

Flynn, E. E. (1992). The graying of America's prison population. The Prison Journal, 72, 77–98.

French, S. and Gendreau, P. (2006). Reducing prison misconducts. What works! *Criminal Justice and Behavior*, 33(2), 185–218.

Gavin, S. (2009). What happens to the Correctional System When a Right to Health Care Meets Sentencing Reform? *The National Academy of Elder Law Attorneys Student Journal, 7* (2), 249–267.

Gendreau, P., & Keyes, D. (2001). Making prisons safer and more humane environments. *Canadian Journal of Criminology*, 43, 123–130.

General Accounting Office Report (2012). *GAO-12-807R Incarceration costs and elderly offender pilot results.* Available at http://www.gao.gov/assets/600/593089.pdf.

Harrison, M. (2006). True Grit: An innovative program for elderly inmates. *Corrections Today*, 68(7): 44–49. Available at http://www.aca.org/fileupload/177/prasannak/Stewart_dec06.pdf.

Harrison, M. & Benedetti, J. (2009). Comprehensive geriatric programs in a time of shrinking resources. Available at https://www.aca.org/fileupload/177/ahaidar/Harrison_Benedetti.pdf.

Human Rights Watch (2012). *Old behind bars: The aging prison population of the United States.* Available at http://www.hrw.org/sites/default/files/reports/usprisons0112webwcover_0.pdf.

Johnson, B., Larsen, D. & Pitts, T. (1997). Religious Programs, Institutional Adjustment, and Recidivism among Former Inmates in Prison Fellowship Programs. *Justice Quarterly*, 14 (1), 145–166.

Kim, K. & Peterson, B. (2014). *Aging behind bars: Trends and implications of graying prisoners in the federal prison system.* The Urban Institute. Retrieved from http://www.urban.org/research/publication/aging-behind-bars-trends-and-implications-graying-prisoners-federal-prison-system.

Kozlov, E. (2008). *Aging while incarcerated: A qualitative study of geriatric prisoners in America.* A Thesis submitted to Wesleyan University.

LaMere, S., Smyer, T., and Gragert, M. (1996). The aging inmate. *Journal of Psychosocial Nursing Mental Health Services*, 34 (4), 25–29.

Laub, J. H. and Sampson, R. J. (2003). *Shared beginnings, divergent lives*. Cambridge, MA: Harvard University Press.

Loeb, Susan J., and Steffensmeier, Darrell. 2006. Older male prisoners: Health status, self-efficacy beliefs, and health-promoting behaviors. *Journal of Correctional Health Care*, 12 (4), 269–278.

Loeb, Susan J.; Steffensmeier, Darrell; and Lawrence, Frank. (2008). Comparing incarcerated and community-dwelling older men's health. *Western Journal of Nursing Research*, 30 (2), 234–249.

Loeb, S. J., and AbuDagga, A. (2006). Health-related research on older inmates: An integrative review. *Research in Nursing & Health*, 29 (6), 556–565.

Lovell, D., & Jemelka, R. (1996). When inmates misbehave: The costs of discipline. *Prison Journal*, 76, 165–179.

Mara, C. (2002). Expansion of long-term care in the prison system: An aging inmate population poses policy and programmatic questions. *Journal of Aging & Social Policy*, 14 (2), 43–61.

Marquart, J., Merianos, D. & Doucet, G. (2000). The health related concerns of older prisoners: Implications for policy. *Ageing and Society*, 20: 79–96.

McCarthy, K. (2013). *State initiatives to address aging prisoners. OLR research report*. Retrieved from http://www.cga.ct.gov/2013/rpt/2013-R-0166.htm.

Miller, D. (2009). Sentencing elderly criminal offenders. *National Academy of Elder Law Attorneys Student Journal*, 4, 25–48.

Morton, Joann Brown. (2001). Implications for corrections of an aging prison population. *Corrections Management Quarterly*, 5 (1), 78–88.

Office of Inspector General (2015). *The impact of an aging inmate population on the federal bureau of prisons*. U.S. Department of Justice, Evaluation and Inspection Division. Retrieved from https://oig.justice.gov/reports/2015/e1505.pdf.

Osborne Association (2014). *The high costs of low risk: The crisis of America's aging prison population*. Retrieved from http://www.osborneny.org/images/uploads/printMedia/Osborne_Aging_WhitePaper.pdf.

Rapaport, E. (2013). *You can't get there from here: Elderly prisoners, prison downsizing, and the insufficiency of cost cutting advocacy*. Retrieved from SSRN: http://ssrn.com/abstract=2254691 or http://dx.doi.org/10.2139/ssrn.2254691.

Rikard, R. V., and Rosenberg, Ed. 2007. Aging inmates: A convergence of trends in the American criminal justice system. *Journal of Correctional Health Care*, 13 (3), 150–162.

Scott D. Camp, Dawn M. Daggett, Okyun Kwon and Jody Klein-Saffran (2008). The effect of faith program participation on prison misconduct: The Life Connections Program, *Journal of Criminal Justice*, 36(5), 389–395.

Serin, R. (2005). *Principles for enhancing correctional results in prisons*. National Institute of Corrections. Retrieved from http://static.nicic.gov/Library/023360.pdf.

Steffensmeier, D. J. et al., (1989). Age and the distribution of crime. *American Journal of Sociology*, 94(4), 803–831.

Thomas, D., Thomas, J. & Greenberg, S. (2005). The graying of corrections-The management of older inmates. In S. Stojkovic (Ed.), *Managing special populations in jails and prisons*. Kingston, NJ: Civic Research Institute.

Virginia Department of Corrections. (2008). *A Balanced Approach. Act Chapter 879 Item 387-B.*

Washington State Engrossed House Bill Report (2009). HB 2194.

Whitney, E. (2009). Correctional rehabilitation programs and the adoption of international standards: How the United States can reduce recidivism and promote the national interest. *Transnational Law & Contemporary Problems*, 18, 777–809.

Williams, B. & Abraldes, R. (2007). Growing older: Challenges of prison and reentry for the aging population, in Robert Greifinger, ed., *Public Health Behind Bars: From Prisons to Communities*. New York: Springer.

Williams, B., Sudore, R., Greifinger, R., and Morrison, S. (2011). Balancing punishment and compassion for seriously ill prisoners. *Annals of Internal Medicine*, 155(2), 122–125.

Winterfield, L., Coggeshall, M., Burke-Storer, M, Correa, V. & Tidd, S. (2007). *The effects of postsecondary correctional education*. Urban Institute Justice Policy Center. Retrieved from http://www.urban.org/uploadedpdf/411952_pse_final_5_29_09_webedited.pdf.

Court Cases

United States v. Carey, 895 F. 2d 318, 324 (7th Cir. 1990)
United States v. Harrison, 970 F. 2d 444, 447 (8th Cir. 1992)
United States v. Tolson, 760 F. Supp. 1322, 1330–31 (N.D. Ind. 1991)

Chapter 8

An Ethic of Care

> Simply seeing a need for care is not enough to make care happen; someone has to assume the responsibility for organizing, marshaling resources or personnel, and paying for the care work that will meet the identified need (Tronto 1998: 17).

The 'get tough on crime' movement, through its focus on increased punishment, had a foreseeable legacy which resulted in increases in the prison population and escalating costs. Consequently, many academics now question its continuing utility. For correctional scholars such as Francis Cullen (2013: 645), "The punishment paradigm has reached the point of exhaustion. After three decades of mean-spirited rhetoric, efforts to mandate harsh sanctions, and prison populations surpassing record highs annually, this approach has achieved all it is going to achieve." This punishment orientation contrasts starkly when compared to the original purpose of the penitentiary. At its inception in the United States, prisons by design were created to provide a place where wrongdoers could do penance and be afforded an opportunity for reformation or rehabilitation. Current research literature undeniably indicates that punishment alone does not work and in fact potentially causes more harm than good (Chen and Shapiro 2007; Gendreau et al. 2000). Even our finest empirically driven studies at best suggest a negligible impact on recidivism from punishment-oriented offender programs (Lipsey 1999; MacKenzie 2006; Petersilia and Turner 1993; Petrosino et al. 2003). More important, the public, just as the Quakers intended in the beginning, has consistently indicated that they want prison to **punish** and **reform** (Cullen and Moon 2002; Cullen et al. 2007). To some, we are set on a path which keeps older prisoners incarcerated well beyond their ability to be released back into society as productive citizens. So unless the singular purpose of prison is retribution, it makes little sense to keep older offenders imprisoned until either life's end or almost life's end if the original goal was penance (i.e., to provide an opportunity for reflection and ultimately earn forgiveness) or rehabilitation (i.e., to eventually re-socialize them to become productive members of society).

What we know about the elderly prison population is that 1) whether as a result of lifestyle or their experience during incarceration, they prematurely exhibit geriatric medical and mental conditions; 2) the population of elderly inmates is growing; 3) we are not at present adequately meeting their needs; and 4) current policies are not cost effective. Such issues call into question the entire purpose of prison for elderly and aging prisoners. Moreover, this becomes more than just a philosophical argument because it has long been established that prison inmates have a constitutional right to adequate and appropriate care and that the government is obligated to provide such care (see *Estelle v. Gamble 1976* or *Brown v. Plata 2011*). Following this line of reasoning, deliberate indifference to the needs of elderly prisoners constitutes a violation of the Eighth Amendment's protection against cruel and unusual punishment.

Yet, many correctional organizations appear incapable of providing adequate levels of medical care and other related services to prison populations (Williams et al. 2013). This fact is especially salient for the elderly in prison who are less healthy and have greater needs than their younger counterparts (Habes 2011). The elderly prisoner, as a practical matter, has historically been ignored by society. Correctional administrators and corresponding policies have tended to focus on younger prisoners rather than to assess and mold practices for the old. This focus led to disparate treatment that places elderly prisoners at a distinct disadvantage during incarceration and upon release; and has as is currently the case in California led to entire correctional systems being placed under receivership (Habes 2011). The lack of attention given to elderly prisoners' concerns is often referred to as a 'latent form of ageism' (Wahadin 2004: 11) or abuse.

Extant literature indicates that elderly prisoners develop unique mental, physical, and behavioral problems behind prison walls that should elevate the amount of attention they receive. For example, elderly prisoners exhibit much higher rates of diabetes, high-blood pressure, cancer, heart disease, liver disease, and the like which has increased the cost of providing for their care to astronomical levels (Aday 2003; Baillargeon et al. 2007; Binswanger et al. 2009; Williams et al. 2012). They are also more likely to have significant mobility challenges, age-related sensory degeneration (eye sight and vision problems), to have trouble accomplishing daily routine tasks such as eating, dressing, and bathing (Williams et al. 2012). Moreover, recent research indicates that institutionalized elderly men require more time in bed in order to recover from injury or illness than men of the same age in general population (Curtin 2007).

Additionally, the elderly in prison experience age-related psychological decline at a much greater rate than found in the general population (Curtin 2007). It is not uncommon to find dementia among the oldest of the incarcerated. This psychological decline can also be attributed to the damaging nature of the prison experience on the psyche itself. According to Crawley and Sparks (2005) the elderly and long-term inmate prison experience is equivalent to the damage experienced by a survivor of a disaster. Some, the long-term elderly prisoner to be sure, have been incarcerated so long as to have become institutionalized and perhaps are incapable of returning to society as productive citizens. Release problems are compounded by the fact that many of the long-term and elderly prisoners have had limited contact with the outside world (Kerbs 2000; Davies 2012).

Given all of these needs, it is not surprising that such prisoners cost more to incarcerate, upwards of $70,000 per year according to the ACLU (2012). One would think that state and federal governments would give considerable attention to prevention and creative programming to offset cost. Rather than focus or prevention, many states have turned towards fee systems for economic relief. California is probably the best example of this. In 1994, California began charging prisoners five dollar co-pays for each medical visit, a figure far too high for inmates earning fifteen cents per hour at their jobs (Habes 2011). In addition, to charging a co-pay for medical services, California prisons "take forty percent out of each prison worker's wages in order to pay for devices such as wheel chairs, glasses, and dental implants" (Habes 2011: 403). A few states have explored early release options. Unfortunately, such states despite having changed their statutes to allow early release fail to grant release to the majority of those eligible (Chiu 2010). Early release is a rarely used option and consequently, does little to alleviate the ever increasing ranks of the elderly and infirm behind bars.

We have reached a crisis point, where more than 124,000 state and federal prisoners were aged 55 or older as a result of an over reliance on a punitive, retributive system (Human Rights Watch 2012). An approach deemed rational and one which demands punishment to satisfy justice. Regrettably, we never answered the question about how much punishment is enough. For the elderly, infirm, and long-term inmate, it is safe to say that perhaps we have punished them to the point where they no longer have the capacity to be contributing members of society. Moreover, what should be clear by now is that we cannot continue with the current treatment (long-term incarceration well beyond the need to do so) of elderly prisoners. Their needs are too great, their care too expensive, and the end state of being with regard to punishment under the current system is questionable. The majority of advocates who call for transformation of the system rely on cost to justify early release and alternative living arrangements for elderly prisoners. As Rapaport (2013) rightly points out, cost alone is an insufficient justification for change. Neglected in this exchange is that there is an underlying moral and ethical imperative related to our relationships with each other and the drive for caring that makes us human which can and should drive transformations of our correctional policies and practices.

An Ethic of Care Perspective

Applied ethics, the study of how we ought to behave in situations involving human care, provides a framework for analyzing and improving the level of service and care provided to elderly prisoners during and upon release (Holsten and Mitzen 2001). Care is (an) "activity that includes everything that we do to maintain, continue, and repair our 'world' so that we can live in it as well as possible" (Fisher and Tronto 1990: 40). Traditionally, the concept of care refers to a feeling of empathy, sympathy, and concern for others. But care is also about the actions and practices that we take as a result of those concerns. From the ethic of care perspective, how we care for one another is an essential feature of what makes us human and gives us a meaningful life by focusing on the actions and practices that constitute the ethics of care. Moreover, the ethic of care paradigm provides a moral compass for decisions and aids in discerning right from wrong policies. Caring, at the same time, is a process that can occur in a variety of settings; yes, even within the institutional setting of prison.

Caring requires judgment and making the best judgment becomes the moral task of engaging in care. For people working in positions where they must provide care the ethic of care perspective provides a framework for analyzing the process of care and making moral and ethical decisions about how to care. The failure to provide care represents an abuse of power which harms us as individuals and as a collective society. Simply seeing a need for care is not enough to make care happen; someone has to assume the responsibility for organizing, marshaling resources or personnel, and paying for the care work that will meet the identified need. (Tronto 1998: 17).

Tronto (1994) also posits four elements that are necessary for effective caring. Effective caring and good care require action, awareness, and a unified, holistic approach to care reflected within the elements themselves. The dimensions are:

Box 8-1. Questions that Arise from Dimensions of the Ethic of Care

Attentiveness:
What care is necessary? Are there basic human needs? What types of care now exist; how adequate are they? Who get to articulate the nature of needs and to say what and how problems should be cared about?

Responsibility:
Who should be responsible for meeting the needs for care that do exist? How can and should such responsibility be fixed? Why?

Competence:
Who actually are the caregivers? How well do they their work? What conflicts exist between them and care receivers? What resources do caregivers need in order to care competently? Who pays attention to changes in care receivers' needs?

Responsiveness:
How do care receivers respond to the care that is given? How well does the care process, as it exists, meet their needs? If their needs conflict with one another, who resolves these conflicts?

Source: Modified version of Figure 5 in Tronto (2001).
Note: Modified Figure 5.1 presented in Tronto (2001, p. 66).

---

(1) Attentiveness, a proclivity to become aware of need;
(2) Responsibility, a willingness to respond and take care of need;
(3) Competence, the skill of providing good and successful care; and
(4) Responsiveness, consideration of the position of others as they see it and recognition of the potential for abuse in care (1994, 126–136).

The elderly are one of the most vulnerable populations in need of care. It is well recognized that because the process of aging through mental and physical degeneration that many of the elderly are placed in situations where they are forced to rely on the assistance of others, where their sense of power in relation to their independent ability to care for themselves shifts to others. This process of needing and providing care is a natural part of human life regardless of whether the person is institutionalized or free in the outside world. An ethic of care need not diminish our goal to punish wrongdoers. Instead, it can serve as an analytical, ethical guide about how and whether we should continue to punish during that most vulnerable period towards the end of human life.

The Application of an Ethic of Care for the Elderly in Prison

Intending to provide care … but then failing to provide good care, means that in the end the need for care is not met (Tronto 1993: 133).

The review of the literature contained in this volume has four primary implications. First, correctional administrators and politicians must recognize that elderly and long-term inmates are likely to prematurely exhibit geriatric medical conditions. Second, we have to accept that current practices are not meeting elderly prisoner's most basic needs and that we need to do a better job. This is not a choice but the provision of better medical, mental health, and structural care is a constitutional obligation. Third, our failure to provide adequate care has driven costs up rather than down. Last, to address the misdeeds of the past we must consider reasonable alternatives to decrease the elderly prison population such as compassionate release and unconventional living arrangements for older prisoners. If we address these issues effectively, caring institutional environments for the elderly prisoner will become the norm rather than the exception.

Unfortunately calls for caring institutional environments and caring dispositions, whilst undeniably sensible, do little to suggest how they are to be realized. According to Tronto good institutional care will be 'highly deliberate and explicit about how to best meet the needs of the people they serve' (2010: 169). The way forward has already been identified by others. There has been an explosion in the literature detailing the challenges of the elderly and long-term prisoner (ACLU 2012; Aday 2003; Kozlov 2008; Rikard & Rosenberg 2007). My goal here is to frame the research in terms of the moral dimensions of an ethic of care for the elderly who are incarcerated. Good care requires the implementation of an integrated holistic approach to elderly prison practice in which those who care about the issues associated with elderly and long-term prisoners and are charged with their care take responsibility, provide care, and modify practice as necessary.

Attentiveness—Effective caring requires that we be attentive to the needs of elderly prisoners. Caring involves becoming aware of and paying attention the need for caring. We must understand the elderly prison population and its needs.

- Attentiveness starts by defining the population of interest. There is little consensus as to what age constitutes older, geriatric, elderly or long-term (Williams et al. 2012a; Williams et al. 2012b).

- Define prison-based functional impairment (Williams et al. 2012a; Williams et al. 2012b).
- Expand research on the specific needs of elderly prisoners (Williams et al. 2012b).

Responsibility—Good care call for correctional systems and workers to assume responsibility to meet a need once identified. Simply recognizing that elderly prisoners have unique needs is insufficient; someone has to assume the responsibility for "organizing, marshalling resources or personnel, and paying for the care work that will meet the identified needs" (Tronto 2001: 63). Responsibility is an essential moral dimension of care.

- Improve classification and assessment (Habes 2011; Osborne Associations 2014; Office of the Inspector General 2015);
- Develop a dementia screening tool (Williams et al. 2012b);
- Expand palliative care which focuses on providing guidance and symptom control for seriously ill people (Mara 2002; 2004; Sterns, et al. 20008; Wahidin 2004; Williams et al. 2012b);
- Expand other health care programs to meet needs of the agency, example, physical therapy, special diets, preventive care, and end of life care (Granse 2003; Habes 2011; Mara 2002; 2004; Snyder et. al 2009; Sterns, et al. 2008; Yates & Gillespie 2000);
- Utilize alternative living arrangements within institutions (Gavin 2009; Habes 2011; Rikard & Thompson 2007; Snyder et. al 2009; Williams et al. 2012b);
- Ensure prison facilities are ADA compliant and meet the needs of the elderly. For example, ensuring wheel chair access, ramps, hand rails, shorter walks to dining hall (Kerbs 2006; Mara 2002; Office of Inspector General 2015; Sterns, et al. 2008; Snyder et al. 2009);
- Implement programs that address the social and emotional needs of elderly and long-term prisoners (Sterns, et al. 2008; Snyder et. al 2009);
- Increase the number of companion programs and develop guidelines for their implementation (Office of Inspector General 2015);
- Provide recreational and work opportunities for the elderly (Office of Inspector General 2015; Sterns, et al. 2008; Snyder et. al 2009);
- Consider implementing early release mechanisms (Bunting 2012; Chiu 2010; Gavin 2009; Habes 2011; Human Rights Watch 2012; Office of Inspector General 2015; Snyder et. al 2009; Williams et al. 2012a; Williams et al. 2012b); and
- Provide release preparation programming (Davies 2012; Habes 2011; Office of Inspector General 2015; Sterns et al. 2008).

Competence—Competence refers to the actual meeting of the caring need. It is the act of individuals and organizations performing the requisite caring tasks to meet needs. From this perspective, incompetent care is a moral failing.

> Good care requires the competence to individualize care—to give care that is based on the physical, psychological, cultural, and spiritual needs of the patient and family (Vanlaere and Gastmans 2011). Good care is aimed at helping the person be as independent as possible, yet safe. Good care needs to be delivered competently, while considering the patient's context (Lachman 2012: 114).
> - Consider placing more social workers in institutions (Office of Inspector General 2015).
> - Train staff and health care providers on aging (Gavin 2009; Sterns, et al. 2008; Williams et al. 2012).
> - For specialized facilities, hospice for example, hire staff that specializes in geriatric care (Gavin 2009).

Responsiveness—The elderly in prison are vulnerable to the action or lack of action of correctional officials. "Responsiveness is complex because it shares the moral burden among the person, thing, or group that has received the care, but it also involves the moral attention of the ones who are doing the caring work and those who are responsible for care" (Tronto 2001: 63). Being responsive means also recognizing that needs are not static but dynamic. Consequently, any single caring act has the potential to create new needs which will require attention. There is an inherent reciprocal relationship between the elderly inmate and the state. The state is obligated to provide adequate care; and that care when provided should meet the needs of the prisoner. The elderly in prison have many needs which evolve over time. To provide good care will require constant monitoring and adjusting of the system to ensure good care.

- Monitor the geriatric population behind bars (HRW 2012; Virginia Department of Corrections).
- Ensure that a senior official has the specific responsibility for monitoring, assessing, and pressing for improvements in confinement conditions for older prisoners (HRW 2013: 13).

Conclusion

A critique of the approach recommended here is that there will always be far more needs among elderly offenders than the state can address. Conflict over whether and how to meet the needs of elderly prisoners remains; yet, we must recognize that coming to some resolution of this conflict is part of the "essence" of caring and requires thoughtful judgment about what constitutes moral and ethical care for those who are aging behind bars. The next step is for correctional administrators and policy-makers to integrate theory, research and practice to develop a more holistic approach to the provision of care to those most vulnerable towards the end-of-life and who reside behind institutional walls. Such an approach is not merely the fiscally responsible thing to do; it is a morally and legally justifiable course of action. An ethics of care approach does not deny our need to punish wrongdoers. Instead, this approach demands that we ask ourselves what is the right thing to do towards the end of human life for prisoners. And once we arrive at an ethically sound decision some action follows. The path to ethical care for elderly prisoners has already been prescribed within the literature. It is time now to move beyond rhetoric and translate this body of work into practice.

Perhaps as Doron and Love (2013: 323) assert the place to begin is with the UN adopting a specific human rights convention for older persons. While Article 1 of the UN 1990 Basic Principles for the Treatment of Prisoners states that "all prisoners shall be treated with respect," the concept of respect is not defined for specific prisoner populations. A declaration from the UN might prove to be the additional incentive that is needed to move American penal policy forward from rhetoric to reality. As a society we are aging and now is the appropriate time to recognize that the older population is multidimensional in nature and require special handling during incarceration and upon release.

Websites

For more information on the United Nations and human rights, visit http:// www.un.org.

For more information on the American Civil Liberties Union and aging in prison, visit https://www.aclu.org/.

For more information on the Osborne White Paper, visit http://www.osborn-eny.org/.

For more information on responding to the needs of elderly prisoners, visit http://nicic.gov.

References

ACLU (2012). At America's expense: The mass incarceration of the elderly. Retrieved March 9, 2013 from https://www.aclu.org/files/assets/elderlyprison report_20120613_1.pdf.

Aday, R. (2003). Aging prisoners: Crisis in American corrections. Westport, CT: Praeger Publishers.

Bailargeon, J., Soloway, R. Paar, D., Giordano, T., Murray, O., Grady, J., Williams, B., Pulvino, J., & Raimer, B. (2007). End-stage liver disease in a state prison population. *Annals of Epidemiology,* 17(10), 808–813.

Binswanger, I., Krueger, P., & Steiner, J. (2009). Prevalence of chronic medical conditions among jail and prison inmates in the USA compared with the general population. *Journal of Epidemiology Community Health,* 63(11), 912–919.

Bunting, W. (2012). A more cost effective way to deal with the elderly prisoner boom. Retrieved April 11, 2013 from http://www.aclu.org/blog/ prisoners-rights-criminal-law-reform/more-cost-effective-way-deal-elderly-prisoner-boom.

Chen, M., Shapiro, K., & Shapiro, J. (2007). Do harsher prison conditions reduce recidivism? Does prison harden inmates? A discontinuity-cased approach. *American Law and Economic Review,* 9(1), 1–29.

Chiu, T. (2010). *It's about time: Aging prisoners, increasing costs, and geriatric release.* New York: Vera Institute of Justice.

Crawley, E. & Sparks, R. (2005). Older men in prison: Survival, coping and identity. In A. Liebling and S. Maruna (Eds.) *The Effects of Imprisonment.* Cullompton: Willan Publishing.

Cullen, F. & Moon, M. (2002). Reaffirming rehabilitation: Public support for correctional treatment. In Harry E. Allen (Ed.), What Works—Risk Reduction: Interventions for Special Needs Offenders. Lanham, Md.: American Correctional Association.

Cullen, F., Vose, B., Johnson, E. & Unnever, J. (2007). Public support for early intervention: Is child saving a "habit of the heart"? *Victims and Offenders,* 2, 109–124.

Curtin, T. (2007). The continuing problem of America's aging prison population and the search for a cost-effective and socially acceptable means of addressing it. *Elder Law Journal,* 15, 473–502.

Davies, M. (2012). The reintegration of elderly prisoners: An exploration of services provided in England and Wales. *Internet Journal of Criminology.* Retrieved May 10, 2013 from http:www.internetjournalofcriminology.com.

Doron, I. & Love, H. (2013). Aging prisoners: A brief report of key legal and policy dilemmas. *International Journal of Criminology and Sociology*, 2, 322–327.

Fisher, B. & Tronto, J. (1990). Toward a feminist theory of caring. In E. Abel and M. Nelson (Eds.) *Circles of Care*, SUNY Press (pp. 36–54). Albany: New York.

Gavin, S. (2009). What happens to the correctional system when a right to health care meets sentencing reform? *The National Academy of Elder Law Attorneys Student Journal*, 7 (2), 249–267.

Gendreau, P., Goggin, C., Cullen, F., & Andrews, D. (2000). The effects of community sanctions and incarceration on recidivism. *Forum on Corrections Research*, 12, 0–13.

Granse, B. (2003). Why should we even care? Hospice social work practice in a prison setting. *Smith College Studies in Social Work*, 73, 359–376.

Habes, H. (2011). Paying for the graying: How California can more effectively manage its growing elderly inmate population, *S. CAL. INTERDISC. L.J.*, 20, 395–423.

Holstein, M. & Mitzen, P. (2001). Elders in the community: Moral lives, moral quandaries. In Martha Holstein (Ed.) *Voices of Community Care: Ethics, Aging, and Caring Practice* (pp. 3–18). New York: Springer Publishing Company.

Kerbs, J. (2000a). Arguments and strategies for the selective decarceration of older prisoners. In M.B. Rothman, B.D. Dunlap, & P. Entzel (Eds.), *Elders, Crime, and The Criminal Justice System* (pp. 229–250).

Kerbs, J. (2000b). The older prisoner: Social, psychological, and medical considerations. In M.B. Rothman, B.D. Dunlap, & P. Entzel (Eds.), *Elders, Crime, and The Criminal Justice System* (pp. 207–228).

Kozlov, E. (2008). *Aging while incarcerated: A qualitative study of geriatric prisoners in America.* A Thesis submitted to Wesleyan University.

Lachman, V. (2012). Applying the ethics of care to your nursing practice. *Ethics, Law, and Policy*, 21(2), 112–116.

Lipsey, M. (1999). Can intervention rehabilitate serious delinquents? *Annals of the American Association of Political and Social Science*, 564, 142–166.

MacKenzie, D. L. (2006). What Works in Corrections: Reducing the Criminal Activities of Offenders and Delinquents. New York; Cambridge University Press.

Mara, C. M. (2002). Expansion of long-term care in the prison system: An aging inmate population poses policy and programmatic questions. *Journal of Aging & Social Policy, 14(2)*, 43–61.

Mara, C. M. (2004). Chronic illness, disability, and long-term care in the prison setting. In P. Katz, M.D. Mezey, & M. Kapp (Eds.). Vulnerable Populations in the Long Term Care Continuum (pp. 39–56). New York: Springer.

Petersilia, J. & Turner, S. (1993). Intensive probation and parole. In Michael Tonry (Ed.), *Crime and Justice A Review of the Research*, 17. Chicago, IL: University of Chicago Press.

Petrosino, A., Turpin-Petrosino, C., & Buehler, J. (2003). Scared straight and other juvenile awareness programs for preventing juvenile delinquent: A systematic review of the randomized experimental evidence. *Annals of the American Academy of Political and Social Science*, 589, 41–62.

Rikard, R. V. & Rosenberg, E. (2007). Aging inmates: A convergence of trends in the American criminal justice system. *Journal of Correctional Health Care*, 13 (3), 150–162.

Rikard, R. & Thompson, M. (2007). The Association between aging inmate housing management models and non-geriatric health services in state correctional institutions. *Journal of Aging & Social Policy*, 19(4), 39–56.

Snyder, C., Wormer, K., Chadha, J., & Jaggers, J. (2009). Older adult inmates: The challenge for social work. *Social Work*, 54(2), 117–124.

Sterns, A., Lax, G., Sed, C., Keohane, P. & Sterns, R. (2008). The growing wave of older prisoners: A national survey of older prisoner health, mental health, and programming. *Corrections Today*, 70, 70–76.

Tronto, J. (1993). *Moral Boundaries. A Political Argument for an Ethic of Care*. New York: Routledge.

Tronto, J. C. (1998). An ethic of care. *Generations: Journal of the American Society on Aging*, 22(3), 15–19.

Tronto, J. C. (2001). An ethic of care. In Martha Hostein (Ed.) *Voices of Community Care: Ethics, Aging, and Caring Practice* (pp. 60–68). New York: Springer Publishing Company.

Vanlaere, L., & Gastmans, C. (2011). A personalistic approach to care ethics. *Nursing Ethics*, 18, 161–173.

Virginia Department of Corrections (2008). *A Balanced Approach. Virginia Department of Corrections 2008 Appropriations Act Chapter 879 Item 387-B "Assisted Living Facilities for Geriatric Inmates.*

Wahadin, A. (2004) *Older Women in the Criminal Justice System: Running Out of Time*, London: Jessica Kingsley Publishers.

Williams, B., Stern, M., Mellow, J., Safer, M. & Greifinger, R. (2012a). Aging in correctional custody: Setting a policy agenda for older prisoner health care. *American Journal of Public Health*, 102(8), 1475–1481.

Williams, B.; Sudore, R., Greifinger, R., & Morrison, R. (2012b). *Responding to the Needs of an Aging Prison Population*. Retrieved May 12, 2013 from http://nicic.gov/Library/026453.

Yates, J. & Gillespie, W. (2000). The elderly and prison policy. *Journal of Aging & Social Policy*, 11(2), 167–175.

Court Cases

Brown v. Plata, 563 U.S. (2011)
Estelle v. Gamble, 429 U.S. 97, 103–104 (1976)

Index

adaptation, 38, 41, 42, 80, 114, 167
adjustment, 38, 41, 42, 45–47, 58,
   71, 72, 155, 166, 188, 191, 192
   maladjustment, 41, 132
administrator, 49, 51, 52, 121
admission, 77, 112, 129, 165
African-American, 33, 35, 63, 140,
   159–161
age cutoff, 21, 55
age out of crime, 19, 43, 178
age-related, 4, 67, 73, 111, 168, 196,
   197
AIDS, 17, 58, 77, 81, 82, 85, 87, 90,
   92, 93, 104, 113–115, 117, 120, 198
alcohol, 58, 80, 94, 104–106, 144, 151
alternative reimbursement, 109
alternative sentencing, 20
Alzheimer's Disease, 79, 134, 135,
   147, 149, 152
Americans with Disabilities Act, 54
Anti-Drug Abuse Acts, 6
anxiety, 39, 51, 67, 121, 127, 129,
   136, 137, 143, 144, 147, 148, 152,
   168, 170, 182
   prevalence in correctional settings,
     95
arrest, 52, 127

assessment, 49, 70, 111, 115, 117,
   145, 148, 149, 151, 201
assisted living, 79, 190, 206
Asthma, 93, 96, 97, 112, 114, 163
attentiveness, 199, 200
behavior, 41, 45, 47, 49, 50, 72, 80,
   82, 90, 114, 117, 120, 125, 138,
   144, 145, 148, 150, 166, 176, 181,
   192
bereavement services, 189
best practices, 110
blindness, 80, 83, 96–98
Brown v. Plata, 196, 207
Bureau of Justice Statistics, 7, 12, 13,
   23–25, 31, 36, 45–48, 59–65, 69,
   71, 76, 89, 91–93, 99, 101–107,
   112, 113, 118, 119, 121, 126, 127,
   129, 131, 147, 149–151, 158, 161,
   162, 165, 172–174
California, 15, 32, 34, 38, 48, 50, 63,
   73, 78, 87, 88, 111, 117, 159, 173,
   184, 187, 191, 196, 197, 205
cancer, 66, 93, 96, 97, 104–106, 131,
   142, 184, 196
Centers for Disease Control, 82, 85–
   87, 90, 91, 94, 95, 97–99, 112–
   114, 117, 133, 138, 139, 147

Central Florida Reception Center, 189
Chlamydia, 81, 82, 85, 86, 113
Chronic Illnesses, 17, 96, 100, 104
    Asthma, 93, 96, 97, 112, 114, 163
    Diabetes, 3, 66, 93, 96–98, 101,
        113, 130, 136, 196
    Heart Disease, 66, 96, 98–100,
        104–106, 120, 122, 131, 133,
        136, 196
    Hypertension, 93, 96, 97, 99, 113,
        114, 163
classification, 57, 201
Colitis, 163
Communicable disease, 81, 110, 112,
    122
    Chlamydia, 81, 82, 85, 86, 113
    Gonorrhea, 81–83, 85, 113
    Hepatitis, 77, 80–82, 93–96, 113,
        114, 117, 118, 120, 163
    HIV, 77, 81–83, 85–87, 90, 92,
        93, 95, 113–120, 122, 144, 163
    Sexually Transmitted Disease, 82,
        85, 86
    Syphilis, 81–84, 113, 120, 122
    Trichomoniasis, 81–83, 86
    Tuberculosis, 77, 81, 82, 91–94,
        112–114, 116–118, 121, 122
competence, 199, 202
confinement conditions, 202
co-payments, 108
coping strategies, 142, 146
costs, 3, 7, 12–16, 17, 20, 22, 23, 26–
    28, 38, 44, 47, 48, 51, 53, 54, 68,
    75–79, 84, 90, 97, 104, 108–111,
    117, 166, 171, 177–180, 183, 187,
    192, 193, 195, 200, 204
    high cost of incarceration, 12–16
    reducing costs for medical care,
        108–109
crime rate, 27, 42
criminal career, 48
cruel and unusual punishment, 45,
    108, 196

deafness, 97
Deerfield, 190
degeneration, 67, 133, 135, 196, 199
dementia, 17, 67, 83, 111, 125, 129,
    131, 133–136, 147, 148, 168, 173,
    184, 190, 197, 201
    prevalence in correctional settings,
        95
depression, 39–41, 67, 96, 121, 123,
    127, 129, 132–134, 136, 142–144,
    146, 147, 149, 151, 166, 168, 170,
    186, 190
    prevalence in correctional settings,
        95
deprivation, 38, 40, 121, 149, 167
determinate sanctions, 28
deterrence, 4, 5
Diabetes, 3, 66, 93, 96–98, 101, 113,
    130, 136, 196
discharge planning, 110, 111
disciplinary infractions, 39, 41
do nothing, 179, 190
drug, 5–7, 20, 25, 31, 32, 34–36,
    46, 58, 62, 76, 80, 104–106, 117,
    148, 164
drug offenders, 6
early release, 22, 52, 108, 109, 125,
    177, 179–184, 190, 191, 197, 198,
    201
Eighth Amendment, 196
elderly, 3–27, 51–73, 75–81, 96, 104,
    108–112, 114, 119, 120, 122–124,
    133, 134, 142, 145, 146, 148, 155,
    158, 163, 166, 168, 170, 171, 173,
    175, 177–180, 182–193, 196–206
    defining elderly, 53, 55
    elderly in prison, 17, 18, 51, 66,
        70, 155, 168, 180, 186, 196,
        197, 200, 202
    female elderly, 63, 65
    national estimates, 29, 54
    needs of elderly, 22, 65, 68, 69, 76,
        78, 186, 189, 196, 200, 201, 203

profile of elderly, 68
types of elderly prisoners, 57–58
eligibility criteria, 183–185
Estelle v. Gamble, 80, 114, 196, 207
ethic of care, 20, 21, 195–207
  application, 152, 184, 200
  attentiveness, 199, 200
  care definition, 20
  competence, 199, 202
  elements of effective caring, 198–202
  perspective, 20, 24, 29, 70, 80, 112, 121, 147, 175, 178–180, 186, 198, 202
  responsibility, 125, 147, 148, 195, 198–202
  responsiveness, 199, 202
evidence, 22, 43, 90, 94, 95, 101, 104, 110, 119, 123, 126, 142, 145, 165, 170, 206
  age out of crime, 19, 43, 178
  emotional support, 141, 142
  HCV, 95, 114
  HIV/AIDS, 81, 82, 85, 87, 90, 92, 93, 114, 115
  mentally ill serve longer in prison, 52, 123, 125
  older inmate victimization, 171
  poor health, 142
  tuberculosis, 77, 81, 82, 91–94, 112–114, 116–118, 121, 122
  victims higher rates of depression, 170
fear, 28, 38–40, 133, 136, 137, 140, 141, 143, 158, 163, 168, 169, 174, 180, 184
Federal Bureau of Prisons, 6, 12, 28, 184, 185, 193
first time offender, 58
Florida, 14, 32, 34, 38, 63, 70, 71, 78, 87, 88, 90, 114, 186, 188, 189, 192
frustration, 170

Georgia, 3, 14, 32, 34, 37, 44, 88, 113, 115
geriatric, 3, 20, 27, 33, 52, 53, 63, 65–67, 75, 79, 101, 136, 146, 151, 155, 165, 166, 168, 169, 172, 177–179, 182–184, 186–190, 192, 193, 196, 200, 202, 204–206
geriatric prison units, 79
geriatric release, 177, 182–184, 192, 204
get tough, 27, 52, 195
Gonorrhea, 81–83, 85, 113
handicap accessible, 186, 190
Hearing Impairment, 97
Heart Disease, 66, 96, 98–100, 104–106, 120, 122, 131, 133, 136, 196
Hepatitis B, 81, 82, 93, 94, 113, 114, 117, 118, 120
Hepatitis C, 80, 93–96, 114, 118, 120
heterogeneous, 29, 57
Hispanic, 7, 33, 35, 63, 64, 102, 107, 131, 160, 162
HIV, 77, 81–83, 85–87, 90, 92, 93, 95, 113–120, 122, 144, 163
home detention, 185
Hospice, 187, 189–191, 202, 205
housing, 38, 42, 67, 78, 79, 144, 145, 148, 185, 186, 188, 189, 191, 206
  segregation, 144
Human Rights Watch, 17, 20, 24, 35, 47, 51, 52, 59, 60, 67, 71, 123, 126, 148, 155, 178–180, 192, 197, 201
Hypertension, 93, 96, 97, 99, 113, 114, 163
imprisonment, 7, 9, 10, 14, 15, 25, 27, 28, 33, 35–38, 40, 41, 44, 45, 48–50, 60, 61, 63, 70, 110, 114, 172, 175, 204
imprisonment rate, 9, 14, 15, 27, 33, 35, 36, 60, 61, 63
incapacitation, 4, 5, 191
incarcerate, 18, 22, 27, 28, 44, 47, 67, 75, 117, 178, 197

incarceration rate, 4, 8, 9, 13, 27, 28, 35
incidence, 81, 92, 95, 112, 118, 124, 126, 142, 155, 158, 159, 171
indeterminate sentencing, 5, 48
inmate code, 169
institutional context, 144
interpersonal conflict, 141, 143
isolation, 39–41, 49, 124–126, 140, 141, 144, 172, 186
Laurel Highlands, 189, 190
life-course-persistent, 19
lifestyle, 53, 57, 58, 80, 115, 148, 196
long-term incarceration, 5–7, 20, 21, 28, 29, 38, 39, 41, 43, 44, 46, 47, 140, 141, 146, 197
  consequences, 6, 39, 41, 43, 44, 48–50, 116, 125, 126
  costs, 3, 7, 12, 13, 16, 17, 20, 22, 23, 26–28, 38, 44, 47, 48, 51, 53, 54, 68, 75–79, 84, 90, 97, 104, 108–111, 117, 166, 171, 177–180, 183, 187, 192, 193, 195, 200, 204
long-term inmate, 28, 29, 76, 78, 197
  defining long-term, 29
  men and long-term, 38–40
  minorities long-tem, 33–35
  needs of long-term, 21, 41, 43, 124, 145
  release of long-term, 41–43
  women and long-term, 41
male, 7, 21, 22, 36, 38, 39, 41, 42, 54, 57, 69, 70, 72, 86, 87, 90, 101, 102, 104, 107, 113, 116, 118, 122, 123, 131, 151, 158–162, 166, 167, 170, 171, 173–175, 187, 193
mandatory minimums, 5, 6, 49
Maryland Hospice Program, 189
masculinity, 163, 167, 169, 172
medical, 4, 17, 21, 22, 33, 52, 54, 57, 69, 71, 72, 75–122, 133, 136, 140,

141, 143, 144, 146, 149–151, 177, 182–192, 196, 197, 200, 204, 205
  medical conditions, 69, 77, 79, 96, 97, 112, 113, 115, 182, 200, 204
medicine, 69, 79, 115, 119–122, 130, 140, 149–153, 182, 191, 194
mental health, 4, 20, 22, 27, 40, 42, 67, 70, 75, 79, 81, 100, 103, 111, 112, 118, 121–153, 158, 168, 173, 186, 189–192, 200, 206
  age and prisoner mental health, 128
  characteristics of mentally disorder prisoners, 126–128
  communicable diseases, 40, 77, 81, 82, 110, 121, 163
  effective approaches, 108, 145
  most common mental illnesses among inmates, 128
  why focus, 76, 124
mentally disordered, 45, 69, 124–126
Michigan, 14, 32, 34, 88
minorities, 27, 33, 35, 36, 61, 82, 87, 90
mobility, 17, 19, 66, 96, 186, 196
mortality, 57, 90, 91, 101, 104–107, 112–114, 119, 151
NAMI Board of Directors, 124, 125, 127, 128
national trends, 44
needs, 3, 4, 7, 13, 19, 21, 22, 27, 33, 41, 43, 51, 52, 57, 65, 68–70, 73, 75–78, 115, 123–153, 172, 181, 185–187, 189, 190, 196, 197, 199–204, 206
New York, 15, 23, 24, 26, 44–49, 61, 69–72, 87, 89, 94, 112, 114, 115, 117–122, 147, 153, 159, 172, 174, 175, 183, 192, 194, 204–206
Newman v. Alabama, 80
nonviolent offender, 17, 52, 140
North Carolina, 15, 32, 34, 79, 89, 170, 177, 183

nothing works, 4, 5, 23
nursing home care, 79
obesity, 97
Oklahoma, 14, 32, 34, 89, 148, 160, 183
Older American Act, 53
overcrowding, 20, 124, 145, 149
pains of imprisonment, 38, 40, 41, 172
palliative care, 111, 189, 201
parole, 5, 9, 13, 17, 24, 32, 37, 48, 52, 119, 125, 181–184, 189, 191, 206
passive, 39
penal harm, 5, 122
personal victimization, 156–158, 166, 168
personality disorders, 123, 146, 166
The Pew Center on the States, 10, 32, 38, 49, 75
pharmaceutical costs, 109
physical decline, 67, 168
policy, 3, 5, 6, 8–11, 18, 20–23, 25, 26, 28, 29, 44, 46–48, 50, 71–73, 91, 108, 109, 116, 117, 119, 122, 124, 125, 148, 153, 169, 173, 184, 191–194, 203, 205, 206
policy maker, 21, 51, 57, 58, 110, 169, 203
predators, 28, 58
preferred provider organizations, 109
pre-prison, 80, 136, 166, 171, 181
prevention, 68, 87, 110, 112–114, 117, 119, 147, 149–151, 153, 173, 197
prison population, 4, 8–11, 17, 22, 24–27, 32, 33, 43, 46, 51, 55, 59–65, 70–72, 78, 79, 98, 119, 126, 134, 136, 141, 145, 177, 179, 187, 189, 192, 193, 195, 196, 200, 204, 206
Prison Rape Elimination, 155, 158, 174, 175
The Prison Rape Elimination Act, 155, 158

privatization, 108
profile, 22, 37, 44, 58, 68, 70
programs, 21, 22, 42, 47, 108, 109, 126, 141, 145, 147, 149–151, 161, 162, 165, 171, 172, 177–195, 201, 206
    Florida programs, 188
    Laurel Highlands, 189, 190
    Louisiana, 11, 14, 88, 183, 189
    Maryland, 15, 88, 94, 95, 118, 120, 151, 183, 189, 191
    True Grit, 71, 188, 192
    Virginia, 11, 14, 32, 34, 89, 183, 190, 194, 202, 206
Project for Older Prisoners, 181
projections, 12, 54, 57, 68, 69
property victimization, 156–158, 168, 169
protocol, 111, 148
psychological decline, 197
PTSD, 40, 127, 136, 137, 163, 166, 171
rape, 15, 31, 40, 155, 157, 158, 163, 166, 173–176
recidivism, 4, 24, 43, 45, 69, 178, 192, 194, 195, 204, 205
reentry, 46–48, 115, 119, 121, 149, 150, 172, 191, 194
referral, 120, 184
rehabilitation, 3, 4, 23–25, 45, 68, 72, 126, 174, 194–196, 204
release, 4, 5, 10, 22, 28, 29, 39–43, 47, 52, 53, 56, 58, 69, 77, 94, 108–111, 125, 126, 137, 143, 177–185, 190–192, 196–198, 200, 201, 203, 204
residential, 46, 51
responsibility, 125, 147, 148, 195, 198–202
responsiveness, 199, 202
retribution, 180, 195
retributive, 197

Schizophrenia, 122, 127–132, 146, 149, 150, 153
  prevalence in correctional settings, 95
screening, 84, 85, 110, 117, 118, 145, 148, 201
segregating, 171, 186
senior, 53, 79, 119, 202
sentence length, 33, 41, 49, 62, 141, 164
Sentencing Project, 6, 25, 33, 36, 37, 47–49
sexual victimization, 42, 147, 156, 158–165, 167–170, 172, 174, 175
skills, 130, 134, 188, 190
snapshot, 29, 54, 176
social support, 41, 140–142, 145, 148, 149, 151, 191
solutions, 20, 81, 171, 178
Southern Legislative Conference, 61
staff competencies, 146
stress, 40, 73, 114, 130, 136, 137, 163, 166, 170, 190
subculture, 117, 167
substance abuse, 42, 57, 118, 127, 136, 144, 152, 153, 188, 190
suicidal ideation, 138, 142, 144, 151, 170
suicide, 105, 106, 133, 138–145, 147–153
  attempt, 138–140, 143
  causes, 44, 48, 50, 93, 96, 104–106, 115, 140, 151, 161, 169, 195
  effective approaches, 108, 145
  prevalence, 138, 149–151, 153
  rate, 4, 8–11, 13–15, 22, 26–28, 33, 35, 36, 42, 54, 60, 61, 63, 76, 85–87, 90, 92, 95, 97, 98, 100, 104, 110, 135, 136, 138–141, 143, 158, 160, 168, 178, 197
Syphilis, 81–84, 113, 120, 122

telemedicine, 108
terminally ill, 68, 108, 109, 177, 180
Texas, 14, 24, 32, 49, 70, 87, 89, 97, 115, 145, 149, 172, 183
time served, 30, 32, 34, 38, 41, 46, 49, 52, 62, 183
training, 110, 130, 151, 185, 190
transmission, 83, 84, 90, 113, 116–119
trauma, 40, 134, 155, 163, 166, 167, 171
trend, 10, 16, 20, 54, 65, 75, 90, 161, 190
Trichomoniasis, 81–83, 86
True Grit, 71, 188, 192
truth-in-sentencing, 5, 183
Tuberculosis, 77, 81, 82, 91–94, 112–114, 116–118, 121, 122
ulcers, 163
United States v. Carey, 181, 194
United States v. Harrison, 181, 194
United States v. Tolson, 181, 194
unreported, 86, 168
utilization review, 109
victimization, 22, 40, 42, 125, 126, 140, 141, 147, 155–176, 186, 187
  consequences, 6, 18, 39, 41, 43, 44, 48–50, 116, 125, 126, 161, 163, 169, 170
  defining, 21, 29, 52, 53, 55, 156, 200
  extent, 52, 78, 134, 169, 183
  prevalence, 155, 158, 159, 171, 173, 175, 204
  sexual victimization, 42, 147, 156, 158–165, 167–170, 172, 174, 175
violence, 19, 38, 40, 47, 72, 120, 123, 124, 136–139, 143, 144, 155, 157, 158, 160, 163, 167–169, 172–174, 176, 183, 187, 189

violent, 5–7, 29–32, 34, 40–42, 45, 58, 61, 62, 69, 126, 127, 140, 155, 164, 167, 177, 180, 183
violent crime, 177
violent offender, 5, 127, 140, 180
violent victim, 126
Virginia, 11, 14, 32, 34, 89, 183, 190, 194, 202, 206
vulnerable, 21, 39, 140, 151, 158, 165, 167, 168, 199, 202, 203, 205

war on drugs, 3, 5, 6, 20, 25, 27, 28, 35, 36, 44
women, 17, 27, 36, 37, 42–46, 48, 50, 70, 71, 83–87, 95, 123, 138, 151, 158, 173, 175, 206
young, 4, 29, 42, 44, 50–52, 67, 85, 136, 185
Zephyrhills Correctional Institution, 189